AN ILLUSTRATED HISTORY of GOSPEL

LION

STEVE TURNER

AN ILLUSTRATED HISTORY
of
GOSPEL

Copyright © 2010 Steve Turner
This edition copyright © 2010 Lion Hudson

The author asserts the moral right
to be identified as the author of this work

A Lion Book
an imprint of
Lion Hudson plc
Wilkinson House, Jordan Hill Road,
Oxford OX2 8DR, England
www.lionhudson.com

ISBN 978 0 7459 5339 7

Distributed by:
UK: Marston Book Services, PO Box 269, Abingdon, Oxon, OX14 4YN
USA: Trafalgar Square Publishing, 814 N. Franklin Street, Chicago, IL 60610
USA Christian Market: Kregel Publications, PO Box 2607, Grand Rapids, MI 49501

First edition 2010

10 9 8 7 6 5 4 3 2 1 0

Acknowledgments
Extracts from the Authorized Version of the Bible (*The King James Bible*), the rights
in which are vested in the Crown, are reproduced by permission of the Crown's
Patentee, Cambridge University Press.

A catalogue record for this book is available from the British Library

Typeset in 10/14 Optima
Printed and bound in China

Contents

Introduction

Gospel music, as we have come to know it, is less than a century old, and during that time it has developed and adapted many times. The 'holy hip hop' of some contemporary performers bears little relation to the music produced by the jubilee quartets of the 1930s. Yet the older and newer forms of gospel have at least three things in common. They are committed to expressing the 'good news of Jesus', they have been shaped by the secular music of their time and they have caused outrage in the church.

This book explores through words and images how gospel music developed from the slave cabins of American plantations in the nineteenth century to the vast public arenas of the world in the twenty-first. Space hasn't allowed me to go into intricate detail, or even to mention every single significant gospel act, but I have attempted to explain the history of the genre in a way that provides a good and easily readable introduction.

Although I have aimed to tell the story in a roughly chronological order, my organizing principle has been to produce not a year-by-year account but a study of all the major leaps forward. My premise has been that it's only really possible to understand gospel music if you have knowledge of all the social, technological, artistic and spiritual ingredients that have been added over the years. For this reason I have, for example, devoted chapters to the great songwriters, and also to the rise of record companies and radio stations, even though this interrupted a strict chronological flow.

Most of my research was done from available books, articles and records, but I had the advantage of having been to gospel concerts in America and of having interviewed some of the genre's legendary figures. In 1976 I was the researcher and interviewer for a BBC TV documentary, directed by Norman Stone, which looked at the rise of gospel music. This allowed me to meet people like Thomas Dorsey, Sallie Martin, James Cleveland, Shirley Caesar, Andrae Crouch, Hoss Allen, Jessy Dixon and the Mighty Clouds of Joy, as well as to visit some of the radio stations, churches and record companies that had played a significant role.

I've included transcripts of some of the interviews I conducted while researching that programme, as well as some from later projects, such as accompanying Jessy Dixon on a tour of Israel with Paul Simon to write a report for *Melody Maker*, talking to the songwriter Herbert W. Brewster to find out how gospel affected the rock and roll of 1950s Memphis and seeing the Blind Boys of Alabama in concert as background for a book I was writing on the evolution of the song 'Amazing grace'. I believe that they provide interesting cutaway shots from the main narrative and allow those who made the music to have their say.

Anyone writing about gospel music today is bound to owe a debt to Anthony Heilbut, the author of *The Gospel Sound*. He was the first person to lay out the history of the music, and his book remains a classic. His love for the music and his knowledge of the performers shine through every paragraph, and his assessments are impeccable. I'm especially indebted because he put me in touch with people like Thomas Dorsey in 1976 and kick-started my education in gospel.

This book will have done its job if it sends people back to their record collections or entices those not already familiar with gospel to go on line and check out some of the most outstanding songs. Writing it has certainly had that effect on me. It reintroduced me to many of the classics and turned me on to new singers I had barely heard of. At its best, gospel is a music that not only sings about the joy, release and fulfilment of salvation, but embodies it in a unique way.

The Calvary Baptist Church Choir performs at the Verizon Wireless 'How Sweet the Sound' National Gospel Competition at the Wachovia Center in Philadelphia, Pennsylvania, in 2009.

I Got So Much to Shout About

In July 1966 the Dixie Hummingbirds, one of gospel music's most venerable acts, took to the main stage of the Newport Folk Festival in Rhode Island for a one-hour 'Gospel Battle' with two other groups – the Swan Silvertones led by Claude Jeter and the Gospel Harmonettes led by Dorothy Love Coates. The idea was to re-create the song competitions that had become a feature of the gospel circuit but to do it in a friendly and affirmative way.

The Newport Folk Festival, which had begun in order to preserve and promote the roots music of America, had become dangerously hip and the folk acts of one year became the rock stars of the next. The previous year's sensation had been Bob Dylan, who had surprised and shocked his core audience

A Fender Stratocaster with tremolo arm. Its arrival in 1954 revolutionized popular music.

by using a band with electric guitars. This year the line-up included such blues legends as Muddy Waters, Skip James and Howlin' Wolf, as well as one of the greatest rock-and-roll stars of all time, Chuck Berry.

The Dixie Hummingbirds were not used to performing for young white people in jeans and teeshirts, who were more likely to be holding a lighted joint than an open Bible. It was unfamiliar territory for them. Yet they knew that the style of music they had been perfecting for over two decades had a universal appeal. It could make the sinner envy the saved.

One of their chosen numbers this Friday night was called 'The reason I shout'. It was taken from their 1965 LP on Peacock, *Every Day and Every Hour*. In common with a lot of gospel songs, it was a series of impressions of the life of Christ that were flung out and punctuated with the pumping vocal cry of 'I got so much to shout about'. It was as if the audience were being given a slide show of Christ's majesty and were then being told that this was the source of the group's joy and commitment. Ultimately, this was the source of their music. There would be no point in shouting if there was nothing to shout about.

That night they performed the song to perfection. Everything they did on stage amplified the meaning of its words. The lead vocals were shared between Ira Tucker and James Walker, who used a single hand-held microphone. Behind them stood the impassive-faced figure of Howard Carroll, carefully chopping the beat on his Fender Stratocaster. To their left, clustered around a microphone on a stand, were James Davis, Beachey Thompson and William Bobo. All of them were dressed in dark suits with white shirts and black ties.

Walker would sing a line, throwing down his left arm for added emphasis, and the three-man chorus would follow up with 'I got so much to shout about'. Then the microphone would be passed to Tucker, who'd been clapping his hands and dancing, and he'd add the next line. There were references to Jesus turning the water into wine, visiting the temple, dying on the cross and saving souls from hell. By the end of the eight-and-a-half-minute workout, Tucker and Walker were exchanging the microphone after every word, their heads jerking backwards and forwards in a frenzy. 'Thank you,' Walker would

cry. 'Jesus,' Tucker would add, and on and on it went until the audience was on its feet.

The Dixie Hummingbirds were bringing the musical experience of black religion to mainstream America. 'Let's have a little church,' was what Tucker had said when he introduced the song. In their voices you could hear the suffering of slavery as well as the hope of the spirituals. In their movements you could see the physicality and exuberance of African American worship. In their smart dress you could sense their pride in being free people on the verge of even greater freedoms.

Hearing them gave plenty of clues as to where American popular music had found a lot of its inspiration. You could hear the beat of Motown, the vocal tricks of people like Otis Redding and James Brown and the guitar licks of Bo Diddley. You could also see the dance moves of Mick Jagger and the suave uniforms of groups like the Temptations and the Impressions. This was spectacular gospel full of passion, verve and imagination. And it made most pop and rock look pale in comparison.

THE INFLUENCE OF GOSPEL
Gospel (both white and black), along with country, blues and jazz, was the main musical tributary flowing into rock and roll. It was during the 1940s that some black artists began fusing these sounds and creating a hybrid that the trade papers called 'rhythm and blues'. In the 1950s some white guys did the same, called it rock and roll and started a revolution in popular music that has yet to end.

Yet of all these forms of music, gospel is the least known about and appreciated by lovers of rock. Rock magazines will regularly celebrate the legends of country, blues and jazz, but almost never the legends of gospel. The Glastonbury Festival in Britain has featured country star Johnny Cash on the main stage, as well as blues guitarist Buddy Guy, but never one of the greats of gospel music. Documentary-makers go in search of the ghosts of Robert Johnson, Hank Williams and Charlie Parker, but never for the ghosts of Thomas Dorsey or Clara Ward. When *Rolling Stone* magazine compiled its list of Immortals – 'The 100 Greatest Artists of All Time' – they included two blues singers (Muddy Waters and Howlin' Wolf), two jazz players (Louis Jordan and Miles Davis), and two country artists (Johnny Cash and Hank Williams), but not a single gospel performer. Not even Mahalia Jackson!

At a pinch *Rolling Stone* could claim to have represented gospel with Al Green, Aretha Franklin and Sam Cooke, but the truth is that they were included for their work as soul artists. Al Green returned to gospel after establishing himself with a string of hits in the 1970s. Aretha sang gospel as a child and has recorded gospel albums since, but her reputation is built on her singles of the 1960s. And Sam Cooke's work with the Soul Stirrers is known only to serious students of popular music. If gospel had been considered by the magazine's panel of experts they would have at least short-listed Southern gospel groups such as the Statesmen Quartet and the Blackwood Brothers, singers like Mahalia, Rosetta Tharpe and Clara Ward, or groups like the Swan Silvertones and Dixie Hummingbirds.

Of the 100 artists selected for the list, a third either sang in gospel groups as teenagers or were profoundly affected by gospel. Looking at the top ten alone reveals a whole range of influences.

Five of the artists recorded gospel songs, the same number were raised in the black church and at least four of them have cited specific gospel singers as having a major influence either on their stage performance or on their vocal technique. Ray Charles loved the voice of Archie Brownlee of the Five Blind Boys of Mississippi, Aretha Franklin originally modelled herself on Clara Ward, Little Richard copied his vocal swoops from Marion Williams, and Elvis was inspired by the on-stage antics of the Statesmen Quartet's James 'Big Chief' Wetherington, who used to quiver his legs in a then controversial way.

Even The Beatles, the number-one act on the list, absorbed some gospel style at second hand through the American artists they admired – falsetto from Claude Jeter via Ron Isley of the Isley Brothers (who started performing in a gospel group), harmonies from the Louvin Brothers via the Everly Brothers, head-shaking from the Holiness Church via Little Richard, call-and-response from the plantation meeting houses via Hank Ballard and the Midnighters. In one of the earliest group questionnaires The Beatles had to fill out for a music paper, John Lennon put 'gospel' as one of his influences but didn't specify which artists. When vicars or priests asked them how they could revitalize their church services, The Beatles would always tell them to introduce a bit of black gospel.

British music historian Charlie Gillett argued that The Beatles' style came from an amalgamation of the hard rock and roll of singers like Little Richard and the gospel call-and-response style of groups like the Shirelles and the Drifters. In his book *The Sound of the City* he speculated that their perceived originality in the

A gospel choir sings in Paris.

early years of their career may have been partly due to people's ignorance of the sources.

The gospel-harmony groups had very little success in Britain, and the result for the British audience was a sound with a familiar rhythm and a novel vocal style. The way The Beatles echoed one another's phrases, dragged out words across several beats, shouted 'yeah,' and went into falsetto cries, was received in Britain as their own invention; it seemed that Britain had finally discovered an original, indigenous rock'n'roll style.

Yet, despite this overwhelming influence, gospel is ignored. The average music lover could reel off a list of greats from country, jazz and blues, but would be hard pushed to name more than one or two greats from the field of gospel. This is despite the fact that, if asked whether they liked gospel music, the same people would answer in the affirmative. They may not buy it, they may never go to a gospel concert, and they certainly don't all believe in its message, but whenever

they catch a flash of gospel performance they find themselves won over by the excitement and the emotion. They appreciate the passion of the singers; they're in awe of the vocal power; they're infected by the rhythm.

Rock musicians themselves frequently have a much more informed appreciation of gospel. Mick Jagger, Paul Simon, Van Morrison, Bob Dylan and Bono have all been known to slip into churches to appreciate gospel in performance. Producer Brian Eno (Talking Heads, U2, Paul Simon, Coldplay) is a long-term gospel fan who has been known to pop into Brooklyn's First Baptist Tabernacle of Christ to catch its choir when in New York. He told *Cashbox* magazine that even though gospel music recordings were often technically inferior to pop and rock, 'they absolutely vibrate with life for me'. He concluded: 'My feeling about gospel is that it's about time there was a music that actually moved you enough to make you shed tears again.' It's not as though gospel music has been kept locked in a back room with no access for non-believers. In every decade since the 1930s there have been enterprising attempts to excite the music-loving world about gospel. The legendary Columbia Records producer John Hammond brought gospel to Carnegie Hall alongside blues and swing in 1938 to make the point that this was a heritage to be cherished.

The Golden Gate Quartet, who sang at Franklin D. Roosevelt's inauguration in 1941, and became one of the first gospel quartets to gain international fame.

During the war years there was a vogue for presenting gospel acts in New York nightclubs for patrons who sipped on their vodkas and sucked on cigars. The Golden Gate Quartet even sang at Roosevelt's inauguration in 1941 and appeared in several Hollywood movies, including *A Song is Born* (1948) with Danny Kaye.

During the 1950s there were annual gospel shows at Madison Square Garden that brought the house down, and some gospel artists began touring the world, playing not only in Europe and Scandinavia but in Korea and Japan. The generation most likely to spurn the music of the church, the countercultural experimenters of the 1960s, were faced with gospel on the Civil Rights marches, and even at some of the great outdoor music festivals, where gospel acts would perform on the same stage as Miles Davis, Bob Dylan or the Paul Butterfield Blues Band.

In the decades since then, there have been repeated opportunities to keep gospel visible. Paul Simon recorded with the Dixie Hummingbirds and the Jessy Dixon Singers in the 1970s, U2 cut a track with the New Voices of Freedom in 1988, Kirk Franklin had a US chart hit with the gospel choir God's Property in 1997, and the London Community Gospel Choir backed Madonna on her Live 8 appearance in 2005 before an estimated global TV audience of 2 billion. Few music fans can say they've been denied the opportunity of ever hearing the music.

The downplaying of gospel has ideological roots. People outside the church can appreciate its authenticity, excitement, vocal skills and musical inventiveness, but they are left cold, or possibly even offended, by the point of view of the lyrics. If a singer is expressing passion for Christ, uninitiated listeners can't relate to it in the way they could if the passion was for Johnny or Diana. The music historian Michael Gray expresses this view well in his biography of Blind Willie McTell. 'Gospel music has been much ignored by most blues-fan writers,' he admits. 'Like me, they tend to be on the atheistic left and often find the whole gospel agenda essentially a turn-off.'

Rock shared the worldview of the blues as well as its musical style. The emphasis was on letting go of all inhibitions and indulging the appetites to the full. There was no God to please, no promise

Paul Simon on stage in Israel with the Jessy Dixon Singers, July 1978.

of heaven and no threat of hell. The fully realized person was the one who could successfully repel the forces of repression and satisfy the natural instincts. The message of gospel, which was hard to ignore because the words demanded attention, opposed this premise.

The only overlap was in the passionate expression of gospel artists. When gospel singers were 'in the Spirit' they seemed to achieve that sense of freedom that rock artists aspired to. James Brown used to mimic the performance of an ecstatic preacher, dropping to his knees and pleading in almost sobbing tones. Yet the point of gospel was not to abandon oneself to instinct but to hand oneself over to God. What looked like freaking out and going wild was, they would explain, captivity by the Holy Spirit.

Another difference with gospel was that, unlike jazz, blues and country, it didn't originate as entertainment or spectacle. The other music forms were designed to amuse, stimulate and bring pleasure in the midst of hard times. Gospel, on the other hand, came into being as a vehicle for instruction, praise and communal worship. It was made by, and for, a special-interest group. It wasn't meant to captivate outsiders or even to divert insiders but to facilitate devotion and spiritual growth. Originally, there was no thought even of evangelizing, of trying to cajole or persuade, and certainly not of making money, although some songs were addressed to the lethargic believer who was in danger of straying from the straight and narrow.

'LET'S HAVE A LITTLE CHURCH'

Gospel music has always struggled when taken out of the church and made to compete with other forms of entertainment. The tendency has

Sister Wynona Carr straddled the worlds of jazz, blues and gospel. She is best known for a series of imaginatively titled songs that drew comparisons between God's power and such newsworthy events as the atomic bomb and the TV series *Dragnet*.

been to accentuate the more physical elements – dancing, clapping, swaying, shrieking – and play down the spiritual. Otherwise, of course, gospel seems completely opaque to someone unfamiliar with the worship, praise and instruction it was intended to promote. In the words of Michael Gray, it's just a 'turn-off'. It feels like reading an internal memo between people you have no knowledge of or interest in.

Because of its origin in the life of the church, gospel music tends to speak only of the spiritual. Its focus is on the relationship between the individual and God and, traditionally, it rarely discusses the commonplace things of life. If it talks about a car it's only because a car is like faith ('Christian's automobile' by the Soul Stirrers). If it talks about the nuclear bomb it's because Christ has an explosive effect on our lives ('Jesus is God's atomic bomb' by the Swan Silvertones). If it talks about baseball it's because life is like a sporting game ('The ball game' by Sister Wynona Carr). Every subject tackled has to have its resolution in the Father, Son or Holy Spirit. (Sister Wynona Carr took this to amusing extremes with songs like 'Dragnet for Jesus' and '15 rounds for Jesus' in the early 1950s.)

This may have worked well in church. After all, you don't expect to hear a sermon about how to fix a boiler or prepare a nutritious salad. A pastor's job is primarily to look after the spiritual welfare of a congregation. But when gospel began to go out of the churches and into the concert halls and clubs it meant that it was presenting subject matter that didn't resonate with a secular audience. There were no experiences for the ordinary listener to relate to. The problems presented – temptations from the devil, waiting for answers to prayer, keeping your mind fixed on God – were not ones grappled with by non-believers. Gospel singers appeared to be exempt from broken romances, unpaid bills, unfulfilled expectations and political instability. They didn't even seem to live in the world of glorious sunsets, twinkling stars and breaking waves.

The primary audience for gospel music, on the other hand, became suspicious if gospel strayed away from overt theology. When Sam Cooke recorded the love song 'Wonderful' he had to use a pseudonym, and when his ruse was discovered his career as a gospel singer ended. Other singers have been reprimanded for airing personal doubts, singing about political issues or introducing the word 'God' too late in a song. Singing about the stuff of daily life would be regarded as either a concession to secular culture or a cowardly avoidance. There was no concept of being implicitly Christian in a song; of appreciating romantic love as a divine gift, for example. Everything had to be spelled out and drawn to an unambiguous conclusion.

Rock music imitated blues in both musical style and lyrical attitude. The Rolling Stones, for example, covered songs written by Jimmy Reed, Willie Dixon and Muddy Waters, but also wrote their own material about murder, slavery, debauchery and the devil that were heavily influenced by the blues singers they admired. When it came to gospel, they would generally keep the tune but rework the lyric to expunge any reference to God or coming judgment (exceptions included 'I just want to see his face').

Their first self-written hit, 'The last time', was a reworking of 'This may be the last time', recorded by the Staple Singers ten years before. In its original form it was the words of a father to his children, telling them that in the light of the promised return of Jesus Christ this may be the last time they meet together. The Jagger–Richards version is a misogynistic ultimatum warning a woman that if she doesn't try harder to please, she could be kicked out.

Soul music openly plundered gospel in this way. Charlie Gillett, in *The Sound of the City*, makes an interesting observation about how this may have been so effective. Gospel, like blues, was concerned with emotion, but the emotions explored in blues are to do with relationships and experiences between people. Gospel, on the other hand, explored the emotions of loving the divine. The object of love in gospel music was elevated. Gillett commented: 'The abstract nature of the relationship in gospel songs between the singer and God was rare in the blues, but it was close to the ideal conception of love which adolescents often have.'

In other words, the approach of gospel and the passion with which it was sung were well suited to songs where the object is believed to be perfect, transcendent and otherworldly. Many teen songs of the 1950s were of this nature. Whereas the relationships in blues songs were generally messy, and bodily functions were described with frankness (albeit often symbolically), the relationships in teen songs were ethereal. Women were goddesses or earth angels who would take you to heaven. They didn't sweat, grunt or cheat.

The next step was to exploit the know-how of gospel by marrying it to the love song. Gillett observed:

> Between 1948 and 1952 the potential connection between the emotions of gospel singing and the expectations of adolescent listeners of popular music occurred to various singers, record company executives, and composers. Indirectly and directly, gospel styles and conventions were introduced into rhythm and blues – and constituted the first significant trend away from the blues as such into black popular music.

They try to buzz me but they can't break me
Cuz I'm down with Christ Darkchild and Nu Nation Make you feel alright.
'Revolution', Kirk Franklin

Surveying the story of spirituals and gospel music that goes back over at least two centuries, it's possible to see that this question of whether the songs should remain in the church or be sent out of the church, and what constitutes a compromise, has been central. It bothered the Fisk Jubilee Singers in the 1870s when they became the first black singers to take spirituals into concert halls. It bothered Thomas Dorsey when he tried to amalgamate jazz, blues and church music. It was an issue that faced Mahalia Jackson, Clara Ward, Rosetta Tharpe and the Golden Gate Quartet.

What is gospel music for? Who is it for? What should be the parameters of its subject matter? These are the questions that percolate through this music, which, as a performing art, began with men in dark suits and women in long dresses, standing in fixed positions and singing slave songs in voices schooled in the European tradition, and has now reached a point where men and women in teeshirts and jeans rap over heavy beats, spin in the air and sing, 'They try to buzz me but they can't break me.'

To understand gospel music you have to understand its history, and to understand its history you have to go back to slavery, Protestant hymns and the antebellum plantations of the American South, where some of the key characteristics of contemporary popular music were forged in an atmosphere of joy, pain and hope.

I Thought I Heard My Saviour Cry

THE ROOTS OF GOSPEL

In one of the early scenes in Harriet Beecher Stowe's 1852 novel *Uncle Tom's Cabin*, the slaves working for Mr Shelby gather in Tom's 'small log building' to have 'a meeting'. It was the closest thing they had to a church, and Tom, 'a sort of patriarch in religious matters', was the closest thing they had to a minister. They sang, they prayed and they had the Bible read to them by one of the few literate slaves in their company. They took cheer from the promise that history was in God's hands rather than in those of their white masters.

Beecher Stowe was writing from personal experience. She had interviewed slaves and visited their homes. She was writing in order to change minds about slavery, and one of her most poignant observations was that these poor slaves had more genuine Christianity in their lives than did those who oppressed them. In the long run the Bible stories that the masters thought might make their slaves more compliant actually emboldened them because they taught them about justice, freedom and human dignity. They also taught them the virtue of longsuffering and the value of performing right actions even when you are despised and forsaken for doing so.

The mid-nineteenth-century snapshot she offered of African American worship in a Kentucky slave cabin captured gospel music in its foundational stage. She commented on their 'evident delight', 'great energy' and 'naturally fine voices' as they sang songs that they had either heard in white churches or picked up in open-air revival gatherings. Their style, she observed, was 'at once wild and spirited'.

She noticed their preference for songs that used repetition and ones that made mention of the banks of Jordan, the fields of Canaan and the New Jerusalem. 'For the negro mind, impassioned and imaginative, always attaches itself to hymns and expressions of a vivid and pictorial nature,' she wrote. 'And, as they sang, some laughed, and some cried, and some

clapped hands, or shook hands rejoicingly with each other, as if they had fairly gained the other side of the river. Various exhortations and relations of experience followed, and intermingled with the singing.'

Most of the characteristics Beecher Stowe saw almost 160 years ago remain in the black church: the outstanding singing voices; the obvious joy; the love of repetition, hand-clapping, exhortation and personal testimony. Whenever singers plead, 'Lord, have mercy!' or 'Can I get a witness?' they are showing their connection to this period of history. Whenever someone uses the images of wading in the water or heading for the Promised Land, they are identifying not just with the Children of Israel in the Old Testament but with the children of Africa who unwillingly came to America in chains and dreamed of escape.

OUT OF AFRICA

The four great determinants of spirituals were West African tribal culture, the experience of slavery, camp meetings and Protestant theology and hymnody. It's a music that appears to endorse the religious values of the dominant culture but actually offers a commentary on them. This was why spirituals became such an effective weapon in the Civil Rights movement of the 1960s. Campaigners were able to take the words of the Bible and shove them in the faces of their apparently Bible-believing oppressors.

Because the original slaves arrived long before the advent of recorded sound, it's all but impossible to know what musical memories they brought with them and how they directly affected the music of America. Musicologists have carried out extensive research in West African countries, but it can't be assumed that the musical styles

that exist today have any resemblance to what existed 200–300 years ago. Colonization created countries where none existed, tribal cultures have surely lost some of their distinctiveness in the modern world, and European culture has had centuries of shaping influence on modern-day Africa.

The closest we can get to imagining that original sound is through contemporary descriptions recorded by travellers, participants in the slave trade and the slaves themselves. From these accounts we know that music played a vital role in the communal life of a typical African village, that it was most often inseparable from dance and that the most popular instruments were percussion (drums) and strings (an instrument variously described as being like a guitar, violin or banjo).

Olaudah Equiano, one of the few slaves to write an account of his life in Africa before captivity, said: 'We are almost a nation of dancers, musicians, and poets. Thus every great event, such as a triumphant return from battle, or other cause of public rejoicing, is celebrated in public dances, which are accompanied with songs and music suited to the occasion.' He goes on to mention drums, 'a piece of music which resembles a guitar', and another instrument that was like a xylophone.

Equiano was probably born in 1745 in what is now known as Nigeria. At around the same time, Nicholas Owen, a British slave-dealer, was resident in Sierra Leone, buying slaves initially captured by Africans and selling them on to the captains of European ships cruising the Windward Coast. Of the natives he commented: 'Their chief diversion is playing upon a certain instrument of wood that sounds like a bad fiddle. This instrument is called a bangelo. They have likewise drums and other games or exercises of diversion.' He also noted that the men's favoured leisure activities were pipe-smoking, wine-drinking and dancing.

White slave-owners didn't particularly care what tribal nation their workers came from. All that mattered was that they were strong, healthy, hard-working and obedient. But to the slaves the separation from their tribe with all its customs and beliefs was traumatic. It meant being severed from everything that had given their lives meaning and dignity and being plunged into experiences they were unable to interpret. Most of them had never seen the sea before, let alone stepped on a ship. The sailors, with their white faces, seemed to be devils, and the power of the wind to move the vessel could only be understood as a hitherto undiscovered form of magic. Life took on the form of an extended hallucination.

Once settled on plantations in the West Indies or North America, they couldn't even communicate with their fellow slaves who were from other tribes and spoke different languages. Their speech was instantaneously deprived of all power. There could be no comfort offered, no anguish expressed. This suited their owners' needs, because it significantly reduced the chances of insurrection. Over time the slaves accommodated to the white man's words, and African ritual, celebration and entertainment became submerged. But dance and play, the love of rhythm, patterns of call-and-response, the use of low moans and high-pitched shrieks, were common to all African slaves. They

Sweet potato planting on Cassina Point Plantation on Edisto Island, South Carolina, USA, during the Union occupation in April 1862.

crossed the boundaries of tribe or kingdom.

This musicality aligned to dance and ecstatic expression caught the attention of the Americans and Europeans who watched them on their plantations or in public spaces, such as New Orleans' Congo Square, with a mixture of fascination and fear. They were impressed by their ability to keep rhythms and to dance fluidly, but they were apprehensive about the apparent lack of inhibition, which seemed to prove that they were inherently wild and therefore in need of taming.

TEACHING ABOUT HEAVEN

The slaves' experiences of Western religion were either in white churches, where they were segregated and made to sit quietly in galleries, or in gatherings such as that described in *Uncle Tom's Cabin*. The masters naturally thought that religion was good for the Africans. Christianity, they thought, would instil good values. It would encourage them to be obedient and to be content with their lot. 'Servants, obey in all things your masters according to the flesh; not with eyeservice, as menpleasers; but in singleness of heart, fearing God' (Colossians 3:22). The teachings about heaven could be used to divert their minds from any discomfort they were experiencing in this world.

It was in the plantation 'praise houses' that a distinctly African American Christianity began to take shape. Away from the eyes of their owners the slaves were able to give expression to their longings and anxieties. Church became a place where news could be exchanged and where, for the first time, slaves could find social status within their own community. The preachers took up a role that Equiano would have recognized from his African childhood, where 'we had priests and magicians, or wise men', who were 'held in great reverence by the people'. Black preachers became much more than religious leaders. They became advisors, social commentators, prophets, seers, counsellors and arbitrators.

Harriet Beecher Stowe noticed that their main sources of music were white hymnbooks and the songs used at camp meetings. When slaves were taken to the churches of their owners, it was most likely to be either a Baptist or a Methodist church. The hymns they learned there in the eighteenth and nineteenth centuries would predominantly have been written by British hymn-writers such as Isaac Watts, Charles Wesley, John Newton and William Cowper.

Although these hymns would be considered old-fashioned today, when they were introduced they were as controversial as gospel music would be in the 1930s. Isaac Watts (1674–1748) and his contemporaries challenged the prevalent belief that the only words that should be sung in a church were those taken directly from the Psalms. He introduced the then novel idea of writing songs that embraced the events of the New Testament (you could sing about the life, death and resurrection of Jesus) as well as the personal response to salvation by the individual believer. Songs could be autobiographical as well as historical.

'When I survey the wondrous cross', one of Watts's most successful hymns, did both of these things. It portrayed the crucifixion ('See, from his head, his hands, his feet / Sorrow and love flow mingled down'), but led up to a personal conclusion ('Love so amazing, so divine / Demands my soul, my life, my all'). This was vastly different from strict adherence to the actual words of the Psalms.

His work became so popular in America that 'Dr Watts's hymns' became a generic term for Protestant hymnody. Worshippers saw his name attached to the foot of so many lyrics that they assumed he had written the entire book. His words, with their powerful visual images and expressions of strong emotion, are still sung in churches across the world. There can be few Christians who aren't familiar with 'Joy to the world', 'O God, our help in ages past', or 'Come, ye that love the Lord'.

John Wesley (1703–91) was another church radical. Instead of waiting for people to come into the church to hear the gospel, he took the message out into the streets and fields of eighteenth-century England, travelling thousands of miles on horseback and preaching in fields, streets and private houses, rather than in churches. His methodical approach to personal holiness led people to call him a 'methodist', and although he never left the Church of England, his followers eventually did, and the denomination they founded became known as Methodism.

His brother Charles (1707–88) wrote thousands of hymns to help him in his ministry, many of which are still included in hymnals. His words were designed to summarize complex truths in pithy phrases that even the illiterate could understand and memorize. His hymns were mini-masterpieces that, like those of Watts, linked doctrine to personal experience. Among his best-known and most enduring compositions are 'And can it be', 'Hark! The herald angels sing', 'Jesu, lover of my soul', 'Gentle Jesus meek and mild', 'Love divine, all loves excelling' and 'O for a thousand tongues to sing'.

Isaac Watts (1674–1748) was an English non-conformist minister and hymn-writer, born in Southampton, UK. His songs would become foundational to the early spirituals.

Wesley's hymns struck a balance between admission of sin and enjoyment of forgiveness. They were neither so apologetic that they wallowed in the misery of the human condition nor so exultant that they overlooked sin. He often used the metaphor of freedom from captivity when looking at salvation, a metaphor that would have had particular resonance among slaves.

> *Long my imprisoned spirit lay*
> *Fast bound in sin and nature's night;*
> *Thine eye diffused a quickening ray,*
> *I woke, the dungeon flamed with light;*
> *My chains fell off, my heart was free,*
> *I rose, went forth, and followed thee.*
> **'And can it be', Charles Wesley**

The hymns of John Newton (1725–1807), who was influenced by both Wesley and Watts, also spoke of release. He knew more about it than most because he had personal experience of slavery, both as a trader on the ground in West Africa and as a slave captain plying the notorious triangle between Britain, Africa and America. When in Africa, the jealous black wife of the trader he was working for on an island off Sierra Leone had held him in captivity while he was suffering from malaria, an experience that he would allude to in his epitaph when he referred to himself as having been the 'slave of slaves'. His best-known hymn, 'Amazing grace', was, like the hymns of Wesley, chock-full of Christian doctrine, but it was also autobiographical. He was the lost person who'd been found. He was the blind man who'd been made to see.

His conversion started in the middle of the Atlantic when the ship on which he was returning to England was caught in a vicious gale and was expected to sink. He survived and vowed that he would live his life for God. He continued in the slave trade as a captain, not seeing any inconsistency between his new-found faith and his old trade, but eventually became a minister in the Church of England and then a high-profile abolitionist. It was his friendship with William Wilberforce (1759–1833) that led the MP to campaign so vociferously for the ending of Britain's slave trade.

THE SECOND GREAT AWAKENING

The camp meetings that Harriet Beecher Stowe referred to were open-air services that started during the religious revival known as the Second Great Awakening at the beginning of the nineteenth century. This was a time when a primitive form of Christianity gripped the imaginations of millions of ordinary Americans, often in spectacular and dramatic ways. Many of the meetings where the message was spread took place in open fields where preachers performed from flat wagons, and the services would go on for hours if not days. They became notorious for the manifestation of strange phenomena such as people falling prostrate on the ground or dancing wildly or croaking like frogs. These were explained as workings of the Holy Spirit.

The unusual locations and the large crowds affected the type of music that could be sung. There could be no handing out of books with words, and preachers couldn't expect people to remember the words of hymns with many verses. 'And can it be', for example, has five six-line verses with no repeated lines. The solution was to take a few lines that could be retained – usually the first verse – and then to develop an extended chorus from it that contained a lot of repetition.

The camp meetings therefore bred a new type of Christian song that had fewer words and more repetition. They also encouraged physical participation. Those who attended would shout, gesticulate, clap and even dance. To the slaves permitted to attend these events it gave legitimacy to some of the practices that white Christians had tended to hold in contempt. Shouting had been deemed inconsistent with reverence towards God and dancing was a worldly practice, yet here were people dancing in the Spirit and shouting words of praise.

This style of music was particularly suited to the slaves because it required improvisation, and since being uprooted from Africa they had relied on the ability to construct meaning out of available material. Their habit of coming up with interjections, of riffing on phrases that caught the imagination, and of stretching and bending the sounds of words, was an artistic equivalent to what they had learned to do with their very existences. 'The concept of improvisation is a part of all American life,' says contemporary jazz musician Wynton Marsalis. 'If you were a slave you had to learn how to improvise. You couldn't speak the language, you had kinds of food you were not used to eating, you had a whole other system to deal with, and if you couldn't improvise you were going to be in a world of trouble. You weren't going to be able to survive.'

SPIRITUALS

The religious songs that were not to be found in hymnbooks were later known as spirituals. Because they were not written down, no one can be sure when or where they originated; but the first definite mentions by observers came in the second and third decades of the nineteenth century along with comments on the mournful melodies, the passion and the repeated use of certain phrases. Some musicologists date the origins to an earlier time, based on the survival of certain spirituals in Caribbean islands where slaves had been transported in the eighteenth century.

The spirituals are not only the foundation of gospel music and also of blues. They are exquisite examples of true folk art; none of the authors are known, nothing is recorded about how the songs were composed, and their preservation is due to their relevance and continuing usefulness. The humanity and spirituality they revealed were to become arguments in the case for abolition. How could people with longings like these be treated as though they were chattels?

The structure of each spiritual was fairly simple. They typically started with a chorus where the first line was repeated in the second, followed by a new line and then a final repetition of the first line. Then came a verse that would perhaps use some of the same repetition, before returning to the chorus. Besides being easy to memorize, and therefore to sing along to, the repeated phrases had a percussive effect. A random example would be 'I got a home in-a dat Rock'. This spiritual is also typical in that the central image of a rock as a place of shelter was most likely taken from a Protestant hymn, 'Rock of ages', written by Augustus Toplady in the eighteenth century, which contains the lines 'Rock of ages, cleft for me / Let me hide myself in thee'. Although the Bible refers several times to God as a 'rock' (for example, 2 Samuel 22:2; Psalm 18:2), it is as an image of a secure foundation rather than a place to hide. It was Toplady who came up with the image of

> I got a home in-a dat Rock, don't you see?
> I got a home in dat Rock, don't you see?
> Between de earth an' sky, thought I heard my Saviour cry
> I got a home in-a dat Rock, don't you see?
>
> Poor man Lazarus, poor as I, don't you see?
> Poor man Lazarus, poor as I, don't you see?
> Poor man Lazarus, poor as I,
> When he died he foun' a home on high
> He had a home in-a dat Rock, don't you see?
>
> I got a home, etc.

Christ as a protective rock when he was caught in a thunderstorm in Cheddar Gorge, England, and took refuge in the fissure of a huge rock. It was then that he thought of himself as being encircled by Christ, the Rock.

The spiritual then moves to the story of Lazarus as told by Christ in the Gospel of Luke (not Lazarus the brother of Mary and Martha, whom Jesus raised from the dead, but a poor man who lives a righteous life). This was a consoling story for slaves because it told of a role reversal in the afterlife. In this world Lazarus is a beggar at the gate of an unnamed rich man, yet when he dies he will be 'carried away by the angels into Abraham's bosom' (Luke 16:22). When the rich man who has ignored the plight of Lazarus dies, he goes to Hades, where he suffers torment. He can see Lazarus and so he calls to Abraham to allow Lazarus to 'dip the tip of his finger in water, and cool my tongue' (verse 24). Abraham can't bridge the gap between heaven and hell. He turns to the rich man and says: 'Son, remember that thou in thy lifetime receivedst thy good things, and likewise Lazarus evil things: but now he is comforted, and thou art tormented. And beside all this, between us and you there is a great gulf

fixed: so that they which would pass from hence to you cannot; neither can they pass to us, that would come from thence' (verses 26–27).

> Rich man, Dives, he lived so
>   well, don't you see?
> Rich man, Dives, he lived so
>   well, don't you see?
> Rich man, Dives, he lived so
>   well,
> When he died he foun' a home
>   in hell.
> He had no home in-a dat Rock, don't you see?

(The rich man isn't named in the Gospels, but traditionally he is known as Dives because *dives* is the Latin for 'rich man' and appears in the Vulgate, the ancient Latin version of the Bible.)

The song ends with a reference to the Old Testament story of Noah and the ark, which illustrates the ability of the narrators to see parallels between Old and New Testament redemption stories. Lazarus is safe in the Rock; Noah is safe in the ark. What they clearly loved were narratives rather than stand-alone doctrines. The stories of Noah, Jacob and his ladder, Joseph and Pharaoh, Joshua and the battle of Jericho and Moses crossing the Red Sea were gripping to them, as were the parables, the death and resurrection of Jesus and the visions of John as told in the book of Revelation.

THE SPIRITUAL AS STORY

The story of Lazarus was a warning. If you accepted salvation, you went to heaven, regardless of your social standing. If you rejected salvation, you went to hell, regardless of your social standing. The teaching of a just God and a final judgment was the ultimate guarantee of equality.

The line 'No mo water but fire next time' has become so embedded in the popular consciousness (the African American writer James Baldwin published an influential book called *The Fire Next Time* in 1963) that it's easy to overlook the deftness of the poet who spliced

> *God gave Noah de rainbow sign, don't you see?*
> *God gave Noah de rainbow sign, don't you see?*
> *God gave Noah de rainbow sign,*
> *No mo water but fire next time.*
> *Better get a home in-a dat Rock, don't you see?*
> **'I got a home in-a dat rock', Traditional**

a reference to a promise made by God to Noah that he would never again punish humanity with a worldwide flood to later references to the earth's final destruction by fire ('But the day of the Lord will come as a thief in the night; in the which the heavens shall pass away with a great noise, and the elements shall melt with fervent heat, the earth also and the works that are therein shall be burned up' 2 Peter 3:10).

When Josh White recorded this spiritual in 1933, the title and structure were the same as notated by James Weldon Johnson in his classic collection *American Negro Spirituals* (1925), but the lead lines of each verse were different. Instead of referring to the story of Lazarus and

the rich man or Noah and the ark, it focused exclusively on the crucifixion.

The second verse became 'Well, they nailed him to the cross, don't you see?' The third verse went 'Well, they pierced him in his side, don't you see?' and the final verse was 'Well, he never said a mumblin' word, don't you see?' Spirituals were that adaptable. There was no definitive text. Singers would personalize a song by keeping the title and structure but filling the verses with their own stories. Often individual lines or whole verses were imported from other spirituals.

The Harlem born writer James Baldwin (1924–87) was the son of a clergyman and became a storefront preacher himself as a teenager. The language of gospel was used to influence his writing style and the title of such novels as *Go Tell It on the Mountain*, *The Amen Corner* and *The Fire Next Time*.

> Well, they crucified my Lord, don't you see?
> Yes, they crucified my Lord, don't you see?
> Just between the earth and sky,
> Lord, my Saviour bled and died.
> I got a home in that Rock, don't you see?
> **'I got a home in that rock', as sung by Josh White**

The line about Jesus never saying 'a mumblin' word' was recognized by Weldon Johnson as coming from a song called 'Crucifixion', which went:

> They crucified my Lord, an' he never said a
>   mumblin' word.
> They crucified my Lord, an' he never said a
>   mumblin' word.
> Not a word, not a word, not a word.

THE SPIRITUAL AS POEM

There was a refreshing flexibility shown by the composers, who were able to see archetypes in the Old Testament and their fulfilment in the New. They thought nothing of bundling Daniel, Jonah, Jesus and a few silver trumpets from Revelation into a single song. The Bible to them was a fluid narrative. They may not even have been conscious of the historical distances between characters as diverse as Moses, David and John the Baptist. What was paramount was the connection they felt with them. They could see themselves in these people and they trusted in the same God. David conquered Goliath, Joshua conquered Jericho, Joseph won over his brothers, Moses overcame Pharaoh's stubbornness. Surely they would overcome too!

The authors of the spirituals loved visual images that captured the imagination. Angels, chariots, swords, trumpets, stars and golden crowns were frequently mentioned, and the Revelation to John, with its description of horses, fire and jewels, was of much more interest than the

The slaying of Goliath by the boy David encouraged slaves to believe that – with God's strength – the weak could overcome the powerful.

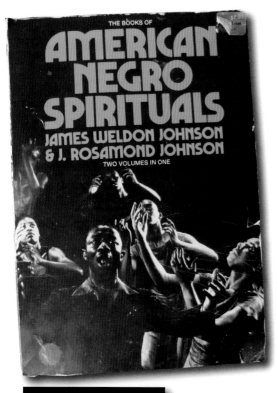

James Weldon Johnson's *American Negro Spirituals* was first published in 1925.

more doctrinally based letters of Paul. They also had a knack of importing new images from the contemporary world. If Isaiah could talk about chariots, why couldn't they talk about trains?

James Weldon Johnson, a celebrated poet who was part of the flowering of African American arts and culture in New York during the 1920s known as the Harlem Renaissance, spoke of their 'lively imagination, not yet wholly dulled by stereotyped ideas'. Giving an example, he cited the train that is used as a symbol for the passage from life to death. 'He [the anonymous composer of the spiritual] does not hesitate to scrap the stereotype and create a new symbol out of his own everyday experiences. He dares to do this, and, what is more important, he does it to the point of perfection.'

Such symbols served a dual purpose. Besides their primary spiritual meaning, there was a secondary meaning that suggested either the fantasy of being sprung from captivity ('Swing low, sweet chariot', 'Climbin' Jacob's ladder') or the real possibility of crossing the border into a state where slavery was illegal ('Deep river', 'Steal away', 'Wade in the water').

The spirituals became the foundation of gospel music. Some of the themes – the longing to be reunited with long-departed mothers, the admiration for Old Testament prophets, the longing for release from captivity, and the assurance that right living contains its own reward – survived the transition. Lyrical devices such as improvisation, repetition and the use of apocalyptic symbolism were developed further. The same combination of rhythm, passion, joy and yearning that characterized spirituals came to characterize gospel.

Most significantly, it was with spirituals that groups of African Americans were first able to present concerts with examples of their own culture. The touring jubilee singers of the late nineteenth century were the forerunners of the gospel groups and choirs who have been entertaining the world ever since. The questions they raised back then, about the commercialization of religious music and the effect of taking church culture into the secular arena for the amusement of non-believers, are still being asked today in the age of gospel brunches, Madonna videos and spiritual tours of Harlem.

Go Down, Moses

'BREATHING FORTH THE SOUL'

On a Sunday night in October 1871 four black men and five black women stood up in Seventh Street Congregational Church in Cincinnati, Ohio, and performed a repertoire of what were referred to at the time by white folks as 'plantation melodies', 'cabin songs' or 'slave hymns'. The men wore dark suits with velvet collars, cloth-covered buttons and waistcoats. The women wore long crinoline dresses over bustles and had their hair scraped back from their foreheads.

When they weren't singing they looked dignified and almost solemn. When they opened their mouths they let loose a sound that the *Cincinnati Gazette* reported as being 'rich', 'clear' and 'touching'. The paper thought that these singers from Nashville were 'breathing forth the soul'. What was remarkable was that this was the first group to take what had for decades been the substance of private worship by slaves and present it as a show for outsiders.

Back cover of *Plantation Melodies* – songs sung by the Canadian Jubilee Singers, the Royal Paragon Male Quartette and Imperial Orchestra during their nineteenth-century five-year tour of the UK and three-year tour of the US.

The heart of their performance was a collection of spirituals they'd learned at their mothers' knees: 'Go down, Moses', 'Singing for Jesus', 'Room enough' and 'Washed in the blood of the Lamb'. Although they didn't strut, dance or wail, they unleashed a form of musical power not previously experienced by white Congregationalists in the North. The voices were strong but sweet, the harmonies perfect. As one minister who saw them at a later appearance wrote: 'With no accessory of dress, with no stage manners, or claptrap of any kind, they have simply thrilled their audiences and left them spell-bound.'

Far from performing in the abandoned way that whites expected blacks to adopt, these men and women were models of physical restraint. They stood close together, their shoulders were straight and they tended to sing with their faces tipped up as though gazing into heaven. Some audience members were disappointed not to find them dressed more gaily. Others didn't think they were black enough.

THE JUBILEE SINGERS

The singing group was initially the idea of a white music teacher, George Leonard White, who was looking for a way to increase funding for his school, Fisk Free Colored School (later Fisk University), in Nashville. Founded after the Civil War by Northern missionaries with the specific aim of educating freed slaves, Fisk had started its life in disused army barracks. However, the buildings had fallen into disrepair and debts had begun to mount.

White already had an interest in the songs that he'd heard slaves singing on plantations, and had tried to encourage Fisk students to perform

them alongside the anthems, hymns and other songs he practised with them, but there was little appetite because plantation songs reminded the young black students of their people's harrowing past. After emancipation they wanted to forget dungarees, log cabins, servitude and all the musical expressions that had been born out of pain, exile and frustration. They wanted to wear smart clothes, straighten their hair and emulate the sophistication of their former masters.

Eventually White was able to persuade them, and in 1871 they set out on their first fundraising tour. The plan was to follow the route taken by escaped slaves, known as the 'Underground Railway', performing in churches and other public places, either charging an entrance fee or taking up an offering. The money collected was not specifically for the education of the singers in the group. It was funnelled back to Nashville to decrease the school's debt and ensure its survival.

Even though slavery had been abolished and the Northern states had led the way, the Fisk singers encountered prejudice as soon as they moved out of Tennessee. At times this was in the form of being patronized. The 'niggers' were looked on as if they were children, ignorant adults or primitives. Some people laughed at them for wearing fine clothes, believing they were over-dignifying themselves. Reviewers would occasionally compliment them on their sound but then add that they'd do better with a bit more European melodic influence. The worst expressions of racism came when they were turned away from hotels and restaurants or forced to ride in the caboose of a train.

They made very little money when they started. At times this was because they weren't able to attract large enough

Late nineteenth- or early twentieth-century stereoscopic card image of Oberlin College, Ohio, where the Fisk singers were seen by the influential Thomas Beecher.

audiences, but at other times it was because even the most generous offerings weren't enough to produce a profit for the group. They had to pay for transport, food and accommodation, and when this was subtracted from their takings there was often nothing left to send back to Nashville.

It was at Oberlin College in Ohio, when they were performing for the National Congregational Council, that things took a turn for the better. One of the attending ministers was Thomas

The Jubilee Singers of Fisk University, USA, captured here during a tour of the UK, looked a picture of Victorian propriety but when they performed they left audiences amazed at their emotional power. *Front row (left to right)*: Jennie Jackson, Mabel Lewis, Ella Sheppard, Maggie Carnes, America W. Robinson. *Back row (left to right)*: Maggie Porter, E. W. Watkins, H. D. Alexander, F. J. Loudin and Thomas Rutling.

Beecher, brother not only to Harriet Beecher Stowe, author of *Uncle Tom's Cabin*, but to Henry Ward Beecher, the minister of Plymouth Church in Brooklyn and one of the best-known preachers of the day. Plymouth Church was wealthy and influential. Thomas Beecher was so impressed with the singers that he promised to recommend them to Henry.

George White saw this as a great opportunity to raise not only money but the profile of his singing group. He realized that he needed what today would be called 'brand identity'. Until then, the singers had been advertised simply as 'colored students from Fisk University, Nashville, Tennessee'. Being the deeply religious man that he was, he prayed about the matter after a performance in Columbus, Ohio, and was rewarded with an idea. He would name them the Jubilee Singers, after the Jewish practice of celebrating a year of jubilee.

White's idea came from chapter 25 of Leviticus, where God instructed Moses in the practice of leaving agricultural land fallow one year in every seven. Then, he was told, after seven of these Sabbaths (i.e., after forty-nine years had passed), the whole of the next year was to be a jubilee, heralded by the blast of a trumpet on the Day of Atonement. A jubilee year was to be a time of forgiveness, restoration and cancellation of debts. It was a scheme that sought to avoid the accretion of debt, power, bitterness and, ultimately, corporate sin. It introduced the concept of a fresh start.

It was a fitting choice, because Leviticus was often the Bible book used by slave-owners to justify the practice of slavery, and also because the year of jubilee illustrated the biblical commitment to freedom from oppression. White

could see the clear parallels between the liberties offered to the Jews once they had entered their Promised Land and the liberties that America had promised to its population of former slaves.

And ye shall hallow the fiftieth year, and proclaim liberty throughout all the land unto all the inhabitants thereof: it shall be a jubilee unto you; and ye shall return every man unto his possession, and ye shall return every man unto his family. A jubilee shall that fiftieth year be unto you: ye shall not sow, neither reap that which groweth of itself in it, nor gather the grapes in it of thy vine undressed. For it is the jubilee; it shall be holy unto you: ye shall eat the increase thereof out of the field. In the year of this jubilee ye shall return every man unto his possession ... Ye shall not therefore oppress one another; but thou shalt fear thy God: for I am the Lord your God.
Leviticus 25:10–13, 17

However, White didn't appear to be aware of the musical origins of the Hebrew word *yobel* (jubilee). It referred to the blast of a horn, especially the signal given by silver trumpets, the instrument so often referred to in spirituals. Because he named his group the 'Fisk Jubilee Singers', 'jubilee' became a description for that style of singing; the earliest gospel music was known as 'jubilee singing' and the groups were 'jubilee quartets'.

TO NEW YORK AND THE WHITE HOUSE
The breakthrough performance for the group took place at Beecher's church in Brooklyn on 22 December. The distinguished preacher asked his congregation to 'hear the songs that have been sung by generations of benighted souls, on the plantation, by day and by night – songs that

have enabled the captive to endure his chains, the mother to hope against hope and keep her soul up when all looked black and dark; when she had parted from all she loved, and the iron had entered her soul'.

The Jubilee Singers performed for over twenty minutes. The worshippers had never experienced anything like it. One member compared hearing them to St Paul's ecstatic experience of being caught up into the third heaven. Beecher had tears flowing down his cheeks. The collection plate was filled with over $250, and the invitations started rolling in from other churches. They were invited back to Plymouth Church for a concert, and the American Missionary Association, which had previously maintained a distance from the tour, stepped in to endorse it, asking supporters to seek to raise $20,000

for Fisk. 'Success is sure,' an extremely pleased George White was able to write in his journal. 'It is only a matter of time.'

Not everyone was as enthusiastic as Beecher and his church. Some more sophisticated New Yorkers thought the music was too wild and untutored. In the same way that the advent of rock and roll caused some to fear a descent into barbarism eighty years later, there were those who thought that the Jubilee Singers marked a coarsening of culture. 'Their performance is a burlesque on music, and almost on religion,' commented a critic from the *Musical Gazette*.

We do not consider it consistent with actual piety to sit and be amused at an imitation of the religious worship formerly engaged in by ignorant but Christian people; and as for calling their effort a concert, it is ridiculously

Reverend Henry Ward Beecher, brother to Harriet Beecher Stowe, at Plymouth Church in Brooklyn, where he ministered between 1847 and 1887. He was one of the best-known figures of nineteenth-century America.

absurd. We regret to see that … the appreciation of music is at such a low ebb that [New Yorkers] can enjoy the 'singing' of these well-meaning but unmusical people.

What was beyond doubt was that the Jubilee Singers were creating an impact. For the first time ever, white Americans were able to have a first-hand experience of black American music, and, increasingly, they liked what they saw and heard. The tour progressed into New England, and at Hartford, Connecticut, the great journalist, novelist and wit Mark Twain was in the audience.

Born and raised in the South by a father who owned slaves, Twain knew that the Jubilee Singers were the genuine article, not to be confused with the 'negro minstrels' who tried to entertain white people with a sweet and sanitized version of black music.

It was the first time for twenty-five or thirty years that I had heard such songs, or heard them sung in the genuine old way – and it is a way, I think, that white people cannot imitate – and never can for that matter, for one must have been a slave himself in order to feel what that life was and so convey the pathos of it in the music.

From New England they travelled to Washington DC, the first time any of them had seen such sights as the White House (which they toured) and the then unfinished Washington Monument. They performed at the Lincoln Hall before an audience that included important ambassadors, clergymen and politicians. One of the clergymen commented afterwards: 'They sing the most touching of Christian melodies, full of Jesus, and of heaven; the most wild of plantation melodies, full of sorrow and aspirations for freedom … Their demeanour is graceful and unassuming, and, before they close, the coldest audience is in enthusiasm, and never tires of encoring.'

The day after this conquest they were invited to the White House to sing for President Ulysses S. Grant. It was a brief encounter. Grant welcomed the singers he'd 'read so much of' and wished them a 'glorious success'. They sang 'Go down, Moses', a spiritual with such obvious resonance with the abolition cause. Grant, no great aficionado of music, thanked them politely and explained that he had planned to see them in concert the night before but his vice president, Schuyler Colfax, had gone ahead without taking him.

From Washington the tour headed north back

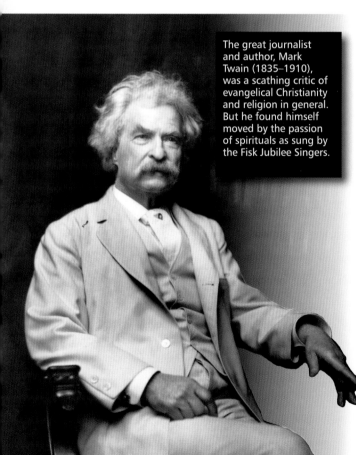

The great journalist and author, Mark Twain (1835–1910), was a scathing critic of evangelical Christianity and religion in general. But he found himself moved by the passion of spirituals as sung by the Fisk Jubilee Singers.

9.
©
A.F. BRADLEY.
N. Y.

through New York and on to Rhode Island, Maine and Vermont. By the end of the six-month tour they had not only paid off Fisk University's debts but raised $20,000 for a site on which to build a permanent new building, to be known as Jubilee Hall. Their return to Nashville was triumphant. They were met at the station by crowds banging on drums and waving banners.

THE FIRST TOUR TO BRITAIN

The Jubilee Singers were only allowed a matter of days to rest before they were taken off on a ten-month tour, which again attacked New England before moving to the unconquered territories of the mid-West. The next big step in their career came in April 1873, when they crossed the Atlantic on a Cunard steamer ship for a tour of Britain. They docked in Liverpool on 23 April, stayed overnight and the next day took a train to London.

Their reception in London illustrated just how far they had come. On their first outing they performed before more than 600 powerful English people – aristocrats, politicians, church leaders – all personally invited by the Duke and Duchess of Argyll. They were introduced on the platform by Lord Shaftesbury, the best-known and most revered reformer of the Victorian age. He, like them, was a fervent Christian, and much of the legislation he introduced into parliament as an MP stemmed from his beliefs. His passion was for the excluded and downtrodden. He campaigned on behalf of the poor, the mentally

Setting the capstone of the Washington Monument. Magazine illustraton, after a sketch by S. H. Nealy. On 6 December 1884, workers placed the 3,300 pound (1.3 t) marble capstone on the Washington Monument, and topped it with a pyramid of cast aluminium, completing the construction of this Egyptian-style obelisk.

ill, animals, slaves, exploited factory workers, the unemployed and the sick. He founded over 200 organizations to improve conditions and was known as 'the social conscience of England'.

The following day they were invited to the home of the duke and duchess, where they were offered the privilege of singing for Queen Victoria, the most powerful leader in the world at that time. They sang 'Steal away' and a chanted version of the Lord's Prayer. The Queen, who would communicate to commoners only through a royal intermediary, then requested another song.

According to one account it was the Civil War song 'John Brown'. According to another it was 'Go down, Moses'. Whichever song it was, she conveyed her delight at their singing. That night, in her private journal, she wrote that the Jubilee Singers had sung 'extremely well together'.

These contacts at the highest levels guaranteed their success in Britain. They sang at the homes of the rich and powerful, at influential churches and cathedrals, at orphanages, temperance meetings and concert halls. William Gladstone, the British prime minister, had them sing at his home on two occasions. When they sang 'Oh how I love Jesus', Gladstone, a religious man, was in tears. 'Isn't it wonderful?' he would ask his guests. 'I never heard anything like it!'

The rest of the tour was equally successful. At the Metropolitan Tabernacle, just south of the River Thames, they sang in front of over 6,000 people. The minister, Charles Spurgeon, the best-known British evangelist and teacher of his era, later said that he had never enjoyed music as much as he had done that day. 'Our friends seem to sing from the heart; their souls are singing right cheerfully, and this gives fire to their music that cannot be in it under other circumstances. They have touched my heart.'

To evangelists they were an invaluable asset: a performing act that was making waves in the news, impacting on everyone from royalty downwards and unashamedly Christian. People who would never normally step inside a church would come to a meeting out of curiosity to see the strange phenomenon of a group of negroes singing their home-grown songs.

American evangelist, Dwight Lyman Moody (1837–99), preaching at the Agricultural Hall in London in 1875. He pioneered large-scale religious meetings and encouraged the use of music to prepare listeners for the sermon.

WITH MOODY AND SANKEY

As they travelled north to cities such as York, Hull and Glasgow, they were invited to take part in open-air revival meetings and evangelistic church services. The most significant of these meetings was in Newcastle, where they met with the American evangelist Dwight L. Moody and his singer Ira D. Sankey. Moody was the first preacher to conceive of mass evangelism, a phenomenon made possible by such new developments as the railways and the first transatlantic cable. He wanted his events to be as appealing as anything show business had to offer.

The group appeared on stage with Moody at a huge revival service, and sang 'There are angels hovering 'round' as the appeal was made for

Their and Mr. Sankey's deep sympathy with the sentiments they utter so melodiously, will elevate the conception of Christian song among us, not as hallowed amusement merely, but elevated and elevating worship. Mr. Moody pronounced the benediction, and Mr. Sankey and the sweet Jubilee Singers burst out from supercharged hearts into joyous, triumphant praise, the likes of which have never been heard.

The Jubilee Singers returned to America in December 1873, but the pattern of intense touring would continue for many years to come, sinners to repent. Moody had no reservations about working on the emotions of a crowd. His relationship with Sankey, the most dominant Christian singer and songwriter of his day, had developed because he believed that music had the power to move people and make them vulnerable, preparing their hearts to receive the gospel.

Moody had already said that the Jubilee Singers had 'stolen his heart' with their music. That night in Newcastle it also did something to the heart of Mabel Lewis, the only member of the group not to have had a conversion experience. She later said that the Holy Spirit overtook her as she sang, and she was reborn.

The Fisk Jubilee Singers crossed paths with Moody and Sankey many more times while they were in Britain. In Edinburgh they stood on the same stage and sang 'Steal away to Jesus', 'There are angels hovering 'round' and 'Depths of mercy'. Rufus Clark, who wrote a book about the campaign, said:

Ira David Sankey (1840–1908) was an American singer and hymn-writer who composed over 1,200 songs and hymns. He accompanied Dwight Moody on his major evangelistic campaigns.

37

with a rapidly changing line-up as singers repeatedly became ill through the strain of travelling or damaged their voices. At the end of their second British tour there was dissension in the ranks. The young vocalists had been so feted and praised in Britain that fame had started to go to their heads. Factions were being created and some of the singers were reckoning that they could either go it alone or form quartets to earn money for themselves rather than for Fisk University.

TOURING THE WORLD

Their third overseas tour, which started in May 1875, took them not only to England, Scotland, Ireland and Wales but to Holland, Switzerland and Germany. While they were in Newcastle, on 1 January 1876, the Jubilee Hall was dedicated in Nashville. It was the largest building in America devoted to the education of black students. The singers didn't return to their home soil until July 1878.

By this time the Jubilee Singers consisted of a pool of musicians rather than a fixed line-up. The novelty value had worn off in America, but the group still toured. In 1886 it set off on its most ambitious tour – six years of travelling around the world. They started in Australia, where, instead of moving from town to town as they had done in Europe, they played long residencies in the major cities – twenty-five nights in Melbourne, sixty in Sydney, forty in Adelaide, and thirty in Brisbane.

They sailed to New Zealand, then to India, Burma, Hong Kong and Japan. The end of the tour marked over twenty years of constant travelling and performing. The music that had been forged in the crucible of slavery had been displayed to the world. The Fisk Jubilee Singers would continue but never again with the novelty value and cultural impact they had enjoyed in the late nineteenth century.

The fundraising task had been completed. Over the first three tours alone they had raised more than $150,000, which, as Andrew Ward calculated in his book *Dark Midnight When I Rise*, represents $2.5 million in today's money. It helped keep the American Missionary Association solvent, built Jubilee Hall (still in use) and contributed to the building of Livingstone Hall, named after the Scottish medical missionary and African explorer David Livingstone (1813–73).

The phonograph, developed by Thomas Edison in 1876, heralded a revolution that would transform the way people consumed music. It would also change the way musicians composed, and the function of music in people's lives. It would create stars and trends, it would enable listening to be a completely private experience

> The invention of the phonograph changed the way in which spirituals could be listened to. What had been created for communal worship was now part of home entertainment.

and it would eventually take spirituals further away from the context of praise and worship and closer to entertainment and business.

The Fisk Jubilee Singers were not among the first artists to be recorded. They didn't make a record until 1909, when a quartet bearing their name recorded for Victor. The group's tenor by this time was John Wesley Work Jr, a pioneering collector and promoter of African American folk music, who was also chairman of the Latin and History departments at Fisk.

The resulting recordings, even though featuring only four voices, are the closest we can get to hearing how the Fisk Jubilee Singers may have sounded thirty years before. What seems striking, to contemporary ears, is how formal the vocals are. The songs are slow and mournful and the enunciation is so perfect that no traces of plantation fervour can be heard. On faster numbers, such as 'Little David, play on your harp' and 'My soul is a witness', there's more release and a suggestion of the style that would later be popularized by groups like the Golden Gate Quartet. Otherwise it's hard to hear what caused so many tears to flow and so many hearts to soften back in the late nineteenth century.

Part of the reason for this must be that we've been exposed to so much more music. We not only have a reasonable idea of how those plantation meetings sounded, but we've experienced jazz, blues, doo wop and rock and roll, forms of music which all, to some degree, owe something to the spirituals but which have dispensed with the old-fashioned sense of restraint.

Yet the Fisk Jubilee Singers were the pioneers who took African American music from the camp meeting to the stage and from the United States to the world. Everyone who has followed, from Mahalia Jackson and the Dixie Hummingbirds to Jessy Dixon and Kirk Franklin, is following in their golden shoes.

Cover page of the *Fisk University News* Jubilee Singers special issue.

CHAPTER

4

Denomination Blues

Not surprisingly, the success of the Fisk Jubilee Singers spawned imitators. By 1872 Gustavas Pike of the American Missionary Association was looking to see if the term 'Jubilee Singers' could be registered as a trademark, and George White was concerned about the existence of a group calling itself the Canaan Jubilee Singers in the New York area. The following year the legendary circus impresario P. T. Barnum proudly added a 'jubilee group' to his Great Travelling World's Fair, boasting that he was 'the first man who has

ever engaged a full Band of Southern Negroes'.

Over the last quarter of the nineteenth century, jubilee groups proliferated, many of them raising money for their colleges and universities as the Fisk Jubilee Singers had done, some of them even embarking on European tours. In 1889 the *Indianapolis Freeman* commented: 'Every college nowadays has its jubilee singers. The latest entry is the Tuskegee Jubilee Singers.' Five years later an advert in a New York newspaper promoted an appearance of 'Asbury's Sunny South Company of Jubilee Singers' at a curio hall in Harlem.

MINSTRELSY

At least four other strands of American music were beginning to coalesce with spirituals to create what would one day be known as gospel music. The first was minstrelsy. In the first half of the nineteenth century, white entertainers 'blacked up' and performed songs that imitated music the writers had heard on the plantations. Often done in a way that mocked the appearance, speech and way of life of the slaves, this was a new form of theatrical

Left: A troop of minstrels at the Empire Theatre, New York, USA, 1904.

Right: A banjo player in a minstrel show. By creating pastiche spirituals, minstrels helped keep the tradition alive at a time when former slaves were seeking greater musical sophistication.

entertainment, the first to have been conceived on American soil. The minstrels' portrayal of black culture was a revelation to most customers, who had no first-hand experience against which to measure it.

After the Civil War, black entertainers and writers got in on the act. After all, if white Americans appreciated this music, why not hear it from those whose culture it was? Again the success of the Jubilee Singers had an impact. Minstrel groups that hadn't previously featured many spirituals in their shows suddenly increased the number of them post-Fisk. Before 1875, for example, the Georgia Minstrels didn't present any religious material, but by 1876 they were featuring a jubilee group interlude and mock spirituals such as 'Oh, Rock o' my soul'.

The African American writer James Blank, whose best-known song was 'Carry me back to old Virginny', parodied 'Golden slippers', a spiritual from the Fisk repertoire, and his comic version, 'Oh, dem golden slippers', became better known than the original. His contemporary Sam Lucas, born to a free black family in Ohio, wrote pastiche songs such as 'Put on my long white robe' and 'De old ship ob Zion'.

Significantly, the jubilee groups and minstrel troupes kept the form of the spiritual alive at a time when black churches were moving away from them. The vogue for personal improvement and self-advancement among blacks meant that European culture was seen as the pinnacle to aspire to, and all things African or reminiscent of slavery days were discarded. The belief was gaining ground that white people appreciated spirituals only because they presented blacks as childlike, naïve, dependent and uncomplicated. They admired them as one would admire a child's painting – not because it was technically proficient but simply because it was created. Those who wanted to get ahead preferred the stirring Protestant hymns or even European sacred music over the spirituals.

When the great vocalist Paul Robeson began performing spirituals in the mid-1920s, much of the form's primitivism had already been expunged. Robeson was an educated man – he'd trained as an attorney – and he had a distinctive bass-baritone voice. His collaborator, the composer and pianist Lawrence Brown, developed new, sophisticated arrangements that transformed these folk songs into material that white middle-class concert-goers felt comfortable with.

But Robeson was no Uncle Tom figure. He was a passionately political man who fought for social justice throughout his life. He saw spirituals as weapons against segregation, because they illustrated the dignity of black people and accurately recorded their hopes and frustrations. He once wrote:

The power of spirit that our people have is intangible, but it is a great force that must be

The bass-baritone singer Paul Robeson brought spirituals and the stories of their origins to the broad American public.

unleashed in the struggles of today. A spirit of steadfast determination, exaltation in the face of trials – it is the very soul of our people that has been formed through the long and weary years of our march toward freedom… That spirit lives in our people's songs – in the sublime grandeur of 'Deep River', in the driving force of 'Jacob's Ladder', in the militancy of 'Joshua Fit the Battle of Jericho', and in the poignant beauty of all of our spirituals.

Robeson played an important role in disseminating spirituals and in broadcasting the story of their origins. His commanding presence, his accomplishments as an actor, athlete and activist, and his acceptability to white audiences contributed to the widespread popularity of such songs as 'Sometimes I feel like a motherless child', 'Nobody knows the troubles I've seen', 'Go down, Moses' and 'Balm in Gilead'.

BARBERSHOP QUARTETS

A second influence contributing to the formation of gospel music was the rise of barbershop quartets. In African American neighbourhoods the barbershop was the place where men and boys would hang out, and they would often go into a back room to sing songs in harmony. The division of lead, soprano, tenor and bass that developed through these sessions was to become the basis of the gospel quartets.

The Dinwiddie Quartet was one of the first such quartets to record. It was founded in 1898 in Dinwiddie County, Virginia, to raise funds for the Dinwiddie Normal and Industrial School, but later performed in vaudeville shows. In October 1902 its four members – Sterling Rex, J. Clarence Meredith, Harry B. Cruder and J. Mantell Thomas – went into the studios of the Victor Talking Machine Company and recorded a selection of six songs: 'Down on the old camp ground', 'Poor mourner', 'Gabriel's trumpet', 'My way is cloudy', 'We'll anchor bye and bye' and 'Steal away'.

Quartet recordings flourished in the first decade of the twentieth century as newly established recording companies scoured America for singing talents to showcase in the developing medium. It was during this time that Victor began recording the Fisk Jubilee Singers. Columbia, the other major record label of the era, answered back by recording the Apollo Jubilee Quartette. They entered a New York studio and cut two tracks – 'Little David' and 'Camp meeting' – but the label's music committee rejected them. They returned and recorded 'Swing low, sweet chariot' and 'Shout all over God's heaven', both of which were accepted; they were released in August 1912.

Quartets developed the style that would characterize gospel singing – the interplay of voices, the intricate harmonies, the pumping bass and the call-and-response structure. Its influence would later extend to harmony groups such as the Mills Brothers and the Ink Spots in the 1930s and 1940s and doo-wop groups of the 1950s such as the Flamingos.

PENTECOSTALISM: THE HOLINESS MEETINGS

A third influence was Pentecostalism. Following emancipation, many black Baptist and Methodist Episcopal churches were established in the South. These tended to be formal, like their white ancestor churches, but within them an ecstatic group flared up and eventually went its own separate way.

The Holiness movement, which, like Methodism, would cite the English preacher John Wesley as its inspiration, emphasized not just personal salvation but personal sanctification. Being 'saved' was the beginning of the process, but what was then needed was a life of obedience towards God that resulted in increased perfection. Some believed that absolute perfection could be achieved. The agent of the process of 'sanctification', or 'holiness', was the Holy Spirit. A focus on the Holy Spirit developed, particularly a focus on the evidence of the presence of the Holy Spirit as described in the biblical account of the Day of Pentecost: 'And they were all filled with the Holy Ghost, and began to speak with other tongues, as the Spirit gave them utterance' (Acts 2:4).

The idea of speaking in another 'tongue', of prophesying, dancing in the Spirit and making a 'joyful noise to the Lord', was congenial to the African American sensibility. The religious rituals of Africa had almost always involved dance, music, prophecy and forms of ecstatic experience, and this movement came closest to supplying a Christian approximation.

The defining moment for the Holiness movement was a series of revival meetings that took place on Azusa Street, Los Angeles, in 1906. At these largely black meetings, which were attended by key Holiness figures, all the restraints broke down. Devotees believed it was the 'pouring forth of the Spirit' referred to in the Old Testament book of Joel, where it was predicted that 'Your sons and your daughters shall prophesy, your old men shall dream dreams, your young men shall see visions' (Joel 2:28). Secular observers thought it was madness.

The Los Angeles Times ran a front-page story on 18 April headlined 'Weird Babel of Tongues'. 'Breathing strange utterances and mouthing a creed which it would seem no sane mortal could understand,' it announced,

the newest religious sect has started in Los Angeles. Meetings are held in a tumble-down shack on Azusa Street, near San Pedro Street, and devotees of the weird doctrine practice the most fanatical rites, preach the wildest theories and work themselves into a state of mad excitement in their peculiar zeal. Colored people and a sprinkling of whites compose the congregation, and night is made hideous in the neighborhood by the howlings of the worshipers who spend hours swaying forth and back in a nerve-racking attitude of prayer and supplication. They claim to have 'the gift of tongues,' and to be able to comprehend the babble.

These meetings are now regarded as the beginning of the American Pentecostal movement. New churches and denominations were started as a direct or indirect result, the Assemblies of God and the Church of God in Christ being two of the best known. The significance for gospel was that the music developed within Pentecostalism wasn't as restricted as that of the Baptists and Methodists. Musical instruments weren't divided into those that could be used for sacred service and those that were of the devil. Pentecostals used pianos, drums, guitars and tambourines. (The Church of God in Christ went on to produce an extraordinarily high percentage of the key gospel music performers.)

Church services could go on for three hours or longer, depending on how the Spirit moved, and there would be clapping, stomping and 'falling out' (collapsing on the ground as a result of spiritual fervour). Rather than being someone who lectured from notes, the Pentecostal preacher was a man of action who sweated, groaned, sang and generally orchestrated the emotions of his congregation. He would wipe his brow with a handkerchief, and his people would urge him on with cries of 'Preach it!' and 'That's right!'

Some of these preachers were so popular that they were asked to record tracks for the same labels that were recording the jubilee quartets. There was not enough time on one side of a 78 r.p.m. disc to preach a normal sermon, so they truncated their speeches and gave them titles that sounded like songs.

One of the most popular of these singing preachers was the Reverend J. M. Gates. His style was to chant extemporaneously in a call-and-response style. At the end of each line there would be some 'Amens' from a small group in the studio, and then at the end of the equivalent of a verse some girls would sing a chorus. Among his better-known tracks were 'Dry bones', 'One thing I know', 'Dying gambler' and 'Death's black train is coming', mini-sermons that often had the melodrama of a cheap novel and the imagery of the blues.

THE ADVENT OF THE BLUES

Indeed, the final ingredient in the gospel mix was the parallel development of the blues. The African American churches took a pretty strict line about what was appropriate for followers of Christ to sing. The word 'spirituals' had been taken from a biblical command to speak to each other using 'psalms and hymns and spiritual songs'(Ephesians 5:19), and it seemed to them that if you were expressing yourself musically yet not in one of these categories, you were sinning.

The difficulty arose because St Paul, the author of the command, was addressing church members and how they should behave in community. The issue under discussion was not personal expression. He certainly was not considering how Christians should act if they found themselves in the business of entertainment or the world of the arts. But in the America of the twentieth century, where the words of songs were often used to capture snapshots of an emotional life or merely to bring a smile to a face, the categories seemed restrictive to some. It meant that songs about such everyday matters as love, weather, injustice, delight, birthdays, food, frustration or injustice were deemed 'worldly'.

This resulted in a division between those who wanted to sing only church songs and those who wanted to sing about life in all its rawness. The black novelist Richard Wright (*Native Son*), in his foreword to Paul Oliver's classic study *The Meaning of the Blues*, surmised that the spirituals were created by 'house slaves', those living and working closest to the plantation homes and therefore more easily influenced by the manners, values and religion of their masters, whereas the blues originated with the slaves working in the fields, who were not so closely involved with white culture.

If the plantations' house slaves were somewhat remote from Christianity, the field slaves were almost completely beyond the pale. And it was from them and their descendants that the devil songs called the blues came – that confounding triptych of the convict, the migrant, the rambler, the steel driver, the ditch digger, the roustabout, the pimp, the prostitute, the urban or rural illiterate outsider.

It appears that the blues grew out of work songs,

field hollers and ballads. When and how this happened, no one can be absolutely sure. The first blues songs were recorded in the 1920s, and if they are representative of the blues as it developed in the early twentieth century, it's a form of music devoted almost exclusively to the 'pleasures of the flesh' – drinking, dancing, fornication – and the downside of those adventures – addiction, exhaustion, rejection, betrayal.

Just as spirituals were an expression of life lived in the presence of God, with the promise of forgiveness and glory ever present, the blues were an expression of life lived without reference to God and often with the threat of hell or the devil. Life is full of problems – cheating partners, poor living conditions, sickness, mistreatment, harassment – but there is no Lord to turn to, so you are faced with the choice of either drinking or weeping.

It could be argued that blues was as much a creation of Christian culture as was gospel. It was the church, after all, that dictated what was sinful and what was righteous. To a great extent the blues accepted that a life of wickedness exacted a price. If being treated mean by a low-down woman was perfectly natural and acceptable, why would a blues singer expect sympathy? The symbols of the devil and hell were also taken from Christian theology, although they may have been built on precedents from West African religions.

The originators of the blues would almost certainly have had a church education. It would have been their introduction not only to music but to the vocabulary of the Bible and the teachings that you reap just what you sow, that judgment falls on the wicked and that the devil prowls around like a roaring lion looking for people to devour. The blues men and women may have lived outside the church, but there was always a bit of the church that lived on inside them.

Charley Patton, one of the first blues artists to record, would sometimes use the word 'Lord' in his songs, but as a rhetorical device rather than a form of address. In 'High Sheriff blues', for example, he concludes that 'It takes booze and blues, Lord, to carry me through'. Bessie Smith, perhaps the greatest female blues singer of the period, says in 'Bleeding heart blues' that she's 'sad', 'lost', 'disgusted', 'blue' and 'heartbroken', but rather than taking her burdens to the Lord she believes that it's time to 'hang your head and begin to cry'.

The blues didn't reflect on a life lived in obedience to God, so it didn't find a home in the church. Blues music became the music of

Bessie Smith (1894–1937) was orphaned at the age of nine but went on to become one of the most influential blues vocalists.

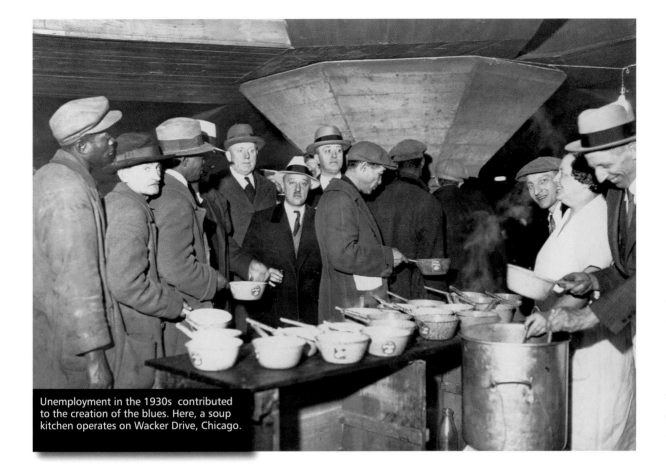

Unemployment in the 1930s contributed to the creation of the blues. Here, a soup kitchen operates on Wacker Drive, Chicago.

those outside the church. It was played in barrel houses, taverns, honky-tonks, brothels, cribs and bars, and so, not surprisingly, the activities that took place in these establishments – drinking, carousing, gambling, dancing and fornicating – came to inform the lyrics. No one goes to a bar wanting to hear a song about repentance or fidelity.

In *The Meaning of the Blues* the great blues expert Paul Oliver collected parts of 350 blues songs to explore their themes. He concluded that the dominant characteristics of the worldview of the blues were guilt, passivity and down-heartedness. Spirituality, family and home – three of the great foci of spirituals – go uncelebrated. Otherworldliness, says Oliver, 'is banned'. Although loved ones are referred to, the family is given 'little or no mention'. Home is 'seldom hymned or celebrated'. Redemption, in the blues, comes instead from the 'sheer force of sensuality'.

The blues faced up to the hardships of life, specifically the life of the poor black person in America, but refused to take refuge in religion. It saw the absence of consolation as a harsh reality. You just had to make good with what you had. The trick was to find enough pleasure to minimize the pain, and then, if you were lucky, there might be just enough left over to make living worthwhile.

'THE DEVIL'S MUSIC'

By the 1920s the division between the blues and spirituals was clear. The blues was for worldly people and those who had fallen away from the church. Spirituals and hymns were for the redeemed. It was this more than any specific belief in an occult connection that led to the blues being referred to as 'the devil's music' and the guitar as 'the devil's instrument'. When bluesmen dabbled in religious songs because of their commercial potential, they would often use a pseudonym. For 'Prayer of death', Charley Patton called himself Elder J. Hadley, and Blind Lemon Jefferson's first two recordings – 'I want to be like Jesus in my heart' and 'All I want is that pure religion' – were released under the name Deacon L. J. Bates. Josh White, one of the few people to have a repertoire that ranged from folk and blues to spirituals and gospel, initially recorded only religious material and was advertised as 'Joshua White – The Singing Christian', because his mother refused to sign his record contract if he sang blues. But once he'd recorded all the spirituals he knew, he started making blues records as Pinewood Tom.

ROBERT JOHNSON AND THE DEAL WITH THE DEVIL

It's possible that when singers were labelled 'the devil's musicians' they developed a curiosity about occultism that they wouldn't have had otherwise. Alan Lomax, who began travelling around America in the 1930s with his father John,

making recordings of different forms of folk music that they feared would die out as radio became more popular, met the mother of legendary blues singer and guitarist Robert Johnson during a trip in 1942. Johnson, perhaps the best-known blues master to refer repeatedly to the devil in his songs, apparently died of poisoning, but fortunately had recorded some tracks for Columbia that were produced by John Hammond (later to play a significant role in introducing gospel music to mainstream audiences).

According to Johnson's mother, the author of 'Hellhound on my trail' and 'Me and the devil blues' developed his early love of music sitting on her knee at church, but as he grew up began hanging out with older boys who didn't belong to the church. They introduced him to the guitar. 'I used to cry over him,' she told Lomax, ''cause I know he was playin' the devil's instruments.'

She was with him as he lay dying, poisoned by either a girlfriend or the girlfriend's jealous lover (the rumours about his death are legion), and apparently he gave her his guitar saying, 'Here, take and hang this thing on the wall, 'cause I done pass all that by. That what got me messed up, Mama. It's the devil's instrument, just like you said. And I don't want it no more.'

Christians may have used this confession as proof that he was demonically driven. After all, one of the best-known myths attached to Johnson is that he did a 'deal with the devil' at the crossroads in rural Mississippi, exchanging his soul for the ability to play blues guitar. However, it's more likely that his conscience was deeply affected by his mother's theology, to the point that he ended up interpreting the events of his life according to it.

GUITAR EVANGELISTS: BLIND WILLIE JOHNSON

The only people who bridged the divide between spirituals and blues were a small number of 'guitar evangelists' who created blues-styled songs with religious words. They were very often blind males who were deacons or preachers – making music and preaching being two of the few occupations open at the time to those who were both black and blind. Besides using their abilities in the church on Sundays they would also sing for money on street corners during the week.

The archetypal blind guitar evangelist was Blind Willie Johnson, born in Brenham, Texas, in 1897. He lost his sight at around the age of seven, either by looking directly at a solar eclipse or when his stepmother threw the caustic solution lye into his face during an argument with his father. The details of his life are sketchy. He had an early ambition to be a preacher but earned his living through his teens and twenties by singing and playing guitar. Unusually for a street singer, his repertoire consisted entirely of spiritual songs.

His style combined the vitality and earthiness of the blues with the solid faith and biblical awareness of the spirituals. His voice, which could switch between tenor and bass, was one of the most distinctive in early blues, and his bottleneck guitar-playing was outstanding. There was recognition of suffering ('Lord, I just can't keep from crying', 'Motherless children have a hard time'), but

Promotional advertizement for American singer, musician and Baptist preacher Blind Willie Johnson (1902–47) on Columbia Records in 1927. Johnson was one of a unique breed of singers who played spirituals in a blues style.

BLIND WILLIE JOHNSON

This new and exclusive Columbia artist, Blind Willie Johnson, sings sacred selections in a way that you have never heard before. Be sure to hear his first record and listen close to that guitar accompaniment. Nothing like it anywhere else.

Record No. 14276-D, 10-inch, 75c

I Know His Blood Can Make Me Whole
Jesus Make Up My Dying Bed

Ask Your Dealer for Latest Race Record Catalog
Columbia Phonograph Company, 1819 Broadway, New York City

Columbia
NEW PROCESS RECORDS
Made the New Way - Electrically
Viva-tonal Recording - The Records without Scratch

there was also hope ('God don't never change').

It wasn't Johnson's intention to subvert the blues. When he started recording in 1927, blues

The Reverend Gary Davis (1896–1972) was a blues singer who became a Baptist minister in 1933. He benefited from the resurgence of interest in American roots music in the 1950s and 1960s.

I was out in the darkness and
I could not see,
Jesus came and he rescued me
He claimed me and gave me victory
Glory, halleloo.
'Oh glory, how happy I am',
The Reverend Gary Davis

hadn't been codified. He would simply have been aware of his love for the sound and his need to express his beliefs. However, in their insistence on personal responsibility and the need for repentance, the words of his songs unwittingly went against the grain. In 'Nobody's fault but mine', for instance, he argued that if he ignored the Bible it would be his own fault if his soul was lost. In 'Soul of a man' he eloquently argued against what philosophers would have termed scientific reductionism:

I saw a crowd stand talking,
I just came up in time,
Was teaching the lawyer, the doctor,
Well a man ain't nothin' but his mind.

Well, I want somebody to tell me,
Answer me if you can,
I want somebody to tell me,
Just what is the soul of a man?

Many of the songs recorded by Johnson were not composed by him. He would take the kernel of a spiritual, an old hymn or a contemporary ballad and make it his own. But they come across with such passion that there's no doubting that he was expressing his point of view. It's said that he was raised as a Baptist but later attended a Church of God in Christ, which might explain his ease with the guitar (COGIC was much more liberal towards musical instruments) and also his growing emphasis on the Holy Spirit.

WASHINGTON PHILLIPS

Another innovative singing evangelist was Washington Phillips, who accompanied himself on a homemade zither-style instrument. Like Blind Willie Johnson, he was from Texas and did all his recording in the late 1920s, but his songs were more didactic – 'The church needs good deacons', 'I am born to preach the gospel', 'What are they doing in heaven today?', 'Train your child'. His best-known song was 'Denomination blues', which mocked the Southern churches for bickering over non-essential doctrines while sinners went to hell.

Well, you can go to your college,
You can go to your school,
But if you ain't got Jesus
You'se an educated fool.
And that's all, I tell you, that's all.
But you better have Jesus,
I tell you that's all.

Others working in the genre, such as Blind Joe Taggart and the Reverend Edward Clayborn, were not as lyrically inventive or as accomplished musically. They were probably more motivated by delivering a message than making music. Arizona Dranes, one of the few women evangelists, had the edge on them with her distinctive, powerful voice and barrel-house style of piano-playing. She was resident pianist for a Church of God in Christ in Texas and cut a number of tracks between 1926 and 1928. She would later become an influence on the gospel singer Sister Rosetta Tharpe.

GARY DAVIS

Others who sang spiritual lyrics to blues formats were musicians who'd learned their craft singing in honky-tonks and on street corners but had returned to the church later in life. The Reverend Gary Davis had always included spirituals in his street act in Harlem because he found that it made it harder for the police to stop him singing or move him on. In 1933 he became a Baptist minister, and devoted his music entirely to religious material.

Like Blind Willie Johnson, he adapted traditional hymns and spirituals, but unlike Johnson he managed to live long enough to reap the rewards of his influence. He was warmly welcomed into the folk scene during the 1950s, and in the 1960s became revered by the rock festival crowd, who loved to hear him perform songs such as 'Let us get together right down here', 'Twelve gates to the city', 'You got to move' and 'When I die I'll live again'. To young whites who'd known only preachers with white teeth and grey polyester suits, the appearance of the Reverend Gary Davis in his pork-pie hat and shades, often with a cigarette in a holder jammed between his teeth, was a revelation.

The traffic between forms of African American music was never one-way. The spirituals informed jazz, but then jazz also informed spirituals. Gospel music drew from the blues and then years later the blues would draw from gospel music, creating a new hybrid they called soul.

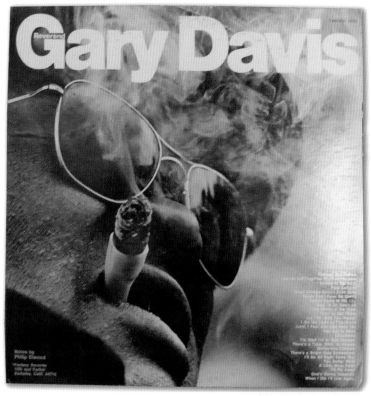

The Reverend Gary Davis combined the rawness of blues with the celebration of spirituals. He was an important influence on white folk musicians of the early 1960s, including Bob Dylan.

CHAPTER

5

Precious Lord

THE FATHER OF GOSPEL MUSIC

Thomas Andrew Dorsey (not to be confused
with the white band leader Tommy Dorsey) is
often referred to as 'the father of gospel music',
a description he revelled in. The ingredients
were all there long before he penned his first
religious number in 1922, but he became the
person who facilitated the mixing.

He didn't coin the terms 'gospel song' and
'gospel singer'. The use of 'gospel' to refer
to music rather than the spoken message is
thought to have originated with the songwriter
Philip Bliss, who in 1874 put together a printed
collection titled *Gospel Songs* to distinguish
them from either psalms or hymns. The year
before, Ira D. Sankey, Dwight L. Moody's music
director, had heard the phrase 'to sing the
gospel' during an evangelistic tour of Britain.

By 1921 the word was
in such common use that
the leading black church
organization, the National
Baptist Convention, published

Thomas
Dorsey,
pictured
at home
in Chicago
in 1976, is
known as
'the father
of gospel
music'.

a song collection with the title *Gospel Pearls*, which included some hymns dating back to Wesley and Watts, some new songs by writers associated with mass evangelism and some spirituals. The aim of the hymnal was to ground people in the best of the old music while stirring

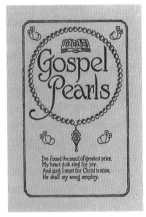

them up with the best of the new. It was in the preface to this collection that the term 'gospel singer' was used for the first time.

But even though Dorsey didn't coin the term he was the person who saw the commercial potential of a form of music that was contemporary in sound and sense, orthodox in theology and capable of being sung in performance rather than only as an act of worship.

What existed before Dorsey were a number of tributaries, often difficult to identify or trace back to a source. What came after him was a mighty river of gospel music, almost all of it owing something to him. From his coaching, writing, performing, directing, organizing and publishing, gospel music grew to be an industry that would soon have its own record labels, publishing houses, writers, conventions, touring circuits, stars and legends. Before Dorsey there were guitar evangelists, singing preachers, jubilee choirs, harmony quartets and sacred soloists, but after Dorsey there was only gospel.

For over sixty years Dorsey presided over the comings and goings of several generations of gospel artists. He was involved in training Mahalia Jackson, who recorded his 'What could I do?' and 'If you see my Saviour'. Marion

Williams had her biggest hit with 'Standing there wondering which way to go'. In 1938 Sister Rosetta Tharpe transformed his 'Hide me in thy bosom' into 'Rock me', a track that anticipated rock and roll by a decade and a half, and the Dixie Hummingbirds started their recording career with a Dorsey song.

Two of his songs – 'Precious Lord, take my hand' and '(There'll be) Peace in the Valley' – became gospel classics and were recorded by almost every gospel act of note, as well as by a few secular artists. 'Precious Lord, take my hand' became the title track of a live album by Aretha Franklin in the 1970s, and Elvis Presley scored a pop hit with 'Peace in the valley' in 1957. Martin Luther King asked for 'Precious Lord, take my hand' to be sung at an evening meal on what turned out to be the day that he died. In recognition of that request, the song was performed at his funeral.

Although Dorsey did make a few recordings his real genius lay not in performing but in organizing conventions, promoting his own song catalogue, and a flair for composition that considered the needs of the listeners and the legitimacy of all forms of popular music. In today's terminology, he saw a gap in the market, and knew enough about showmanship and commerce to be able to fill that gap. He may have been pious in his theological utterances, but when it came down to business he wasn't afraid to exploit his religious songs through all available outlets.

His strength as a songwriter came from the breadth of his musical knowledge. Although he'd been raised in a religious home and knew all the great hymns and spirituals, he was also familiar with vaudeville, jazz, ragtime, country, circus songs and blues, and was able to marry aspects of the secular forms to the sacred content. He knew from experience that the blues addressed people at a deep emotional level, and saw no reason why the observations of a Christian couldn't be matched with a musical style pioneered by people like Charley Patton and Bessie Smith.

UPBRINGING

Dorsey was born in Villa Rica, Georgia, in 1899. His mother, Etta, was a pious woman with musical talent. His father, also named Thomas Dorsey, had trained to be a pastor at Atlanta Baptist College and had become an itinerant preacher, but found he couldn't raise a family on a preacher's income. So, when his son was a small child, Dorsey Sr divided his life between preaching, sharecropping and teaching at a local school.

Dorsey would go on preaching engagements with his father, and this fostered in him a love for the drama of presentation and also a respect for the status then accorded to a preacher in the black community. When alone, he would practise his father's gestures and make up sermons that he imagined delivering. His mother would play the church organ and organize singing sessions at home for neighbours and relatives. Dorsey would later claim that these experiences provided the foundation for his musical career.

In 1909 the family moved from rural Georgia to Atlanta to improve their standard of living, but it didn't work. Dorsey's father's skills as a farm labourer weren't needed in the city and he couldn't find work as a schoolmaster. He ended up doing menial jobs as a gardener and porter. This loss of status had a deep effect on the young Dorsey, who felt he'd known his place in the country but was lost in the city.

He dropped out of school around the age of twelve and began hanging around the theatres on Decatur Street, where the best black entertainers of the day would perform. Here he saw artists such as Bessie Smith (then an unknown teenager), Ma Rainey, Skunton Bowser and Buzzin' Burton, and acquired a taste for show business. His ability to remember tunes meant that after a show he would return home and practise them on his mother's organ. His regular presence on the street led to a job in one of the theatres, selling drinks and popcorn, and this access allowed him to associate with the musicians. He quickly picked up their techniques, and by the age of fourteen he was playing piano at dance halls and bordellos.

He doesn't appear to have commented on whether his parents knew of this work or, if they did, what they thought about it. Although the church was no longer as big a part of their lives as it had been in the country, they still maintained their connection. Dorsey, though, lost all interest in religion at this point. It no longer fitted into his life. 'I felt religion but I didn't want to go to church too often,' he once said. 'I wasn't very religious at that time.'

Michael W. Harris in his study *The Rise of Gospel Blues* conjectures that Dorsey's style of music was formed during this period, since brothels and illegal clubs required performers to play for a long time (three hours was usual), and to keep the music soft so as not to attract the attention of the police and to create a mood of intimacy. The music also had to be mainly improvised.

FROM ATLANTA TO CHICAGO

In 1916 Dorsey left Atlanta for Chicago, the main destination for blacks wanting to escape poverty

The Chicago of the 1930s was a city of hope for displaced Southern blacks. It was also a crucible for blues, jazz and gospel.

and racism in the South. For a while he was unsettled there, returning home frequently, but by 1919 it became his permanent home. As in Atlanta, he began scuffling around music venues offering his services as a piano-player, but also, wisely, now taking lessons in composition and arrangement. He knew that he'd eventually earn more money if he could read and write music. In 1920 he registered his first composition, 'If you don't believe I'm leaving, you can count the days I'm gone'.

It was in the following year that he had the first of a series of religious experiences that would eventually draw him back into the church. An uncle invited him to the National Baptist Convention in Chicago. Dorsey didn't want to go, but was finally persuaded, and found himself taken by surprise during the performance of a song called 'I do; don't you?', performed by W. M. Nix, a member of the convention's music committee.

The song was written by a white hymn-writer, Edmund O. Excell, and was being performed to promote *Gospel Pearls*, the convention's new hymnal. Dorsey was moved not just by Nix's performance, which contained embellishments that he recognized from his experience with the blues, but by the words, that were so simple and direct and yet contained a gospel challenge:

I know a great Saviour, I do; don't you?
I live by his favour, I do; don't you?
For grace I implore him,
I worship before him,
I love and adore him, I do; don't you?

'My inner being was thrilled,' he told Michael W. Harris when recounting the experience. 'My soul was a deluge of divine rapture; my emotions were aroused; my heart was inspired to become

a great singer and worker in the Kingdom of the Lord – and impress people just as this great singer did that Sunday morning.'

In emulation of the contemporary songs in *Gospel Pearls*, Dorsey began composing religious songs and attending New Hope Baptist Church on Chicago's South Side. His fervour, however, was short-lived. His goal – to 'impress people' – was for his own attainment and glory. He'd become his church's director of music, but as soon as something more alluring came along – in this case a job with a group called the Whispering Syncopators – he abandoned it.

He continued writing in the blues genre, and one of his songs, 'Riverside blues', was recorded by King Oliver, a great jazz band leader of the era. It was a tremendous boost for Dorsey and earned him his first press coverage. In April 1924 he joined the celebrated blues singer Ma Rainey, playing with and directing her permanent touring band the Wild Cats. This gave him a unique perspective on contemporary entertainment. Until this time he'd been playing to small audiences, most of whom weren't there for the music. With Ma Rainey he was appearing in legitimate theatres and performing for customers who had paid to see a performance.

MA RAINEY

Ma Rainey, born in 1886 in Georgia, was justifiably known as 'the mother of the blues'. Leroi Jones has called her 'one of the most imitated and influential classic blues singers', and she was responsible for grooming that other great and influential blues singer, Bessie Smith. When she first heard the blues, in 1902, she'd never heard anything like it. She was performing with the Rabbit Foot Minstrels, a vaudeville troupe, in Missouri, when she heard a local girl sing about how her man had left her. Everyone in her group was so stunned by the song that Rainey worked it into her act. She later described it as 'strange and poignant', an indication that even if she wasn't actually present at the birth of the blues, she was one of the earliest singers to recognize it and introduce it to a wider audience.

Rough country blues was made on acoustic guitars. The theatrical urban blues, as with Ma Rainey, involved a jazz band with a director. She would perform the rural blues of Georgia, the city blues of Chicago, and a few vaudeville numbers, and then let her band play instrumentals. This show gave Dorsey the opportunity to hone his abilities not only as a musician but as an arranger. He would stand while playing the piano, something of an innovation at the time, and learned about timing, presentation and stage presence.

Much of what he would later give to gospel music was acquired while with Ma Rainey. Most significantly he saw how the blues connected with an audience who experienced the same feelings but were unable to express them. When people heard songs like 'Jealous-hearted blues', 'Hear me talking to you' or 'Don't fish in my sea', they identified with

Ma Rainey and her band in 1923, with a young Thomas Dorsey leaning over the keyboard.

the sense of injustice, betrayal or infidelity so profoundly that there was a collective sense of release and cleansing. Dorsey saw women so connected with the music that they'd jump up and shout as if they were in church, shouting 'Sing it' rather than 'Amen'. 'What we call low-down in blues doesn't mean that it's dirty or bad or something like that,' he told Michael W. Harris. 'It gets down into the individual to set him on fire, dig him up or dig her up way down there 'til they come out with an expression verbally.'

THE BREAKDOWN

Everything went well with Ma Rainey until 1926, when Dorsey had a breakdown. It started with stage fright but quickly led to an inability to work at all. He was plunged into a deep depression, the end of which came only when he recommitted his life to the spiritual path he had decided on in 1921. One of the results of this change was the writing of his first gospel blues song, 'If you see my Saviour, tell him that you saw me'.

The song, like a blues song, grew out of painful personal experience. His illness had lasted for two years, during which time he'd been nursed by his wife. In the apartment above lived a young taxi-driver, who suddenly fell ill one night. The Dorseys comforted him in his bed, and the next morning the man was taken into hospital. Within hours he was dead. Dorsey found it hard to comprehend that his neighbour had been ill for such a short time and yet had died. 'If you see my Saviour' was his instant personal response, a song addressed to the man he'd briefly nursed.

Dorsey was never conflicted about the legitimacy of the blues. He saw it not as a genre

that could be either all right or all wrong, but as a universal feeling of loss. The saved as well as the unsaved got the blues. The blues was a truth about the human condition and therefore perfectly acceptable in sacred song. 'I don't see anything wrong with the blues unless you use vulgarity in it,' he said. 'But, the blues itself? The music itself? It can't hurt. It can do more good than it can do harm.'

For his gospel songs he took what he called 'the trills, turns, movements, tempo, lilt, expression and feeling' of the blues and matched them with different sentiments. 'You use different words,' he once said, 'and then you take that blue moan and what they call the low-down feeling tunes and you shape them up and put them up here and make them serve the other purpose, the religious purpose.'

Between 1928 and 1932 he continued writing blues while experimenting further with gospel, and not all of his blues songs would escape the charge of vulgarity. His best-known composition from this period, written with Hudson Whitaker, was 'It's tight like that', and this was followed by a number of other *double entendre* songs such as 'Pat that bread', 'You got that stuff', 'It's all worn out' and 'Somebody's been using that thing'. He recorded and performed these songs as Georgia Tom, partnered with Whitaker, who became known as Tampa Red.

THE 1930 NATIONAL BAPTIST CONVENTION

He eventually stopped writing blues songs not because of a crisis of conscience but because he realized his potential for making a mark in religious music was greater. The turning point was the 1930 National Baptist Convention in Chicago. Many of his religious songs were well known by then, and some had appeared in hymnals, but he hadn't been socializing in places where he could bask in the acclaim. At the convention a singer named Willie Mae Fisher sang his song 'If you see my Saviour', and Dorsey was able to set up a stand and sell over 4,000 copies of the sheet music.

From that point on Dorsey's variety of gospel blues seeped into the consciousness of the black church, particularly in his home city of Chicago. But the acceptance didn't come without a struggle. A cultural divide existed between the storefront churches that encouraged the emotional style of worship brought up from the South and the large urban churches that prided themselves on sophistication. These churches wanted to distance themselves from anything that smacked of primitivism.

THE EBENEZER CHURCH AND THEODORE FRYE

In 1931 Dorsey began working with a gospel chorus at Ebenezer Baptist Church along with soloist Theodore Frye. Although Ebenezer was an inner-city church, its minister was sympathetic to the sounds of old-time Southern religion. While the Ebenezer Senior Choir performed more restrained music at the Sunday services, the minister allowed the more informal Ebenezer Gospel Chorus to play in the older style at Friday-night meetings. This provided Dorsey with the opportunity to develop his vision of gospel blues, a music that looked for its inspiration not to the concert halls of Europe but to the plantation huts, Southern churches, jazz clubs, theatres and bordellos of the South.

Frye was the perfect choice to head up Dorsey's experiment because, besides being a singer, he was a preacher with a commanding stage presence. He could strut across the stage in a way that excited a congregation and had a bluesy moan in his voice that turned hymns into songs. News of what was happening at Ebenezer spread to other churches in Chicago. Dorsey was invited to bring the Chorus to Pilgrim Baptist Church, where the minister was so impressed that he poached him. Dorsey became the musical director at Pilgrim, a position he occupied until the end of his long life.

These gospel choruses could explore the new church music that Dorsey was pioneering without interference, while the senior choirs performed the more traditional anthems, hymns and classical pieces. Edward Boatener, director of Pilgrim's senior choir at the time, was one of those who doubted the value of the new gospel style. 'I felt it was degrading,' he told Michael W. Harris over forty years later.

> How can something that's jazzy give a religious feeling? If you're in a club downtown … that's all right. That's where it belongs. But how can you associate that with God's word? It's a desecration. The only people who think it isn't a desecration are the people who haven't had any training, any musical training – people who haven't heard fine religious anthems, cantatas, and oratorios.

THE NATIONAL CONVENTION OF GOSPEL CHOIRS AND CHORUSES

Yet the new gospel was proving to be unstoppable. Gospel choruses were started in churches all over Chicago. In 1932 Dorsey and one of his singers, Sallie Martin, established the Gospel Choral Union, which in 1933 became the National Convention of Gospel Choirs and Choruses, specifically designed to encourage the dissemination of the new music. The first meeting, held at Pilgrim Baptist Church, attracted over 3,000, and the organization became the engine room of the gospel phenomenon.

To the annual conventions would come all the great gospel stars of the future – male and female soloists, choirs, choruses, quartets. It was an opportunity to network, hear new songs, see new acts and receive an education in playing, singing or arranging. By 1937 Dorsey had become such a part of the aristocracy of black church music that he was asked to direct the choir for the National Baptist Convention in Los Angeles. The most popular song of the whole event was 'Take my hand, precious Lord', a song that he'd composed after losing his wife and then his infant son. It was a compelling blend of orthodox religious sentiment and low-down blues that satisfied both the urban sophisticate and the old-time religionist.

In 1937 the first two recordings of 'Take my hand, precious Lord' were made. There was a Decca recording by Elder Beck and one on Bluebird by the Heavenly Gospel Singers. The following year Sister Rosetta Tharpe recorded a version of 'Hide me in thy bosom', which she re-titled 'Rock me'. He hadn't invented gospel music with an eye on the secular recording industry, but many opportunities were opening up.

He had seen himself principally as a writer of songs that would be published and used throughout the black church in America. To that end, during 1932–44 he toured the country putting on events under the title 'An Evening with Dorsey', during which he would introduce his latest songs. He would take with him singers he had trained, principally the vocalists Sallie Martin and Theodore Frye. They would demonstrate his songs, and afterwards the sheet music and songbooks would be sold.

Sallie Martin became indispensable to the whole operation. She had great administrative abilities and established Dorsey's publishing companies and worked out his accounts. Highly committed in her faith and uncompromising in her values, she would later establish herself as one of the most formidable forces in the gospel business. She became head of the largest black-owned gospel publishing company, Martin and Morris, and formed her own group, the Sallie Martin Singers, to sell its compositions.

Dorsey's revolution made everything else possible. It provided the template for a new style of religious song, the publishing houses to market the sheet music, the network of churches keen to experiment with gospel and the convention to hold everything together. Within a short time gospel music would make itself felt in the world of recorded sound.

Interview with Thomas A. Dorsey (1899–1993), Chicago, April 1976

❉ **How did you start in music?**

I was a blues writer, singer and musician. In fact, I was also in bands. I was Ma Rainey's band leader. I was with her while she travelled the country and I wrote quite a number of blues for her at that time. Music has been my business all my life wherever I could get into it or get to it. My mother was an organist in one of the country churches when I was a little fellow and my father was an itinerant preacher travelling from place to place and sometimes he'd take me along as company. In that way I got my experience; quite a bit of it for music, quite a bit of it for travel, quite a bit of it for liking to meet people.

❉ **As church people, did your parents approve of you playing the blues?**

People used to look down on the blues as if it was something bad, naughty or degrading. Anything is degrading if you make it degrading. But blues? My definition of the blues is that it's nothing but a good woman feeling bad or a good man feeling bad. That's all. They're blue! They gave many definitions for the word 'blue' but blues is a good heart broken; a good man or a good woman feeling bad.

❉ **How did your conversion happen?**

I just felt that I needed to be saved! That's all. I couldn't work at it then. I had to work at whatever would pay off but that didn't stop me from treating people right and serving God. I think most people don't understand Christianity. You got to keep your head straight up in the air and keep your toes straight on your feet, but that's not Christianity. Christianity comes from within. If your heart is right, if you're following Christ, you can become a Christian.

❉ **You became a Christian after hearing a song, didn't you?**

Yes. It was called 'I do; don't you?' There was a Baptist convention up the street from where I was living. I was playing rags and blues at parties and things on Saturday nights. There was a fellow who came to the convention by the name of Nix who stayed with my uncle, and he got up one night and sang 'I know a great Saviour, I do; don't you?' After he'd finished, the minister said that anyone could join the church. If you were interested they would send you to a church of your choice. I thought, 'Here's my chance.' I was playing jazz music. In fact, I was working in clubs. So I quit. I walked off my job.

❉ **Your best-known song is 'Take my hand, precious Lord'. Tell me how you wrote it.**

When my first wife was going to become a mother I went to carry out some engagements in St Louis. We were in church one night having a gospel programme when I got a telegram. I read it and it said, 'Your wife just died.' So we left that night after the service and drove back to Chicago. When we arrived I got out of the car and ran to the house and it was so. The body hadn't been moved. I found a baby boy there, a healthy-looking fellow, but the bad part about it is that, that night, the baby died. I was ready to cuss God out, along with anyone else that came my way, but I didn't, and I can see now what all that was for. That was for me. If that hadn't happened I wouldn't be what I am today. I wouldn't have 'Precious Lord'. That's how that song came about. I was rehearsing with Theodore Frye and I was singing 'Blessed Lord, blessed Lord'. I said, 'Come on, Frye. Hear this here. See what you think of it.' He said, 'Oh no. Don't call it "Blessed Lord". Call it "Precious Lord"'. I said, 'That does sound better, doesn't it?' So I called it 'Precious Lord'. And from there I went on to make an arrangement. I had some fly copies printed, went out the next Sunday to churches with it and they went wild. I sold all the copies I had for 10 cents a copy. 'Precious Lord' has been going ever since.

❋ A lot of people write and sing gospel songs today.

I started it. I named them gospel songs. They used to call them hymns or church songs. But gospel means 'good news', and if you read 'gospel' in the modern Bibles it says 'good news'. If it's good news, it's good news for everybody, no matter how it's delivered. You can sing it. I once went into a church and they almost threw me out because I wanted to sing one of my gospel songs. The people accepted it in such a great way that the preacher denounced it, saying, 'You can't sing no gospel! You can only preach it.' I wanted to tell him that that was a lie, but I didn't.

❋ What is the good news?

The gospel! That's why the Saviour came here. He came to bring good news to the world. That's what Christ came for. That's what these songs impart. That's what they convey. The message that we're trying to get into the world is that Christ died for all and that he's alive again for all mankind. It's good gospel wherever you hear it. You hear it and you want to expound it or put it out yourself. You can say 'Christ died for sinners' any way you want to put it.

❋ Are gospel songs for the converted or the unconverted?

They're for everybody. Many of those who are already converted need uplifting. They need a shot in the arm. As far as I know my kind of gospel song has brought folk back to the church, back to Christianity.

❋ Some gospel singers have been criticized for not living the way Christians are expected to live. You wrote a song called 'I'm gonna live the life I sing about in my songs'. Tell me about this.

Many gospel singers, as they call themselves, sing to make a living. They ain't bothered about their souls or the souls of other folks. They sing, they shout and they comment so that they can get part of that cash box. But what if there was no cash box? Would they still do it? I would. It wouldn't make any difference to me. I was so poor I had to work my head off and God blessed me with an idea and the idea swept the world.

❋ What were your favourite hymns when you were a child?

I went to school in a one-room building. They taught three grades in that room. We used to sing all the songs there. That's going back to 1905. I used to like the Watts hymns. He was a good hymn-writer. I loved the meaning and the feeling of hymns like 'Must Jesus bear the cross alone?'

❀ When you started there was no gospel music to imitate?

No. I created the style.

❀ What did you think gospel songs would have that the hymns didn't?

In the first place they had a beat. Some of them had a tempo. Some had simple good news. They weren't written in flowery English that was so high that the ignorant people couldn't understand. It was just time for a change.

❀ Soul music has obviously borrowed a lot from gospel. What is your opinion of soul music?

Soul music? Can you define it for me? Even the man who gave it a name can't define it. They just needed a name to touch the people. What they mean is that it's something that gets deeper inside of you than the ordinary.

❀ Some say that it's like gospel music without God.

Without God you can do nothing. You can't have no music, no soul or no nothin'. If we were to put God in all of our plans it wouldn't be such a hard world to live in. There are so many that don't want God and they have so many different gods.

❀ Aretha Franklin started by singing gospel and now she sings love songs.

I'm not against that, but I think it's done more for the monetary increase in life. I'm glad I came over to the gospel. I know this is the best over here. Without it I'd have been dead a long time ago. If they hadn't worked me to death, I'd have died a natural death. You see, I'm working for myself and God now.

❀ Music is a universal language.

Music has something that will draw; it has something that will soothe; it has something that will attract; it has something that will get inside a person quicker than anything else. It can do you more good than a dose of medicine.

❀ What should I look for if I want to find real gospel?

You have it here with me. I'm real gospel. If you're gonna define gospel, take the King James Version of the Bible and it'll tell you that gospel is good news. That's all it is. It's good news coming to you that makes you happy, helps you be saved and helps you surmount all of life's problems. About all we need is good news. All we get in the newspapers and on radio and television is bad news.

❀ Would it be gospel if the price of gasoline dropped?

No.

❀ It would be good news, wouldn't it?

It's good news, but we're talking about good news coming from the connection with the Saviour. These folks are singing about heaven. There are some good things here too.

DORSEY'S
SONGS WITH A MESSAGE
No. 1
New and Familiar Gospel Songs for All Religious Occasions

DEDICATED
for the love
MAGNOLIA LEWIS BUTTS
mother of the
Convention

Price $1.00

Published by
THOMAS A. DORSEY, Publisher
4154 So. Ellis Avenue
Chicago, Illinois 60653

A Dorsey songbook, given by Dorsey to the author at the time of this interview.

CHAPTER
6

Standing on the Highway

THE TRIUMPH OF THE MALE QUARTET

Four young men stand before a church congregation. They wear identical double-breasted suits, each with a coloured handkerchief in the breast pocket. They have neckties, white shirts and highly polished black brogue shoes. The singer on the left, who is taller than the rest, is singing tenor, while his three friends are chiming in with interlacing vocals. They hardly move from their positions,

This was the type of highway that groups travelled on in the pre-war years. The photo was taken outside San Francisco in 1925.

although they use their hands to underline certain phrases, but the impact of their voices is powerful.

The group is presenting not hymns but a mixture of adapted spirituals and hot-off-the-press gospel tunes. For the church, this is a new experience. The people in the pews are used to singing congregationally and listening to the choir or the chorus, but not to watching an all-male group. Some folks say that the devil is slipping into the church through the back door and that this gospel music is mere worldly entertainment in disguise. Other folks, mostly the young, think it makes church more exciting.

In this Southern city, gospel groups are being formed every week. The singers are mostly in their teens and met each other at church or school. They call themselves the Heavenly this, the Golden that or the Echoes of something else, and get to perform during Sunday services or at one of the 'programmes' organized in an outside venue by several churches. Some of the groups are successful enough to play in other towns and some even travel to neighbouring states. The best of them return home with some money in their pockets.

During the 1930s gospel music was consolidating its style. The focus had initially been on choruses, choirs and soloists, but it would be male quartets who would pioneer the new sound on record and in concert. No one knows exactly when black quartets were developed, but they existed even during slavery. The Swedish author and early feminist Frederika Bremer, who spent two years travelling through America in the mid-nineteenth century to research the effects of democracy, heard slaves singing in Virginia in 1851 and commented that

'they sang quartettes … in such perfect harmony, and with such exquisite feeling, that it was difficult to believe them self-taught'.

The authors of the classic 1867 anthology *Slave Songs of the United States* stated in their introduction: 'The voices of the coloured people have a peculiar quality that nothing can imitate; and the intonations and delicate variations of even one singer cannot be reproduced on paper.' They noted that although the singers didn't sing parts, as in European music, no two singers appeared to sing the same thing. 'The leading singer starts the words of each verse, often improvising, and the others, who "base" him, as it is called, strike in with the refrain, or even join in the solo, when the words are familiar.'

Minstrel troupes, as already mentioned, began to create quartets and after the success of the Fisk Jubilee Singers groups emerged to sing spirituals and were known as jubilee quartets. James Weldon Johnson, the poet and collector of spirituals, could remember the singing groups of his Florida childhood in the late nineteenth century. 'Pick up four coloured boys or young men anywhere,' he wrote, 'and the chances are ninety out of a hundred that you have a quartet. Let one of them sing the melody and others will naturally find the parts. Indeed, it may be said that all male Negro youth of the United States is divided into quartets.'

Jubilee quartets were being recorded at the time of Johnson's reminiscences, but over the next twenty or thirty years the style had hardly developed. They sang unaccompanied, kept close harmony, enunciated clearly and relied on a repertoire of favourite hymns and spirituals. Even though the songs had originated in the fervour of the meeting houses or the sweat and

and Kenneth Morris. Line-ups expanded to include six or seven ('quartet' became a description of the style rather than the exact number in a group), movement on stage replaced the old 'flat-footed' style, singers began to improvise and sing behind the beat, and, over time, the anonymous group appearance would give way to a collection of individuals.

THE MEMPHIS EXPERIENCE

Every city had its top-rated gospel outfits and their individual sound bore regional distinctions. In *Happy in the Service of the Lord*, his detailed study of 'African-American sacred vocal harmony quartets in Memphis', Kip Lornell was able to track down information on eighty-one quartets founded in the city. Seven were formed in the 1920s, twenty-seven in the 1930s, twenty-six in the 1940s, sixteen in the 1950s and only five since then. Of all these, only three could be counted as professional groups, eight were semi-professional and the rest never rose beyond amateur status. Only 25 per cent of the groups ever made a record.

dust of the cotton fields they were delivered with precision and self-control, perhaps with the intention of showing the white folks that they were as capable of great art as any group of white singers.

EVOLUTION

The first gospel quartets were jubilee groups who took the then daring step of supplementing the old material with the new-fangled songs of writers such as Thomas Dorsey, Lucie Campbell

Lornell took six of these acts and looked at their schedules during the 1940s. He found that almost all of their dates were within a 100-mile radius of Memphis, and most were in the northwest corner of Mississippi. When he looked into the birthplaces of thirty-nine singers from Memphis quartets he discovered that most were in the same area, suggesting that groups tended to play in places where there were family connections. Typically an invitation to play would be procured through an old friend or relative.

The majority of the groups (fifty-five out of the eighty-one) were together for ten years or less, but some of the rest had managed to exist for as long as twenty, thirty and even forty years. However, the groups with longevity tended to undergo frequent personnel changes. For example, the most successful Memphis quartet, the Spirit of Memphis, can claim to have been in existence since 1930, yet of seven members photographed together in 1936, only two of them were still in the group in 1983. Three of the most significant members of the group, lead singers Silas Steele, Little Ax (Wilbur Broadnax) and Jet Bledsoe, were with the group only during its peak years in the 1950s. In its thirty-five-year recording career, there were almost twenty changes of line-up.

Memphis quartets, like any others, were affected by the Depression and World War II, which plunged the recording industry into crisis, first through lack of finance and then through the diversion of materials to munitions factories. Of the nineteen Memphis quartets that recorded, only one had done so before the war. The Spirit of Memphis had been around for almost two decades when it first went into the studio in 1949

to record 'Happy in the service of the Lord'.

THE DIXIE HUMMINGBIRDS

The story of the Dixie Hummingbirds, one of the most influential quartets in gospel history, illustrates this period well, and introduces most of the key players. Like so many quartets, its foundation was in the choir of a church, in this case a Holiness church in Greenville, South Carolina. It originally consisted of the founder, James Davis (tenor), Barney Parks (baritone), Fred Owens (bass) and Bonnie Gipson Jr (lead). The group had no uniforms or instruments, and learned its craft by singing at church on Sunday evenings, later being invited by other churches to appear on their programmes. They were known as the Junior Boys because they belonged to the junior choir. Later they changed their name to the Sterling High School Quartet, and then, on leaving school, to the Dixie Hummingbirds.

At first they performed as amateurs and then as semi-professionals, until finally becoming one of the few groups to be able to live entirely from their income as performers. They decided to turn professional after seeing the Heavenly Gospel Singers, a quartet formed in Detroit in the late 1920s, who could command ticket prices of 25 cents when they played Greenville instead of the traditional 15 cents. It made the Hummingbirds aware that a higher fee could actually make a group appear more desirable. (When the Soul Stirrers came to Memphis in 1938 they were able to charge a dollar a ticket.)

The Detroit group was inspirational in another way. Every region had its own style and it was only when groups travelled that they became exposed to these differences. The Dixie Hummingbirds, being from the Carolinas,

The classic Dixie Hummingbirds line-up, c. 1953. *Front row (left to right)*: Howard Carroll, Ira Tucker, James Walker, Thomson Beachey. *Back row (left to right)*: James Davis, William Bobo.

had been raised on close harmonies, but the Heavenly Gospel Singers adopted the Northern, urban style, where lead singers were encouraged to break away from the rest of the group and improvise. Bass

The Heavenly Gospel Singers. A gospel quartet from Spartanburg that competed against the Dixie Hummingbirds.

singers also became stars in their own right. Jimmy Bryant of the Heavenlys clowned around on stage and developed a percussive vocal style that would create hysteria among congregations.

COMPETING FOR GOD

Gospel music had been designed to aid worship and evangelism but from the earliest days there was a parallel incentive to entertain and to impress. Groups would be judged by hearts thrilled rather than by souls saved or spirits refreshed. The wilder the reaction of the listeners, the more successful the group was deemed to have been. There followed a practice

of what were effectively gospel slams. Groups would be given two, possibly three numbers in a tightly scheduled programme, and the winner would be the act that wound the audience up the most.

For some of the more pious groups these contests bordered on the sacrilegious. How could you compete with fellow performers if your shared goal was to bring glory to God? Was it right to whip up the emotions of an audience or a congregation through a highly charged theatrical presentation, claim it was all an act of the Holy Ghost and then gain personal acclaim and reward for your role? Lornell believes that the 'song battles' or 'quartet contests' were the first indication of gospel music adopting secular values, moving away from the ideals of fellowship and ministry towards individualism and competition.

The Heavenly Gospel Singers and the Dixie Hummingbirds would frequently find themselves on the same bills in the Carolinas, and as they competed against each other they developed new crowd-pleasing tricks and gimmicks. The rivalry spurred them on to seek out new songs, more complex harmonies and more dynamic presentation. In 1938 the highly talented Jimmy Bryant left the Heavenlys to join the Dixie Hummingbirds and was replaced by William Bobo. Later Bobo also joined the Hummingbirds.

At this time the Hummingbirds were working mainly with spirituals that they had pulled apart and reassembled – 'Ezekiel saw the wheel', 'Swing low, sweet chariot', 'Motherless children', 'Where was Moses?', 'Moving up that shining way'. The advent of radio meant that everyone could now monitor developments in style that would once have been known only within the regions where they took place. The Hummingbirds began to realize the rich palette of vocal possibilities available to them; bending notes, changing tempos, weaving tapestries from punctuated interjections.

Because they performed *a cappella* they could rehearse anywhere, and some of their most exciting vocal discoveries were made in motel rooms or in their borrowed cars (usually Model A Fords) while travelling between venues. The spreading of their fame meant that work took them away from the small country churches of North and South Carolina and into the nearby states of West Virginia, Georgia, Pennsylvania and the northern part of Florida.

During segregation and before the construction of interstate freeways, travelling was fraught with difficulties for gospel groups. Musicians could be turned away from motels and restaurants or threatened by white racists. Once, in Tavares, Florida, a white man pulled a gun when one of them tried to buy a candy bar from a store. Car journeys were long and uncomfortable, and in the absence of road managers the musicians had to take it in turns to drive.

Only a few promoters specializing in gospel existed in the 1930s. Bookings for the Hummingbirds were the responsibility of baritone Barney Parks. The preferred strategy of the group was to base itself in a major town from which to reach out into the surrounding communities by approaching churches directly. If there was a local radio station, they'd drive up, introduce themselves to the manager and inevitably get themselves a spot that would help broadcast their music and their upcoming performances. Their income at this stage came from collections or tickets sold on the door.

The biggest temptation for a group as vocally accomplished as the Hummingbirds was to forsake gospel for pop, because the audience was bigger and there were more outlets. Black vocal groups were starting to become popular. The best known were the Mills Brothers, who'd started their own radio show on CBS in 1930, and the Ink Spots, who'd made their TV debut in 1936. These groups were championed by the great band leaders of the era – the Ink Spots by Paul Whiteman, the Mills Brothers by Duke Ellington – and their fame was greater than that of any gospel group. But the Hummingbirds held on to their conviction that they were involved in a spiritual ministry.

The Happyland Jubilee Singers, which contained the nucleus of the Blind Boys of Alabama.

CUTTING A RECORD

They weren't against making records. Although they never expected to make money from them, they knew that a recording carried prestige and could advertise them on the radio when they were elsewhere. They were picked up by Decca Records, one of America's major companies, and were invited to New York in 1939 to cut a number of tracks that would be suitable for release as singles.

The choice of sixteen songs that they recorded was indicative of the changes that were taking place in gospel. The bulk of the material was made up of spiritual songs possibly written in the twentieth century. They were neither the spirituals sung by the slaves, nor traditional hymns. For example, they recorded two songs that Blind Willie Johnson had been singing in the 1920s: 'Motherless children have a hard time' and 'Book of the seven seas'. 'Book of the seven seas' should actually be 'Book of the seven seals', as it refers to the scroll held by God in Revelation 5, and Johnson had recorded a version of it known as 'John the Revelator'. 'Wouldn't mind dying' was first performed by the spiritual blues singer Blind Mamie Forehand in 1927, and some credit her as author. 'Joshua journeyed to Jericho' was a song of which James Davis said, 'I don't know where the song came from. I just know we did it.'

But in addition to these old numbers they recorded two songs by Thomas Dorsey – 'When the gates swing open' and 'Little wooden church'. Although they weren't the first group to record Dorsey's songs (the Blue Jay Quartet had cut 'If you see my Saviour' in 1931), they were among the first, and the recordings anticipated the changes that would take place in gospel music after the war. Significantly, 'When the gates swing open' was chosen as the A side of the group's first single.

In style the Hummingbirds were still conforming to their jubilee background. The songs were slow and mournful, sometimes sounding as though they were being played back at the wrong speed, and you could almost hear the lack of movement in their bodies. They sounded as though they had been bolted to the ground. The excitement of their performance at the time was restricted to the intricacies of the vocals and the play between each singer.

IRA TUCKER JOINS

Shortly after this debut, they picked up a new baritone singer, Ira Tucker from Spartanburg. He would bring innovations to the group that would revolutionize gospel quartet singing. Only thirteen at the time, he had absorbed musical influences from a variety of sources. He enjoyed the white country gospel of the Chuck Wagon Gang and Tennessee Ernie Ford, church choirs, the blues played by a local musician known as Blind Simmie, the street-corner singing he heard in his neighbourhood and quartets such as the Norfolk Jubilee Quartet and the Spartanburg Famous Four.

Tucker was particularly impressed by the lead tenors of these groups – Norman 'Crip' Harris of the Norfolks and Buster 'Bus' Porter of the Famous Four. Both men were at the time extending the boundaries of quartet singing – Harris through his sophisticated arrangements and use of barbershop chords, Porter through his note-stretching, moaning, improvisation and ability to switch between tenor and falsetto.

When Tucker began touring with the Hummingbirds another singer began to exert an influence on him. This was Holden Smith of the General Four, a group from Shelby, North Carolina. Tucker could see that Smith had a special relationship with his audiences. He knew how to work them. His voice was capable of tapping into an extensive range of emotions and, on top of these performance skills, he wrote his own songs.

Although hired by the Hummingbirds as a baritone, Tucker began to share leads with James Davis, a move that was to prove crucial in the development of the Hummingbirds' sound. Davis had a high voice, whereas Tucker's was more rhythmic and raw. Together they had the ability to explore a greater range of moods, and over the years they would turn this 'lead-switching' into a spectacle in its own right, passing the mike between them with speed and agility and exaggerating their movements to excite the crowd.

'SWEET' AND 'HARD' GOSPEL

Especially following the war, a difference emerged between the traditional jubilee style of singing and the newer, more expressive style that was the favourite music of the young. The older style became known as 'sweet' gospel, while the new style was 'hard' gospel. Tucker never fully discarded the sweet-sounding songs, but increasingly he would use them as a set-up for the harder approach. Just when audiences were lulled by the familiar harmonies of the jubilee style, he would come in with his

soulful shrieks and wails, and his dynamic style of performance would take them by surprise.

THE GOLDEN GATE QUARTET

The Golden Gate Quartet exemplified the sweet style, making a name for themselves through their complex harmonies and easy-going demeanour. They'd started out in Norfolk, Virginia, in 1934, as the Golden Gate Jubilee Quartet. The Hummingbirds had met them in 1937, when they had a regular radio show broadcast out of Charlotte, North Carolina, and were impressed

The Golden Gate Quartet sang a 'sweet' form of gospel that contrasted with the 'raw' gospel of the Soul Stirrers.

not only with their style but with the way in which they'd been able to make a commercial success of gospel. While sticking with spiritual music, they'd been able to cross over, selling records, appearing on national radio and being heralded by the taste-makers of New York.

Their style was very different from that of the Hummingbirds. They used highly syncopated jazz-influenced arrangements and would retell Bible stories in hip black vernacular. They also had a knack of imitating sounds. In 'Gospel train' they would use their voices to imitate all the parts of a steam engine, from the pumping pistons to the escaping steam, varying the pace of delivery as the journey speeded up and slowed down. In songs such as 'Gabriel blows his horn' and 'Behold the Bridegroom cometh' they would imitate the sounds of horns, trumpets and saxophones.

The newer style was typified by such groups as the Kings of Harmony and the Soul Stirrers. The Kings of Harmony were founded in Birmingham, Alabama, in 1929 as the BYPU Specials (BYPU being the Baptist Young People's Union). They met the Hummingbirds four years later in Cleveland, Tennessee, while on a tour when both groups were singing the jubilee style. They stopped being known as the BYPU Specials after winning a gospel group competition organized by Philadelphia radio station WCAU. They were deemed to be 'the kings of harmony' and so they took it as their name.

R. H. HARRIS AND THE SOUL STIRRERS

A great lead singer named Carey Bradley joined in 1938, but left after a few months and went to Chicago. Here he came across the Soul Stirrers, a Texan quartet who were already perfecting the hard gospel sound. They were singing Dorsey songs, writing their own material and employing two lead vocalists. The Soul Stirrers' main lead, R. H. Harris, was one of the great innovators of quartet singing, but also a deeply religious man who became concerned that gospel music was becoming mere entertainment. He fretted over the emphasis on style, even though his own style had added to the bag of tricks available to gospel singers.

The Golden Gate Quartet broke out of the church and played at nightclubs, and even appeared in Hollywood films.

He claimed to have been the first gospel singer to sing falsetto. He also believed that he'd introduced the idea of ad-libbing lyrics and singing in delayed time. 'I'd be singing half the time the group sang, not quite out of meter,' he told gospel historian Anthony Heilbut. 'The group would start one meter, and I'd be in and out, front and behind, all across there.'

Each innovation was initially a source of controversy. Some Christians didn't feel comfortable with the departure from the self-controlled, clearly enunciated style of jubilee singing. Carey Bradley wasn't one of them. He liked what he saw and heard, and when in 1942 he was invited to rejoin the Kings of Harmony he transformed their sound into hard gospel. Heilbut said of this incarnation: 'It seems as if each member – lead, tenor, baritone, and bass – contributes a sensational phrase or harmonic twist.'

Interviewed many years later by Ray Funk, Bradley explained: 'William Turner [lead] liked the jubilee style of singing, a little bit like the Golden Gate Quartet. You know – fast-paced. When they did try to do a little gospel Turner wasn't doing the lead. They would switch him off and [Walter] Lattimore, the baritone singer, would do the lead. But after I came we reverted more to harmony and to the gospel style of singing.'

World War II created a hiatus in the development of gospel. Record companies couldn't get the raw materials necessary to make records. Touring was affected not only by rationing

The Soul Stirrers, c. 1951 (from left to right): Sam Cooke, R. B. Robinson, Paul Foster, S. R. Crain, J. J. Farley.

75

World War II marked the end of several gospel careers as singers were conscripted into the armed forces.

on fuel consumption and the rubber needed for car tyres but by a travelling restriction imposed by the American Federation of Musicians. No one was allowed to drive for more than 300 miles between shows. This necessarily dampened the entertainment industry.

Then there was the matter of military service. Many of the acts on the cutting edge of gospel were made up of young men of just the right age for call-up. Some people's careers were merely put on hold. For others the break in continuity meant that their gospel singing days were over. Ira Tucker was too young for the draft.

James Davis had too many children. Bass singer William Henry was drafted, as was baritone Barney Parks. Neither of them would return to the Dixie Hummingbirds.

But the war years didn't destroy gospel. In fact, its best years were yet to come. And while the men were away, the women were given an opportunity to play.

CHAPTER 7

Strange Things Happening Every Day

GREAT FEMALE ARTISTS: MAHALIA JACKSON AND ROSETTA THARPE

These two women singers couldn't have appeared more different. Mahalia Jackson was a large-boned Baptist who sang gospel songs in a peerless contralto voice with effortless dignity and an aura of piety, usually accompanied by the piano of Mildred Falls. Rosetta Tharpe was a feisty Pentecostal who played her own guitar, rocked audiences with an early form of R&B and had a reputation for sexual relationships with people of both genders.

They represented two directions in which gospel music was being pulled. On the one hand there were those who thought things had gone too far and that gospel should remain a church ministry delivered in a reverent way. It should not be used to glorify performers. On the other hand there were those who saw no reason why gospel music shouldn't compete

Sister Rosetta Tharpe, seen here in 1957, played the guitar and wrote her own songs.

in the marketplace against jazz, blues and pop. They argued that show-business techniques could be used to hook the otherwise uninterested and that ventures into nightclubs and concert halls were effective ways of reaching the unsaved.

Mahalia and Rosetta biographically had a lot in common. They were both born in the South prior to World War I, moved up to Chicago, were talent-scouted by Decca Records in the late 1930s and enjoyed a string of hit records. Their differences centred on the role they saw for their music. Although Mahalia spent a lot of her career performing in concert halls, she always saw her music as an act of worship. Early in her career she wouldn't sing without her head-covering, and when in later years she played the Newport Jazz Festival she requested that she be allowed to perform on a Sunday so that her spot would become a church service rather than a show. Rosetta, whose background was in the Holiness Church, became increasingly ambivalent as to whether she was primarily a minister or an entertainer. In the 1940s she caused controversy by accepting engagements in a New York nightclub, where she performed in front of patrons who were drinking and smoking.

A CALLING OR A CAREER?

It raised the old questions about the division between secular and sacred music. If gospel music was a calling, was it a rejection of that calling either to sing something that was not explicitly religious or to pursue a musical career where success was measured in income and acclaim rather than in spiritual harvest? In some quarters gospel fans were very unforgiving of singers who appeared to compromise. They

would not welcome the return of someone they considered to have 'sold out'.

Although gospel music would soon create stars out of a select few, there was no comparison between the earnings of an average professional gospel singer and his or her secular counterpart. The financial rewards of leaving gospel for pop were a temptation, and some of the record-company bosses deliberately used it to persuade groups to use their voices for more obviously commercial ends.

Mahalia was born on Pitt Street, New Orleans, Louisiana, in 1912, and was influenced by all the sounds that coursed through that city of music. She heard jazz before it was known as jazz, saw the marching bands that accompanied traditional funerals, sang hymns at Mount Moriah Baptist Church, listened to the music of the local

Rosetta Tharpe.

Holiness church and played blues records at home.

'When did I begin to sing? You might as well ask me when I first began to walk and talk,' she told the legendary Chicago-based interviewer Studs Terkel. 'In New Orleans, where I lived as a child, I remember singing as I scrubbed the floors. It would make the work go easier. When the old people weren't at home, I'd turn on a Bessie Smith record and play it over and over. "Careless love", that was the blues she sang. That was before I was saved. The blues are fine, but I don't want to sing them.'

Bessie Smith recorded 'Careless love' in May 1925. It wasn't long afterwards that a teenage Mahalia Jackson declared that she'd been 'saved' one Friday night during a revival at her church. Shortly afterwards the minister, E. D. Lawrence, baptized her in the Mississippi and she was received into the church as a member. 'Ever since that day,' she would say, 'I promised the Lord that I'd dedicate my life to him in song.'

Rosetta Tharpe was raised in a Holiness church where the music was wilder and where no instruments were thought of as out of bounds for use in worship. The musical policy of the Church of God in Christ had been decided by Psalm 150, which read in part: 'Praise him with the sound of the trumpet: praise him with the psaltery and harp. Praise him with the timbrel and dance: praise him with stringed instruments and organs. Praise him upon the loud cymbals: praise him upon the high sounding cymbals. Let everything that hath breath praise the Lord.' Although the psalmist didn't mention the drums, piano, organ and guitar, he might as well have done, because the message was that anything that makes a noise can be used to praise God.

Rosetta's mother, Katie Atkins (later Bell), played the harmonium, and Rosetta took up the guitar at an early age. After arriving in Chicago, Katie began travelling as an evangelist and by the age of twelve Rosetta was accompanying her and contributing as a singer. An influence on her music was Arizona Dranes, a blind female piano-player from Texas who was also a member of the Church of God in Christ. Although Rosetta never copied her, the singer was an inspiration. Rosetta first saw her perform in Chicago and later at various COGIC conventions.

Interestingly, in the light of her subsequent career, Rosetta wasn't shaped by the emerging blues scene. The Holiness churches, in accordance with their name, emphasized the separation between the believer and the non-believing world. There were the usual prohibitions of alcohol, tobacco, make-up and dancing, but it was also considered sinful to partake of secular entertainment. It was certainly regarded as wrong to sing the sort of songs that entertained people in bars and clubs.

THE INFLUENCE OF THOMAS DORSEY

While Rosetta was making her living by singing for God on the road, Mahalia was washing floors, taking in laundry and doing anything she could to make money to get by. She was a member of Greater Salem Baptist Choir in Chicago and also sang with three brothers from the church in a group called the Johnson Singers. Thomas Dorsey saw them in the late 1920s, and remembered the quartet as being unusual at the time for having one female member and for being significant in that it was getting an emotional reaction by performing in the earthier Southern style. 'They were really rocking them everywhere they went,' he said. 'Mahalia was with this group and was going and killing them off. I mean, she was laying them out.'

Mahalia performed at revivals at Pilgrim Baptist Church, which is where she introduced herself to Dorsey and asked if he could supply her with gospel songs. Until then she had been relying on material from *Gospel Pearls* and other hymnals, and Dorsey knew that this wasn't stretching her enough. He started

tutoring her, teaching her new material and improving her breathing and performance technique. 'I wanted to train her how to do my numbers and do them with the beat,' he later said. '[You have to] shake at the right time, shout at the right time. You don't get up to start off shoutin'. You lose yourself.'

Although she knew Mahalia and the singer Clara Ward, Rosetta didn't meet Dorsey during this period and had no contact with the burgeoning Chicago gospel scene surrounding him. This was due to her schedule rather than to ignorance. While on the road with her mother, she had no time to be a part of what was going on in the city. While Mahalia was being trained by Dorsey, Rosetta was being shaped by the demands of the sawdust circuit.

Rosetta had to learn how to respond to the signals of different preachers and how to make her voice heard over the moaning and crying of worshippers. She had to sense when a congregation's attention was flagging and how to come up with songs that fitted the mood set by the sermon. 'She developed a Sanctified gospel guitar style that emphasized the picking of individual notes as a counterpoint to her voice,' wrote her biographer Gayle Wald. 'Plucking individual notes, and plucking them quickly, served not only as a form of visual entertainment, but also as a way of filling the otherwise dead space between vocal phrases. Rosetta also worked on the technique of embellishing a song with improvised lyrics or vocal interpolations, something which later became one of her trademarks.'

Mahalia was the first to make a record. On Friday 21 May 1937 she cut four tracks for Decca – 'God's gonna separate the wheat from the tares', 'Oh, my Lord', 'Keep me every day' and 'God shall wipe all tears away'. Released on the Coral label, they made no impact, and shortly afterwards Decca dropped her. The label left gospel alone for the next year and a half and then launched another gospel artist – Rosetta Tharpe.

SECULAR AND SACRED

Why did Decca try again with gospel? The answer probably lies in Rosetta's willingness at least to straddle the border between secular and sacred. In 1938 she decided to leave the church circuit and enter show business proper. She got herself an agent, signed a publishing deal and accepted a two-week stint at the celebrated Cotton Club on a bill headlined by Cab Calloway and featuring exotic dancers. Now billing herself as 'Sister' Rosetta Tharpe, she made her gospel background an additional novelty.

She posed for portraits wearing a long dress and cradling a guitar, a striking image that combined the austerity of a chorister with the daring of a blues player. She realized that in the secular marketplace she was an oddball and she used this to her advantage.

Her ambivalence over her position was reflected in her choice of material. Of the first four songs she recorded – 'That's all', 'My man and I', 'Rock me' and 'The lonesome road' – two were not gospel. 'My man and I' was a secular reworking of her own gospel song 'My Lord and I'. 'The lonesome road' was a song written in 1928 by the original crooner Gene Austin and included in the film version of the musical *Showboat* the following year. 'That's all' was Washington Phillips' 'Denomination blues' under a different

title, and 'Rock me' was her version of Thomas Dorsey's 'Hide me in thy bosom'.

The way she reinterpreted Dorsey's song was significant. The discarding of his biblical-sounding title for the raunchier sounding 'Rock me' showed where she was aiming. So did her alteration of key words in Dorsey's text. Where he had written 'hear me singing', she sang 'hear me swinging'; where he wrote 'wash me' she had 'moist me'; where he pictured himself surrounded by a 'world of sin', Rosetta was surrounded by a 'world of love', and, most importantly, where Dorsey beseeched Jesus not to leave him, Rosetta addressed an anonymous 'you'. The saviour in Rosetta's version was not the Messiah but a lover. Dorsey's image of being rocked was of Christ comforting the believer in

A programme for a production of 'Cotton Club Parade', featuring performances by Cab Calloway and the Nicholas Brothers, at Harlem's Cotton Club, 1934.

the cradle of his love. Rosetta's image was of being rocked by an aggressive lover in bed.

She was trying to play it both ways by singing songs familiar to church folk but making them fit secular expectations. When questioned about her controversial move from the church into the world of nightclubs and entertainment venues, she commented that there were more souls out there that needed saving, but all the recorded accounts of her life during this time portray a woman who had little passion for salvation. Although she may have felt a twinge of residual guilt because she knew she had transgressed as far as the Holiness culture was concerned, she got over it pretty quickly.

Once she'd crossed over she enjoyed money, luxury, fame and the high life. Gayle Wald summed up the tension: 'Although she sang about the wages of sinful living, she pursued romantic relationships – primarily with men, but occasionally with women – wore pants before they were the norm for women, and swore like a sailor. She also maintained a lifelong affiliation with a church that regarded all these behaviors as anathema.'

The British jazz singer George Melly, who toured Britain with her twenty years later, observed the same contradiction between the beliefs she sang about and the way she lived.

One of her numbers was called 'God don't like it'. And the words were aimed at the

> The Cotton Club existed on the corner of 142nd Street and Lennox Avenue in Harlem. It was a magnet for fashionable white folk who wanted a taste of black entertainment.

most pleasurable human activities. It became clear to us within the first two days that if she believed in what she was singing, she must realize that she was causing the Almighty almost non-stop displeasure, but that there was no sign it bothered her at all.

CARNEGIE HALL AND CAFÉ SOCIETY

Within two months of recording for Decca she played the Paramount Theater in New York with Count Basie and then the Apollo Theater in Harlem on a bill with Fats Waller, Lionel Hampton, the Ink Spots and Artie Shaw. The most groundbreaking appearance was in John Hammond's landmark Carnegie Hall show *From Spirituals to Swing* in December 1938, an event that would presage the coming together of jazz, folk and gospel a decade and a half later in the form of rock and roll.

The white son of rich parents, Hammond approached music as a social cause rather than a product to be shifted. Blessed with an ear for authentic American music, he despised anything

that was phoney or insincere. During his time at Columbia Records he had a hand in the recorded output of such giants as Benny Goodman, Billie Holiday, Robert Johnson, Aretha Franklin, Bob Dylan and Bruce Springsteen. With *From Spirituals to Swing* he designed an event that would showcase the best of the music he loved with an eye to revolutionizing musical taste in America. Above all he wanted to stress the importance of African American music in mainstream popular music.

The evening was divided into thematic sections, and Rosetta appeared during one called 'Spirituals and holy roller hymns', where she sang 'Rock me' and 'That's all'. Mitchell's Christian Singers, a jubilee group, performed the spirituals 'What more can Jesus do?', 'My poor mother died' and 'Are you living humble?' The significance was that the show presented her music alongside the blues of Jimmy Rushing and Joe Turner, the jazz of Sidney Bechet and Albert Ammons, the boogie-woogie of Meade 'Lux' Lewis and the swing of Count Basie. It was the first time that gospel had been presented to a white audience as part of the continuum of American music.

While Mahalia continued to work in Chicago

and to travel with Thomas Dorsey, promoting his songs, Rosetta was being toasted by the East Coast liberal elite, which discovered that it enjoyed gospel music, especially when it was presented as entertainment. A club had opened

Record producer and music enthusiast John Hammond (1910–87), who led the way in giving spirituals their deserved place in American musical history.

on Sheridan Square in Greenwich Village, where black music acts were presented for the delight of white audiences. With tongue in cheek it was named Café Society. It attracted the Dixie Hummingbirds and the Golden Gate Quartet, and, in October 1941, Sister Rosetta Tharpe.

By now she was working regularly with Lucky Millinder, a white band leader who specialized in what would soon be known as R&B and who employed some of the most capable black musicians around. In June, August and September of that year she cut seven tracks with Millinder, including reworked versions of 'The lonesome road' and 'Rock me'. The recordings were more professional than those she had done three years before, but her style was no longer as earthy as it had been when she still had sawdust on her shoes. She was no longer trying to warn backsliders, inspire believers and put the fear of God into sinners. She was now trying to provide a pleasant listening experience.

THE QUEEN OF GOSPEL

Mahalia didn't return to the recording studio for almost a decade. In 1946 she signed with Apollo, an independent New York record label, and her third single, 'Move on up a little higher', became a million seller. It marked the beginning of a change in status between Mahalia and Rosetta. Mahalia was becoming the undisputed Queen of Gospel, while Rosetta was bouncing between church and nightclub playing the religious freak in front of the secular audience and the repentant sinner when addressing the godly.

She returned to gospel in the mid- to late 1940s with recordings like 'Strange things' and 'Up above my head', but by then the church audience wasn't sure how to take her. Her private life was, to put it mildly, complex. She divorced her first husband, Tommy Tharpe, in 1943, and almost immediately married Foch Allen. That marriage ended four years later, and then in 1951 she married Russell Morrison in front of 22,000 fans at Griffith Stadium in Washington DC.

What was billed as 'the most elaborate wedding ever staged' was an idea hatched by her publicity agent, who thought it would put

Café Society Uptown, which, along with Café Society in Greenwich Village, brought jazz, gospel, folk and blues into mainstream New York entertainment. Here, French singer Lucienne Boyer performs with an orchestra in 1947.

Mahalia Jackson takes part in a live broadcast at New York's WOV.

favourable. Many secular critics thought it crass and unbecoming of someone who was still supposedly representing the gospel.

In the long run it probably helped Mahalia more than it helped Rosetta, because everyone knew that Mahalia would never do anything as tawdry. She was, as Dorsey's song put it, someone who lived the life she sang about in her songs. She was on record as saying that her work was 'a ransom of gratitude for God delivering me from trials', and she resisted overtures to record secular songs. She once turned down an offer that would have guaranteed her $25,000 a performance in Las Vegas, saying, 'I'd rather sing about "old man Jesus" than about some old man some woman has lost.'

Yet, as Mahalia became an international figure, she made other shades of compromise. She allowed Columbia to sweeten up her sound by adding strings, and acceded to their demands to record such standards as 'Danny boy' and 'Summertime', neither of which had anything to do with gospel. Her escalating fees priced her out of church events, and her attention switched from black Christian to secular white audiences. Like Rosetta, she had trouble with her choices in husbands. She divorced two of them but later remarried the second.

her in front of a massive public. Besides a few numbers performed by the bride, the wedding show would feature the Harmonizing Four and prophetess Dolly Lewis. It got all the publicity her agent had imagined, but not all of it was

APPEARING TOGETHER: CHICAGO, NEWPORT AND EUROPE

Despite their differences, there was never any animosity between the two singers. In 1946 they were put on the same bill at Chicago's Eight Regiment Armory, and in 1951 played on the same Carnegie Hall bill together with the Gaye Sisters and Clara Ward. Rosetta met her future partner Marie Knight at a Mahalia Jackson concert in Harlem where Knight was on the same bill.

In the 1950s and 1960s they appealed to a similar market and were both objects of fascination to the baby-boomers, who were rejecting their parents' taste in white music and tuning into black radio stations for alternatives. Television and radio helped bring gospel closer to white audiences. The *Mahalia Jackson Show* was aired on radio in 1954, and in 1962 Rosetta hosted the Chicago-based programme *TV Gospel Time*.

Mahalia first toured Europe in 1951 and Rosetta followed in 1957. This was a time when young Europeans were fascinated by American blues, jazz and gospel because of their perceived authenticity. Miles Davis was celebrated in Paris and Big Bill Broonzy was a hit in post-war London. Music purists who slavered over precious American imports saw Mahalia and Rosetta as manna falling in a cultural desert.

Since the late 1940s Rosetta had been playing electric rather than acoustic guitar, and her wild, expressive style had an impact on the sound of emerging rock and roll. Jerry Lee Lewis chose her song 'Strange things happening every day' as one of his audition pieces when he went to see Sam Phillips at Sun Records. Little Richard saw her

Cab Calloway plays piano and Duke Ellington the guitar, while Rosetta Tharpe (left) joins in the fun. Photo taken at a private party in August 1939.

folk and rock, and further established their relevance to the emerging rock-and-roll music. At the jazz festival in 1958 Mahalia appeared on a bill that also featured Miles Davis, Chuck Berry, Duke Ellington and Louis Armstrong. Her forty-five-minute set was recorded for an album and part of her performance was used in the

The Newport Jazz Festival's temporary headquarters, 1958 (left). Louis Armstrong (below) on stage at Newport in 1958.

perform at Macon City Auditorium, Georgia, in the late 1940s when he was selling Coca-Cola to the crowds. 'Strange things' was one of the first records that Carl Perkins played along to when he was learning guitar.

Asked about his musical influences another former Sun artist, Johnny Cash, said:

I grew up just over 100 miles from Cotton Plant, Arkansas, which was the hometown of Sister Rosetta Tharpe, and she was one of my favourites when I was a kid. I love songs like 'This train'. I think that song could be a rock-and-roll smash, if somebody recorded it right. Another song she did was 'Didn't it rain?' She also did 'Don't take everybody to be your friend'. She had some great songs that were spiritual but still had a universal message. Rock musicians have discovered these gospel and blues roots to an extent, but they haven't gone all the way. They've barely touched the source.

At the Newport festivals Mahalia and Rosetta performed alongside legends from jazz, blues,

influential documentary *Jazz on a Summer's Day*. Rosetta appeared at the jazz festival in 1964 and the folk festival in 1967.

Mahalia Jackson and Rosetta Tharpe were far more than gospel pioneers. They were successful black women at a time when not many women ran business empires and not many black entertainers were openly respected by the white community. They both managed to make it in a white man's world and their music continues to inspire in the twenty-first century.

Interview with Sallie Martin (1895–1988), Chicago, April 1976

❀ **You worked with Thomas Dorsey through the 1930s, performing his songs, establishing his publishing, managing his finances and organizing the National Convention of Gospel Choirs and Choruses. How did you two meet?**

I heard a young lady singing 'How about you?' and I asked her, 'Where did you get that?' She said that it was written by a man called Mr Dorsey and that if I was to go to 59th and Wabash on a Saturday night I could meet him because he came there to sell his music. I went and he was there teaching people how to do gospel numbers. He asked me if I'd like to join a group he was putting together. That's the way I got started. I went for a rehearsal at his home. I noticed that people would come in and buy his sheet music for 10 cents and he'd put the money in a little bag and put it in his desk drawer. I said to him one day, 'Mr Dorsey. You have something here but you don't know what to do with it.' He said, 'Do you think you could do any better?' I said, 'I'm sure I could.' At this time I was working for the City, which was broke, and I didn't receive a salary but I did get board and keep. He said he could pay me $4 a week. I had to decide whether I was going to take a chance to live on $4 or stay where I knew I had room and board. But I knew it was my time. I had always wanted to travel, always wanted to sing. So I said, 'All right. If I sell your music for $5 will you give me $2.50?' That's the way I made up the loss. When he came in one day from the Metropolitan church he said, 'Sallie, do you think that we could have a convention?' I said, 'Sure.' He asked me to write to a number of people including Artelia Hutchins in Detroit and I. J. Johnson in St Louis, and in August 1933 we had the first convention.

❀ **What does a gospel song need in order to be a good gospel song?**

I think it should have a real meaning, not just some words put together to rhyme up or some music to give you a good feeling. I never use a number that I do not feel is part of me. I try to let the words be in my life. Some people will sing anything that has a good tune and a good rhythm, but I wouldn't consider that. There's a song that says 'I'll go where you want me to go, dear Lord.' Before I went to Africa I never did sing that song because I thought maybe I don't want to go. I need to be able to will what the words say.

❀ **Can a gospel singer also sing pop songs?**

Well, you can't be on both sides. There's the rock-and-roll side and there's the gospel side. If you're saved, when you're doing gospel songs you're really singing for Christ. You're singing because the Lord has really saved you. If you're gonna sing rock and roll tonight and then sing gospel tomorrow night – I don't go for that. People change over for the money. What we say is that the Lord has everything; he can supply your needs. What's the meaning of my claiming him if he can't supply my needs and I have to go over to the rock-and-roll side? Let me put it like this. If I got to go over on the devil's side to make it then there must be something wrong with God. If he holds the whole world in his hands, why can't he supply my needs? Aretha Franklin made an album with James Cleveland. I don't appreciate that. I believe that if you're saved you live what you sing about and you just can't be on two sides.

❀ **What is the purpose of a gospel song?**

The purpose ought to be to help. Ministers don't like to hear you say it but many souls get convicted from songs. I had a man who said to me, 'Sallie, I just want to tell you that whatever I have I give the credit to you and God for this reason. I was sitting in First Church Deliverance Choir but I'd never met the Lord. I was just singing. But you came to First Church and you sang "I heard the voice of Jesus saying / Come unto me and rest." I got so convicted I went out of there and I didn't stop praying until I met the Lord.' So that's the thing. I don't know who I'm singing to out there but somebody may be burdened or depressed. There may be a sinner there. So if you sing out of your soul and really mean it then it will maybe touch somebody and that's what it's for. It's like if someone is preaching. They ought to be telling the story so that someone gets the message.

❁ **So wouldn't it be best to take gospel music out of the churches? In church you're literally singing to the converted.**

You'll find almost any kind of person coming to the church and that gives you an opportunity to give the message. That's the reason I have many people going from house to house passing out pamphlets. I feel there is nothing like trying to tell the story to a person directly. I don't like singing when the lights are off. I like to see a person. I like to look directly and see them and I think they realize a little bit better looking at me that I really mean what I'm doing.

❁ **What is the most challenging song that you sing?**

It can depend on who you're singing to. If there are a lot of people there that's unsaved I try to sing something that they can think on. Mr Dorsey wrote a song 'Have I given you anything today?' When you sing that most anybody will start thinking – what have I done today? I always try to sing something that might touch somebody in the audience, not just something with a good rhythm.

❁ **If you have a church audience that is responding physically to your music – maybe dancing or falling out – do you think they might miss the message?**

Sometimes they might not hear it all, but the part they did hear I guess it can touch them. I don't think there's any harm in shouting if you're happy.

❁ **Did you see the quartet style of singing develop during your lifetime?**

Yes. I tell you, the very first quartet group after I started out in gospel was the Soul Stirrers and they were beautiful.

❁ **Was that style of singing completely new at the time?**

No, I don't think it was completely new, because, you see, when I was younger there were barbershop quartets. As a young girl I went to church and they were doing what you call 'shape notes'. I tell you, when you get ten or twelve people doing shape notes they don't miss on it. Everyone sings their part and they know the notes. This really makes them sing it right. It's beautiful when you get a lead, a tenor and a bass all singing and all getting it right. That's the way they used to do it way back. They didn't have any musical instruments.

❁ **How do you feel about growing old?**

Me? I just thank the Lord. So many who started when I started are now gone. I don't worry about it so long as I don't have to be a burden to anyone.

CHAPTER

8

Get Me Jesus on the Line

THE GOLDEN AGE

The Golden Age of gospel music is reckoned to have been 1945–60. Some would shorten it, pointing out that record sales were dipping by 1955. Some would extend it, arguing that the creative surge continued through to the late 1960s. Few would disagree that the end of World War II marked its beginning and that it was the time when gospel was at its most vital, influential and commercial.

Essential to this celebrated period of gospel music history was the rise of small independent record companies willing to take a chance on black music, and the liberalization of regulations regarding broadcasting that allowed local radio stations to proliferate across America. Without the records, gospel would have remained a secret of the church and the black community. Without the radio stations, few people would have had the opportunity to hear the records.

THE RECORD COMPANIES

The major record companies, then as now, were too big and inflexible to respond to grassroots musical movements. Into the gap came a number of labels that started out in bedrooms, attics and the back rooms of record stores but which had their ears to the ground. They were almost exclusively interested in black music and became the crucible for the most exciting post-war jazz, blues and gospel, creating the template for rock and roll, which would itself be properly launched by an independent label in Memphis. The artists were not well paid and the sessions were short and sweet, but so many of the tracks laid down have become enduring works of art.

Window display in 1951 of records on the Specialty label, including 'Lover's prayer' by Jimmy Liggins and 'Doctor Jesus' by Brother Joe May.

The typical owner of a record company specializing in gospel was a white Jewish male who'd been alerted to the potential market through experience with either a radio station or a record store. A personal passion for the music wasn't essential. It was a case of supply and demand. Not only was there a black audience out there that was willing to pay for hard-to-get music, but there was an expanding white audience made up mostly of teenagers who found Caucasian music too anodyne.

HERMAN LUBINSKY AND SAVOY RECORDS

The pioneer was Herman Lubinsky, a former naval wireless operator, who ran a radio station from the attic of his home in New Jersey and owned the Radio Shop of Newark. He formed a record company during the war years, naming it Savoy Records after the Savoy Ballroom in Harlem. Throughout 1943 and 1944 he recruited a selection of gospel acts – the Kings of Harmony, the Johnson Jubilee Singers, the

The Savoy Ballroom in Harlem set musical and dance trends in the 1940s. Herman Lubinsky named his label after it.

Heavenly Four of Alabama, Sister Dorothea Robinson.

He then proceeded to build up one of the most impressive jazz rosters ever. In 1945 he recorded the likes of Dizzy Gillespie, Billy Eckstine, Errol Garner, Slim Gaillard and Charlie Parker. In 1946 it was Stan Getz, Sonny Stitt and Duke Ellington. And so it went on. In 1948 he returned to gospel, recording a female group from Philadelphia, the Ward Singers, who were causing a stir in the gospel world. The group was run by Gertrude Ward and consisted of her talented daughter Clara, an outstanding vocalist named Marion Williams and Henrietta Waddy.

Lubinsky sensed that the Ward Singers represented the future of gospel music. They were commercially minded, wore elaborate gowns rather than choir robes, and had a dynamic musical style that involved a lot of improvisation and vamping. They were colourful and controversial. At the height of their success they would travel in Cadillacs with trailers and do concerts that involved only six songs, the rest of the time being taken up with reprises.

In the 1950s, when many such independent labels turned to rock and roll, Savoy remained faithful to African American music, pumping out even more blues, gospel and jazz releases. The list of gospel artists it recorded reads like a *Who's Who* of gospel during its Golden Age: the Gaye Sisters, the Caravans, Clara Ward, the Staple Singers, Marion Williams, the Davis Sisters, the Roberta Martin Singers, Alex Bradford, Jessy Dixon, James Cleveland and the Blind Boys of Alabama among them.

Although Lubinsky was the owner, the quality

Herman Lubinsky (1896–1974), the founder of Savoy Records, one of the most prolific gospel labels.

of the creative output was down to his A&R (Artistes and Repertoire) men, who in those days were a combination of talent scout and record producer. From 1954 to 1959 his right-hand man was Ozzie Cadena, a music lover from Newark who'd worked with him at the Radio Shop. He was responsible for producing records by, among others, the Ward Singers, Shirley Caesar, the Davis Sisters and Marion Williams as well as such jazz artists as Charles Mingus, Milt Jackson, Cannonball Adderley, John Coltrane and Kenny Clarke. Anthony Heilbut has said of him that 'the sound on those old Savoy albums still transcends any current gospel releases. Virtually every Savoy album produced by Cadena was a masterpiece.

He is, with Art Rupe of Specialty ... probably the most gifted producer in gospel history.'

IKE AND BESS BERMAN: APOLLO RECORDS

Another label named after a Harlem venue was Apollo, started by husband-and-wife team Ike and Bess Berman at their Rainbow Record Shop on 125th Street in New York. Apollo recorded many different forms of music from swing and hillbilly to calypso and Yiddish comedy. Its gospel catalogue wasn't as impressive as Savoy's, but it earned its place in music history by being the label to sign Mahalia Jackson in her prime and get some of her best recorded material.

Bess Berman, the driving force behind the label, wasn't as interested in preserving and promoting gospel music as she was in recruiting vocal talent that had been nurtured in the church. When she signed Solomon Burke in

1955 she is reputed to have commented: 'Let's take this church boy and make him the next Harry Belafonte.' Another of her achievements was taking members of the Selah Jubilee Singers, a well-known New York gospel group that had relocated to South Carolina, and turning them into the Larks, who had R&B success with 'Eyesight to the blind' and 'Little side car'.

The experience of this group illustrates the increasingly thin borderline between sacred and secular music. In October 1950 they came to New York and recorded seventeen tracks for four record companies in a single day, choosing a different group name each time. They recorded gospel for Jubilee, Regal and Apollo as, respectively, the Selah Jubilee Singers, the Jubilators and the Southern Harmonaires, and then recorded risqué blues for Savoy as the Four Barons.

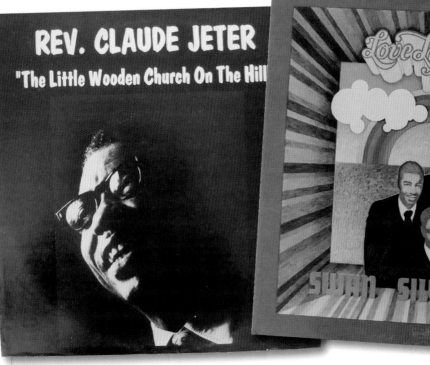

RECORD STORES

It was natural that the owners of record stores would be quick to respond to the demand for recordings of black musicians. They could see what sold and were the first to find out what customers were hungry to get their hands on. Vee-Jay Records, one of the few black-run labels putting out gospel, was created by Vivian and James Bracken (hence Vee-Jay), who realized the need from the sales pattern at their record store in Gary, Indiana. Best known for their success with R&B artists such as Jimmy Reed, Jerry Butler and John Lee Hooker, and for being the first American label to release a Beatles record, they recorded such influential quartets as the Swan Silvertones and the Highway QCs, and were responsible for launching the instrumentalist Maceo Woods, who helped popularize the Hammond organ in gospel music.

King in Cincinnati, Ohio, Aladdin in LA and Dot in Gallatin, Tennessee, were all established by record-store owners (Syd's Record Shop, the Philharmonic Music Shop and Randy's Record Shop respectively). Art Rupe, of Specialty Records in LA, later to sign both Little Richard and Lloyd Price to his label, closely studied the most successful 'race records' to discover what they had in common. He concluded that it was a combination of the big-band sound that characterized the swing music of the time and the feel of the gospel music he'd experienced at first hand growing up near a black church. Besides incorporating his findings into his R&B hits, he produced the Pilgrim Travelers, Brother Joe May, Sister Wynona Carr, Alex Bradford, and the Soul Stirrers, featuring Sam Cooke.

Few of these record-company owners had much to recommend them as custodians of Christian music. They weren't religious, and many of them had bad financial reputations. Don Robey, who founded Peacock Records in 1949, home to the Mighty Clouds of Joy, the O'Neal Twins and Julius Cheeks, had

Art Rupe entering the offices of Specialty Records, on Venice Boulevard in Los Angeles.

been a professional gambler, taxi-cab operator and nightclub manager before getting into music. Syd Nathan's experience before starting King Records was as a drummer, pawnshop clerk, wrestling promoter and jewellery salesman.

The Spirit of Memphis were with both Peacock and King. From King they would get advances as small as $400–$500 and would then see no further royalties. They weren't given financial statements and so couldn't track their sales. They never knew what was owed to them. Their relationship with Peacock was more satisfactory, although other artists found Robey irascible, dishonest and hard to work with. Little Richard claimed that Robey punched and kicked him. When he had a falling-out with the Pilgrim Travelers over payments for their hit 'Stretch out', he pulled a gun on them.

The most prolific producer of gospel records was Nashboro Records, founded in 1951 by Ernie Young, who was the owner of Ernie's Record Mart in Nashville. As well as having a store on 3rd Avenue, he ran a mail-order business that he pushed by sponsoring a show on Nashville's WLAC. It soon occurred to him that he'd make more money if he was also producing the records he sold, so he started Nashboro and, a year later, the R&B label Excello. He never had high production standards (he'd spent most of his life in real estate and was already in his fifties) and was happy recording live in the studio without any time-consuming retakes.

As radio spread, disc jockeys became power arbiters of musical taste. Here, Duke Ellington poses at a radio station turntable.

RADIO STATIONS

Young had been quick to realize the importance of commercial radio in helping to sell records. Even though his list of gospel stars (the Consolers, the Angelic Gospel Singers, the Swanee Quintet, Edna Gallmon Cooke) was nowhere near the calibre of Savoy's, Specialty's or Peacock's the records he released would often outsell theirs because of his market penetration.

WLAC in Nashville was a 50,000-watt station that targeted the black populace with its choice of music and its advertising for baby chicks, hair pomade, skin-lighteners, choir gowns and funeral parlours. However, its reach extended way beyond Nashville. There were listeners in the East and Midwest and, if reception was clear at night, it could be picked up in Canada and Mexico, and the Caribbean islands. At its peak it was said that WLAC was listened to by 65 per cent of America's black population.

It was also being tuned into by white teenagers, to whom the music choice was a revelation. Reared on the white sounds of Perry Como, Guy Lombardo and Frank Sinatra, they were suddenly being introduced to the Dixie Hummingbirds, Sister Rosetta Tharpe, Jimmy Reed, Muddy Waters and Elmore James. It alerted them not only to what was available via Ernie's Record Mart in Nashville but to what could be bought over the counter at their nearest black record store. Small groups of aficionados would form at high schools, where records would be listened to and swapped and lyrics checked.

DISC JOCKEYS

This gave the disc jockeys of WLAC unprecedented power. Four of them in particular – Gene Nobles, John R, Herman Grizzard and Hoss Allen – gained a reputation for being hip and ahead of the times. Although they were all white, they loved the music they played, had deep voices that disguised their racial identity and perfected a line of jive talk that fitted in perfectly with the records they were playing.

Although they would all play gospel tracks, and John R – whose show was sponsored by Nasboro Records' Ernie Young – had a Sunday morning gospel show, it was Hoss Allen who became particularly identified with spiritual music. Known to his listeners as the Hossman, Allen had joined WLAC in the late 1940s and would deputize for Gene Nobles whenever he was off air. He became so integrated with the gospel music scene that he would host local gospel concerts and would eventually present a programme of music and meditations, *Early Morning Gospel Time with the Hossman*.

Another white DJ, Dewey Phillips, was having a similar effect with gospel in Memphis. In 1949 he'd started a show called *Red Hot & Blue* on WHBQ, where he played whatever he felt like regardless of style and regardless of whether it was a new record. This was the show that Elvis Presley most eagerly listened to as a teenager and then as a young man on the cusp of fame. Phillips was doing on radio what Elvis would later do in the studio – mixing up country and gospel, blues and spirituals, swing and pop. Phillips liked Elvis's first single so much that he played it seven times in a row on its release.

Black radio stations were as rare as black-owned record companies. In 1943 only four stations programmed to the African American community, and four years later, out of a total of 3,000 DJs on American radio, only sixteen were black. The first station to feature all-black programming was WDIA in Memphis in 1949. In its publicity during the 1950s it boasted that it had 'pioneered Negro programming and was the first station to devote all of its time to serving Negroes. WDIA had the first all-Negro staff of broadcast stars, "Brown America Speaks" (the first all-Negro forum for the free and open discussion of Negro problems), and the first Negro woman broadcaster in America.'

Music was naturally a large part of its output. It claimed to have discovered B. B. King, Johnny Ace, Rosco Gordon and Bobby Bland.

Every week it featured the local gospel acts the Southern Jubilee Singers, Cleophas Robinson, the Friendly Echoes and the Gospel Writers. The Spirit of Memphis had their own live fifteen-minute show, and on Sundays there was a live broadcast from East Trigg Baptist Church, where the minister was the great gospel songwriter W. Herbert Brewster.

Before the advent of designated gospel DJs, a few favoured quartets had their own radio shows. The first was the Utica Jubilee Quartet, who appeared on WJZ in 1927. The Southernaires had shows on both WMCA and WRNY in New York and would later host *The Little Weather-Beaten Whitewashed Church* on WFIL. The rationale of these programmes was that they appealed to Southern migrants who loved reminders of the country ways they had left behind. In 1937 the Golden Gate Quartet hosted *The Magic Key Hour* on the NBC affiliate WBT in Charlotte, North Carolina, before being given a regular weekday programme on WIS.

Radio stations came to play an increasingly important role in the gospel network. They were an essential link between record company and record-buyer and were able to advertise local events and national tours. When WDIA in Memphis boosted its signal it had an immediate impact on the career of the Spirit of Memphis. 'I didn't think we'd ever get booked 20 miles out of town,' said manager Jethroe Bledsoe, 'but when WDIA went up to 50,000 watts that blew the top! We were getting letters from all over, from as far as the station would reach.'

Radio also meant that, for the first time, gospel music was being heard in private secular situations – driving in a car, drinking

Memphis DJ Dewey Phillips played the gospel music that a young Elvis Presley tuned in to hear.

in a café or sitting in a living room. People who had no allegiance to the message of gospel loved it for its rhythm, its passion and its feeling of authenticity. Those who were in the business of music rather than the ministry of music recognized this as an opportunity for gospel to break out of the confines of the religious black audience and gain widespread acceptance in the marketplace.

EVENT PROMOTERS

Promoters seized the opportunity to stage gospel events in venues associated with entertainment rather than worship. In New York, for example, the key entrepreneurs keen to make gospel more commercial were promoter Johnny Myers, radio presenter Joe Bostic Sr and Thermon Ruth, one-time member of the Selah Jubilee Singers. All three men were black.

Myers had booked dates for Sister Rosetta Tharpe on the church circuit, and after the war he put on gospel programmes at Harlem's Golden Gate Ballroom, best known as a jazz venue. At the time some gospel fans were not sure that it was right to charge people to hear sacred music, let alone present it in a show-business arena. Myers was an aggressive publicist as well, driving around Harlem in a car with speakers on the roof broadcasting news of his forthcoming events. In the end, commerce won. Acts such as the National Clouds of Joy, the Kings of Harmony and the Dixie Hummingbirds became sell-out attractions. 'The people were packed in,' remembered Marie Knight, who

The Spirit of Memphis at WDIA in 1951 (left to right): 'Little Ax' Broadnax, 'Jet' Bledsoe, Robert Reed, James Darling, Earl Malone, Silas Steele.

appeared there with Rosetta Tharpe. 'It was amazing how he did it, but he did it.'

Joe Bostic was already a legend for being the first black announcer on American radio. He moved to Harlem from Baltimore in the 1930s and in the early 1940s started a gospel music show called *The Gospel Train* on WLIB. He became a key person in the promotion of gospel in the New York area and this naturally led on to him promoting concerts and even starting his own small record label. He became best known for bringing the first all-gospel show to Carnegie Hall in 1950 (the Negro Gospel and Religious Music Festival, starring Mahalia Jackson). This became an annual event and introduced such performers as James Cleveland, Norsalus McKissick and J. Earle Hines. Then, in 1959, he mounted the first annual Gospel, Spiritual and Folk Music Festival at Madison Square Garden. It drew a crowd of 11,000.

Bostic's position allowed him to think big. He was responsible for the introduction of gospel to the Newport Jazz Festival when he arranged for the Ward Singers and the Drinkard Singers to appear there in 1957. This would lead to other acts being invited in later years, from Rosetta Tharpe to the Dixie Hummingbirds, and was an attempt in the same spirit as John Hammond's *From Spirituals to Swing* concerts to give gospel an equal standing with jazz, folk, country and blues as one of the foundations of twentieth-century American popular music. In 1958 he told the prolific freelance writer Richard German that gospel music was now big business, with an annual gross of around $15 million.

Therman Ruth, who had a background in vaudeville, gospel, radio and R&B, hosted *The Ship of Zion* on Harlem's radio station WOV.

He became the first promoter to put on an all-gospel show at Harlem's legendary Apollo Theater. This was no easy task, as the Apollo's management was sceptical about gospel and many of the gospel singers were uneasy about taking their message to a venue with such a 'worldly' reputation. However, Ruth convinced the singers that this was just the place where the gospel was most needed, and in December 1955 he mounted the first such show, featuring the Pilgrim Travelers, the Blind Boys of Mississippi, the Caravans, Brother Joe May, the Sensational Nightingales and the Harmonizing Four.

On the West Coast, Art Rupe of Specialty Records had been thinking the same way. In July 1955 he had mounted a concert at the Shrine Auditorium in LA to showcase his most popular gospel acts and record it for a live album. Billed as the Annual Mid-Summer Festival of Gospel Music, it drew a capacity crowd to witness the Soul Stirrers, Ethel Davenport, James Cleveland and Dorothy Love Coates with the Original Gospel Harmonettes.

Those who produced, promoted and exploited gospel music were almost all in the business for reasons other than to spread the message of Christ or to build up the spiritual lives of Christians. They rightly saw that it was music full of dynamism and creativity, worthy of critical respect and the equal of any other music developed by Americans on American soil. They could also see that millions would pay money to participate in the gospel music experience. Their involvement would eventually kill gospel, but for a few years they were the enablers of the Golden Age.

Rosetta Tharpe (piano) and Marie Knight.

Interview with Bill 'Hoss' Allen (1922–97), Nashville, 29 April 1976

❋ **How did the gospel show you are doing now begin?**

A DJ who had been at WLAC for many years, John Richburg, who was known as John R, had for many years done 1 a.m. to 3 a.m. and had played blues and done spots for gutted mufflers, baby chickens, Bibles and weight-loss products. He was retiring after some thirty years at the station. They wanted me to do 1 a.m. to 3 a.m. but I didn't want to be on in the middle of the morning and do blues because I would have to do it live every day and I knew there was this great demand for gospel. I knew there was a big gospel market out there and I knew there were many companies turning out gospel product who had no outlet for it. I felt I could sell the two hours in just a few phone calls to the relevant record companies – to Nashboro here in Nashville, Jewel in Louisiana, Stax in Memphis, who at that time had a gospel label, and King, who were still operating then. So I prevailed on the management of the station. I said I'd do the 1 a.m. to 3 a.m. if they let me tape it and turn it into a gospel show. The record companies paid the station. It wasn't payola. It was a straight time buy.

❋ **You had been doing country music before that?**

No. I had been doing R&B for the past twenty years.

❋ **Then you saw that gospel needed more of an outlet?**

Yes. In the meantime R&B was on the wane. Shortly after I got the gospel show started we had a change in programming at the station.

WLAC had left CBS and gone into middle of the road [music] during the day. Since 1947, we had been playing black music at night and that was the first time in the South or anywhere else that blacks had had a power station playing their music. There had been some stations in New York, Chicago, Philadelphia, Detroit, LA and maybe Atlanta, small stations that practically didn't get out of the city, that were playing black product. We were the first power station. We were a 50,000-watts station with a twenty- to twenty-one-state coverage plus the West Indies. We had a directional signal, 1510 on the dial. We went straight north and south, which is from Bogotá to Montreal, then we went south west almost to El Paso. We covered all the so-called heavy black belt across the Carolinas, Florida, Georgia, Mississippi, Alabama, Louisiana, East Texas. But, back to gospel. The show really took off even though it was in the early morning. It caught on so fast that we were besieged with mail. We promoted gospel records and they sold well and the record companies noticed an immediate pick-up in sales. I started playing sermons or part of a sermon. These sermons are put out as part 1 and part 2. I'm playing one at the moment called 'What the hell do you want?' by Reverend Leo Daniels, and on my Sunday show I'll play about fourteen minutes of a sermon. There will normally be fifteen to eighteen minutes on one side. They are recorded live in churches, and usually in part 2 the preacher is really getting into his act and is getting a reaction from the congregation.

❋ **Are they performances rather than messages?**

Well, it's their form of religion. They work like hell all week and this is one place they can go once a week and completely let go. And they do. They fall out, scream and get carried out. There's an expression that travelling gospel groups use. They say, 'Well, we really turned 'em out tonight,' which means that they had sisters falling out all over the floor, speaking in tongues and this, that and the other. It's very Pentecostal, very exciting, and they have this unusual ability to slough off all their troubles. They go to church to get rid of everything, to forget all their problems. Historically, they've been controlled by white people. They've worked in menial jobs and have suffered indignities, but the church on Sunday belongs to them. It's like charging their batteries for the week to come. A lot of the preachers will take blues tunes. The Reverend Jasper Williams, who has a church in Atlanta, took a tune that Little Milton made famous, called 'If walls could talk', and he made a sermon out of it. The preachers bring the people together with them.

❀ **Who buys the records you play?**

Rural black listeners for the most part. They want basic, earthy gospel as done by the Angelic Gospel Singers, the Swanee Quintet, the Soul Stirrers, the Brooklyn All-Stars, the Bright Stars, the Gospel Keynotes. The Gospel Keynotes have become very popular in the last couple of years. My audience wouldn't buy anything by the Mighty Clouds of Joy, for example. The last album of theirs that I was sent I couldn't find a single track that I could play. My show probably wouldn't go down well in a city like LA.

❀ **Are gospel groups hard to produce?**

You can't really produce them because they've been playing the same way for years and years. The big thing is getting a good sound on them and doing a good mix. You don't want to change it too much from how they actually sound on stage because people buy the record and then they go and see them in concert and they'll wonder why there aren't bongos, conga drums and the organ. You want to keep the same instruments that they would normally play.

❀ **What's your understanding of black religion?**

I think it's a release. What else have they got to look forward to? Everything is like 'when I cross over the Jordan' or 'it's gonna be better over there'. Nothing can be as bad as it is here. Tunes that were traditional and popular in the 1930s are still being done today but by younger groups. So even with all the things that have happened since Martin Luther King's march in Selma in 1963, it's like yesterday as far as they're concerned. They've been in bondage for 400 years. The spirituals grew out of field chants. It was a rhythm they could work to and it was also a way of sending messages from row to row without the foreman knowing what they were talking about. They sang in patois. In the Carolinas there are still blacks who speak geechee, which is from the Angolo tribes which came from Ghana. They came into places like Savannah and Charleston. They still have their own patois in that area, which is a mixture of Spanish, French, English and African influences.

❀ **Are you a Christian?**

Er ... I believe in a higher power. I had a drinking problem for twenty-five years and I went to AA and now I've been sober for five years. I'm a walking miracle. We believe in a higher power which we choose to call God. I'm a Catholic by birth and went to church all my life, but when I went into the army I stopped. Now I go to AA meetings a couple of times a week and I feel like that is my church.

❀ **Where is the geographical heart of gospel music?**

All of the South, of course. It seems to be more popular in the Carolinas and the coastal areas of Florida and Georgia. It's very big in Mississippi, Alabama and East Texas. It's popular wherever you have blacks, but the difference is that in the

Northern cities they go more for choirs. They also go for a smoother sound, whereas the people in the country want their gospel to be earthy.

✤ **Many listeners think that you're black.**

I grew up on a farm surrounded by blacks so that's why I know some of the folkways, mores and clichés. I hadn't played with a white boy until I was eight years old. It was all blacks that worked there so I played with their children. I was eight when I moved to town.

✤ **You not only have a deep voice but you know all the hip phrases and slang.**

When I was doing a blues show I used a lot of blues clichés and did a lot of shouting and talked a lot of trash. I sold Royal Crown hair dressing, which had a lot of products for straightening your hair, negro cosmetics, records and this, that and the other. I'd come on and say, 'Hey, it's get down time with the Hossman', and anybody out there who was black knew that 'get down time' is when the whores hit the streets. I used a lot of *double entendres* that only black people would understand. When I came off the air I'd go to black clubs. When I used to go sailing in the Bahamas I'd meet people who listened to the Hossman, but when I told them I *was* the Hossman they wouldn't believe me because I was white. I'd have to go through a whole routine to convince them. There are jocks that are much bigger than me, like the Wolfman, but the Wolfman would be the first one to tell you that he got his pitch from John R and myself.

CHAPTER

9

Move On Up

MAKING MONEY

The Golden Age of gospel was truly golden. All of the greatest gospel artists were working during this time, record sales were increasing, chart music was being shaped by its influence and there was a growing acceptance that gospel music was great art rather than a primitive cacophony. Gospel was not only on the radio but in movies and on television. It was not only in the churches but on the stages of jazz and folk festivals and some of the most prestigious venues in the world.

This was the time during which female vocalists such as Mahalia Jackson, Marion Williams and Clara Ward did their best work, when groups such as the Swan Silvertones, the Soul Stirrers and the

Mahalia Jackson at the start of her recording career.

Dixie Hummingbirds established their definitive line-ups and when the key innovations in style, composition and performance took place. They were also the years when independent record labels such as Savoy, Chess, Peacock and Specialty began to outsmart the majors by tapping the so-called 'race market' and discovering vital young talent in gospel, blues and jazz.

This once despised music began to be taken seriously by show-business reporters, who couldn't help but notice that gospel was drawing audiences and making money. In 1951 Mahalia Jackson performed to a crowd of 42,000 at the Coliseum in Chicago, and the following year the Soul Stirrers announced a 101-city tour. In 1953 the Pilgrim Travelers played 173 dates and grossed $100,000, while the average gospel single sold 10,000 copies. In 1956 the Ward Singers made over $500,000, and were travelling between concerts in a two-tone Cadillac limousine that hauled a matching trailer for their luggage.

The elite gospel singers began to live and perform very much like their counterparts in jazz, blues and pop. Few of them had ever

Clara Ward and the Ward Singers, 1959.

imagined that they'd be so richly rewarded for playing the music they played in church. The Ward Singers decked themselves out in sequinned gowns and extravagant wigs, the Dixie Hummingbirds (inspired by the Soul Stirrers) began dressing in white tuxedos with tails, and Sister Rosetta Tharpe became the first gospel singer to have her own tour bus. There were agents to book gospel tours, promoters to hire venues and managers to look after their every whim.

Recognizing the potential of making money from tours as well as record sales, the smaller labels established agencies for their artists. Acts on Specialty were dealt with by Herald Attractions, those on Peacock by the Buffalo Booking Agency. The Ward Singers opened their own agency in 1955 and established a publishing company to which they signed the writers of songs they planned to cover. Mahalia Jackson was represented by the prestigious William Morris theatrical agency.

Although there were hundreds if not thousands of gospel acts active during this time, the main innovations, hits and national tours emanated from a core of around twenty-five acts. A list of the top-selling gospel acts published in 1955 included Mahalia Jackson, the Soul Stirrers, the Pilgrim Travelers, Alex Bradford, Brother Joe May, the Swan Silvertones, the Ward Singers, the Spirit of Memphis and the CBS Trumpeteers. Most of the big events would include at least four or five of these names with the addition of one or two local favourites. The majority of the gospel groups of the era, even those that had recording contracts, have long been forgotten.

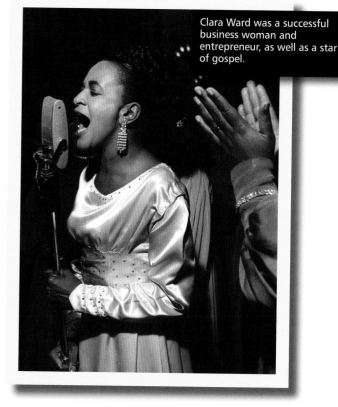

Clara Ward was a successful business woman and entrepreneur, as well as a star of gospel.

THE POST-WAR BOOM

The boom started with the end of the war. Servicemen returned from abroad, record production was no longer hampered by restrictions on shellac, sound reproduction had been boosted by 'high fidelity' and the revived economy meant that more money was available for leisure activities.

It was also the beginning of a shift in mood among America's black community. In the South, still the heartland of gospel music, there was a movement to end segregation and any form of discrimination on the basis of race. The black church, itself forged in the fires of the Civil War, became a powerful force for change, able to argue for the dignity of every human being on the basis of a theology shared with the white oppressors.

THE CIVIL RIGHTS MOVEMENT

The gospel music of the Golden Age was composed and recorded against the background of novels like *The Invisible Man* by Ralph Ellison and *Go Tell It on the Mountain* by James Baldwin, and events like the Montgomery Bus Boycott initiated by Rosa Parks. These gave birth to the Civil Rights movement, organizations such as the Southern Christian Leadership Conference founded in 1957, and the figure of Martin Luther King, a political leader who used the language of gospel music in his writing, the cadences of the gospel preacher in his speeches and the philosophy of the New Testament in his thinking.

'Move on up a little higher', gospel music's first million-selling single in 1948, anticipated the mood. On the surface it was a biblically informed song about going to heaven and indulging in its blessings, but the subtext was one of a racial minority moving up to get some of the things it deserved. It was a song of courage, hope, pride and reward.

Rosa Parks sits in the front of a bus in Montgomery, Alabama, after the Supreme Court ruled segregation to be illegal on the city bus system on 21 December 1956. Parks had been arrested on 1 December 1955 for refusing to give up her seat in the front of a bus.

Gospel music of the Golden Age, though, was largely apolitical, at least as far as the lyrics were concerned. Occasionally a group would drop in a topical song, as the Pilgrim Travelers did with 'Jesus hits like the atom bomb' and the Dixie Hummingbirds did with their Korean War song 'Wading through blood and water', but generally the songs focused on the traditional New Testament themes of redemption, the Christian walk, heaven and the comfort of knowing Jesus.

The political nature of gospel lay in its ability to empower rather than its outspokenness. Gospel music, for example, was one of the few areas of music where black women could gain respect and admiration. This was in part because women found it easy to become music directors in black churches. Of the twenty-five top acts of the 1950s, almost half were female. Sallie Martin, as has already been mentioned, was head of the largest black-owned gospel music publishing company in America.

Gospel music provided stars for the black community. When fans poured into the giant auditoriums to see the likes of the Caravans or the Ward Singers, they felt a sense of unity they had never experienced before, and the fact that the white world was looking on in admiration instilled a sense of pride.

After the war, gospel quartets made the most dramatic departures from the jubilee tradition of 'flat-footed' performances and close harmony singing. There was a fresh emphasis on individualism, self-expression and flamboyance. R. H. Harris, the legendary founder and lead singer of the Soul Stirrers, was credited with many of these changes. He encouraged his group to use the stage rather than to cluster, introduced the 'swing lead', where two vocalists shared the lead duties, and led the movement away from hymns and traditional spirituals towards material written by the groups themselves.

Ira Tucker took the Dixie Hummingbirds to new levels of showmanship by jumping off the stage during performances and running down the aisles, falling onto his knees in a prayer-like position and slapping his thighs for emphasis. The Hummingbirds began to develop ever more sophisticated arrangements that out-dazzled their contemporaries. Singers in the group would take over one another's parts and switch easily from tenor to baritone or from lead to bass. They would also use key words from the lyric that could be chanted to build up a sonic backdrop. Tucker was a master of ad-libbed vocals, which he would slip into available spaces.

These adaptations were made to bring audiences into a state of emotional ecstasy. The language that singers used about this phenomenon involved images of violence rather than tenderness and uplift. They spoke about 'wrecking' or 'tearing up' the house, as if they were agents of destruction who had come to bring chaos out of order. Although these scenes of shaking, dancing, crying and collapsing were always interpreted as a visitation of the Holy Spirit, a more likely explanation is that, like teenage Beatles fans in the 1960s, they were simply responding to music that continually created tension and release.

The Pilgrim Travelers had been a reasonably successful quartet, but their fortunes were transformed when they were taken over by manager J. W. Alexander, a former singer and football player. He realized that the group would have to introduce a show-business pizzazz to cause the sort of mayhem that built reputations.

He encouraged them to loosen up their vocal style, to do the sort of tricks that wowed audiences and to choreograph their movements. Lead tenor Kylo Turner was a responsive student and developed a style of singing that would become highly influential in gospel.

ADDING INSTRUMENTS

The other major innovation for gospel was the addition of musical instruments. Gospel quartets had traditionally sung a cappella, although female vocalists and choirs would be accompanied by a piano or organ.

Mahalia Jackson, for example, made her best music with pianist Mildred Falls, and the Angelic Gospel Singers used keyboardists. Despite the commercial success of Rosetta Tharpe, there was still church resistance to the idea of using guitars with sacred music, and drums conjured up memories of Africa and heathenism.

Guitarists had sometimes played for quartets. George Scott played guitar for the Blind Boys of Alabama, the Dixie Hummingbirds had performed with bands at Café Society and the Swan Silvertones used guitar on a 1946 recording for the King label. The impetus for the development didn't come from within gospel. There was no sudden revelation from Scripture. Record producers simply realized that 'race music' was having more of an impact when drums and guitars were added.

The companies recording gospel music were also recording blues, jazz and R&B. At the same time that Peacock had the Original Five Blind Boys and the Dixie Hummingbirds, it was recording Clarence 'Gatemouth' Brown, Memphis Slim, Johnny Otis and, through an associate label, Bobby 'Blue' Bland and Johnny Ace. The Pilgrim Travelers, Brother Joe May and the Soul Stirrers were with Specialty at the same time as Roy Milton, Joe Liggins and the Honeydrippers, Lloyd Price and Percy Mayfield. Frequently these acts were produced by the same people in the same studio.

R&B singer Johnny Otis, who recorded for the Peacock label, became a preacher in the 1990s and pastored Landmark Community Gospel Church in Santa Rose, California.

Don Robey at Peacock had a passion for pushing his gospel acts towards R&B. He later claimed to have been largely responsible for introducing instrumentation into the quartets. 'I'm the one who put the beat into religious records,' he said. 'I was highly criticized when I started it but I put the first beat – which was not a drum – and then, after the public started to buy the beat, then I put a drum into it. Then a guitar, then a trombone.'

The first beat he introduced was probably the stomping of the Dixie Hummingbirds' feet on a 1952 session. The same year guitarist Howard Carroll joined them playing a large-bodied Epiphone guitar with an electric pick-up. In 1953 they did their first recordings with guitar and drums, as did the Soul Stirrers (the Swan Silvertones had used drums, piano and organ early in 1952). Robey's reference to the use of trombone was probably a 1953 experiment with the Spirit of Memphis. It wasn't one he repeated. As he said, the guitar found acceptance and so they went with it. The trombone was dropped.

The exact chronology of gospel's adaptation to musical instruments is hard to ascertain. Bunny Robyn, chief engineer for Specialty, was putting microphones at floor level to pick up the sound of the Pilgrim Travelers' toe-tapping as early as 1947, and the Original Five Blind Boys (the ones from Mississippi) were known for their heavy drum backbeat in 1951. Robey had employed the guitar of Namon Brown on 'Let's talk about Jesus' by the Bells of Joy a year before the Dixie Hummingbirds first stomped their feet.

The fact is that during a seven-year period (1946–53) gospel quartets added instruments and filled out their sound. They also began to add members, so that by the mid-1950s the term

Promotional portrait of the Dixie Hummingbirds, grouped around a CBS radio microphone, c. 1940.

'quartet' did not always apply strictly to the number of personnel but rather to the tradition. The Soul Stirrers had been a five-man group since the 1940s and became six when Paul Foster joined in 1952. Howard Carroll was a fifth member for the Dixie Hummingbirds.

TAKING THE LEAD

One of the main differences between the post-war gospel groups and the pre-war jubilee quartets was the independence given to the lead singers. In the past the voices melded together and no singer was given prominence over the others. Now the lead singers emerged as performers in their own right and were celebrated for their distinctive styles. Surprisingly, the solo male gospel artist was a rarity. There was no male equivalent to Mahalia Jackson. All the great men singers were embedded in groups.

Archie Brownlee was known alternatively as 'the hardest singing voice in gospel' or 'the baddest man on the road' because of his riveting screams, yells and shrieks with the Blind Boys of Mississippi. Both Julius 'June' Cheeks of the Sensational Nightingales and Claude Jeter of the Swan Silvertones were celebrated for being

Sam Cooke of the Soul Stirrers made the transition from gospel to pop, but fell out of favour with the church for doing so.

able to climb from their normal singing voices (baritone in the case of Cheeks, tenor in the case of Jeter) up to an outrageous falsetto when the emotion of a song demanded it.

Sam Cooke had a lyrical tenor voice that impressed with its sweetness rather than its jaggedness. Instead of ripping audiences up with vocal athleticism, he soothed them, and in doing so he became the first genuine sex symbol of gospel when he joined the Soul Stirrers in 1951. His intimate style and his handsome looks caused women to swoon. He was an unusual choice to replace R. H. Harris, the man who had left the group because he felt gospel music was becoming too full of gimmicks and that the gospel highway had become a road strewn with temptations.

Not as deeply religious as Harris, Cooke had no problem with temptations. He simply gave in to them, while at the same time recording some of the Soul Stirrers' most defining songs, including his debut single as the group's lead vocalist, 'Jesus gave me water', and the incomparable 'Touch the hem of his garment'. He left gospel music behind in 1957 for a career in pop. He started by disguising his identity and recording a secularized version of his gospel song 'Wonderful' (re-titled 'Lovable'), but his voice was too distinctive to hide and his cover as 'Dale Cook' was blown.

He ended up having a string of pop hits, including 'Cupid', 'Wonderful world', 'Bring it on home to me' and 'You send me', before being shot dead in a dispute at a seedy motel in Los Angeles where he had rented a room with a prostitute. There were many people in the gospel world who felt that this was a punishment for having turned his back on gospel music. They

believed that God had given him a voice to sing his praises but that Cooke had used it for mere financial reward and had sold his soul to glamour, lust and wealth.

The female singers of the Golden Age went through parallel changes. Rosetta Tharpe had always been out of step with whatever was conventional in gospel. She recorded with guitar from 1938 onwards and in 1941 was paired with Lucky Millinder and an orchestra which included Bill Doggett on piano and Panama Francis on drums. From 1947 onwards she toured with an electric guitar, playing it in a style that embraced both blues and country. Her 1947 version of 'Didn't it rain?' could stake a claim for being one of the earliest rock-and-roll recordings. She and Marie Knight bounced their vocals off each other, with Pops Foster providing walking bass, Sam Price on boogie-woogie piano and Kenny Clarke on drums.

Mahalia Jackson performed in the more conventional style of gospel but nevertheless developed her delivery. Her favoured style was what was known as 'surging' – a technique of starting a song at a slow pace and building up its intensity over the verses. The excitement was therefore accumulative rather than repetitive. This was particularly effective in songs like 'The upper room', 'How I got over' and 'Move on up a little higher', where the words were describing progress from a lower level to a higher one. Mahalia had the ability to use her voice to transport the listener from low to high.

She also developed physical jerks and verbal interpolations that became a part of the gospel style. At times she would lift up the hem of her long dress and strut across the stage as if mildly possessed and then move back to the microphone stand as if nothing had happened. Her use of phrases like 'Lordy' and 'Oh my Lord', derived from her childhood church experiences in New Orleans, was loved by audiences. She enjoyed slowing down old spirituals so that she could stretch out the syllables and play with them, adding trills and moans wherever appropriate. Bessie Griffin, as lead vocalist with the Caravans, could similarly make a song last up to twenty minutes, enabling her to embellish, increase the pitch and repeat key words and phrases.

The close of the 1950s marked the end of an era. Kip Lornell's study of quartets in Memphis shows that no new groups were formed in the city during the 1960s and only five have been formed since. The fate of quartets was a good indicator of changes that were happening throughout gospel.

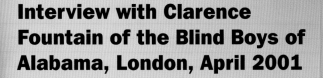

Interview with Clarence Fountain of the Blind Boys of Alabama, London, April 2001

❇ **You were one of the earliest groups to sing gospel.**

There was the Golden Gate Quartet. They were the best of the best. They had a mixed-up show. They could sing the blues as good as they sang gospel. I never liked to do that. I made the Lord a promise that if he let me make my living from gospel I'd go all the way. I had plenty of chances. I was just as good as Ray Charles, just as good as Stevie Wonder, but that ain't the idea. I don't want to go there. I never had the desire to go. See what God'll do for you. What does the Scripture say? He'll take from you what you seem to have. He can do that because he's God and can't nobody do what he can do. The difference between God and the devil is that the devil is mighty but God is almighty. There you have the difference.

● **Today you're popular with secular audiences. What do you think they get from gospel music?**

We had a secular audience there tonight. Now somebody done heard something. Remember this – all of us has a part of God in us. When he made man he breathed into him the breath of life. God did it. You can't get rid of that whether you believe in God or not. He made man in what? In his own image and likeness. So, you can't get rid of that. It don't matter what your age is. You can't get rid of that part that God put in you. That's the part that's going back to him.

● **You sang 'Amazing grace' tonight, but most of the audience would not have been Christian.**

Remember how we sang it twice?

Now, here's the thing. We sang it the way it was recorded [to the tune of 'House of the rising sun'] because the woman that owned the record company was there. Other than that, I wouldn'ta sang it. Not that way. I would have sung it the way we sung it before because we get more out of it that way. Everybody know that's the song and that's the right melody to the song. I sing it because it's a good song. Hey, I could sing it three times and I still wouldn't be tired. It's just a good thing to do.

● **What makes 'Amazing grace' such a good song?**

Listen to the words. See! Listen – 'Through many dangers, toils and snares / I have already come. / It was grace that led me safe so far, / And grace will lead me home.' You gotta be in God to have these things ever happen to you. The average person, believe it or not, when he gets a pile of money thinks it was given by God. Christian businessmen declare that God takes them and gives them grace abundantly. But if you've never been through troubles then you don't know what God can do. I am a witness because I know what he can do. I'm not speaking about what I heard. I'm talking about what I know he can do. That means I can sing the song and know what I'm singing about. I don't have to read about it. I don't have to wonder about it. I know what he has done. I can tell you. I ain't never seen a hungry day yet. And, I mean, we've come through something!

● **So do you need to be older to be able to sing it with conviction?**

Not necessarily. I already know what the words mean and I know that it's a fact of life that if God takes his hand off you, man – you're done. When you just put that

115

together you know whether he's with you or not. One thing God says is: 'I will never leave you or forsake you.' He told them preachers that and that goes for everybody else if he said it. The preacher didn't say it and I didn't say it. God said it. Whether you agree with it or not makes no difference. It'll come out his way anyway. We can't change nothing.

✿ You've been on the road a long time.

We've been together singin' for sixty years. I know for myself I done well servin' the Lord. I ain't got rich but I ain't never seen the righteous forsaken. My mummy and my daddy was good soldiers. I ain't been homeless. I always had somethin' in my pocket that I could get somethin' to eat with. So I know about God. I don't care whether they know it or not. I know. I can only tell you what I know.

✿ Your group was founded at the Alabama Institute for the Negro Blind. Had you been blind all your life?

Just about. Since I was two.

✿ So you don't know what sight is?

Naaah. But I'll see one day! Oh yeah. Everythin' gonna be all right. I ain't even worried 'bout that. That's one thing that has helped me. You see a bunch of people walkin' along the street. Now, if they can't sing – that would have been my fate. But, if you can sing, there's a place to go. You go to the stage. I know the Lord gave it to me. Couldn'ta been nobody else give it to me but him. Ain't no way I could have it on my own. Impossible! I could've sang the blues like Ray Charles and Stevie Wonder, but I didn't want to do that.

✿ How do you feel when you sing the line 'Was blind but now I see'?

That don't mean blind physically. That means spiritually.

✿ But you must understand the line in a different way to me.

I understand it like you do. I was blind in sin but now I see the light and I'm walkin' in it. That's what it all boils down to. I can see the light and I'm walkin' in it.

Music in the Air

THE COMPOSERS

The growth of the gospel music market meant that there was an ever greater need for writers to compose new songs. Although some artists wrote their own material – Ira Tucker and James Davies wrote for the Dixie Hummingbirds, and Sam Cooke, R. H. Harris and Roy Crain did the same for the Soul Stirrers – the majority depended on traditional hymns or spirituals that they could arrange, or newly written songs with hit potential.

CHARLES ALBERT TINDLEY

If Thomas Dorsey was the father of the gospel song, the grandfather was Charles Albert Tindley, one of the first African Americans to compose a new type of religious song that was neither a spiritual nor a hymn. Anthony Heilbut has said that Tindley's 'merger of black folk tunes and sentiments with the music of shabby white evangelism is one of the greatest chapters in American popular music'. His songs took something from both blues and jazz and he became a hero and role model to Dorsey.

Born in 1851 to parents who had been slaves, Tindley was self-educated and became the minister of Bainbridge Street Methodist Episcopal Church in Philadelphia. Under his guidance it became one of the biggest and most active churches in the city, with a membership of 10,000 and a successful programme for helping the poor during the Depression. In 1927 it was renamed Tindley Temple.

Although never able to read music he composed songs in his head, which he then had professional musicians transcribe for him. In 1901 he published a collection of his songs, the first African American ever to do so, and the church began to perform his works. In 1922 he organized a piano-accompanied group to perform them. He named them the Tindley Gospel Singers.

Tindley created the musical and lyrical template for future gospel writers. There was a looseness in the construction of the songs that allowed singers to be creative and playful, and his words drew on biblical imagery in a way that made it relevant to his black inner-city congregation. The twin poles of his songs were the suffering in this present world and the glory of heaven. There was rarely any advice as to how to escape from the former to the latter. It was assumed that the singers were already believers.

Although some eighteenth-century Protestant

hymnody language was retained – 'peace abounds like a river', 'tossed and driven on the restless sea of time', 'naught of this world's delusive dream' – there was a movement towards more colloquial expression – 'when I'm growing old and feeble, stand by me'. A typical Tindley song was not as densely packed with theology as one by Wesley or Watts, but neither was it as sparse and heavily dependent on repetition as the spirituals.

Tindley's songs appealed to the guitar evangelists. In 1927 Blind Joe Taggart recorded 'The storm is passing over', and both he and Washington Phillips recorded 'What are they doing in heaven today?' Gospel musicians had grown up with his songs in their hymnals, and so it was natural that they would plunder his catalogue when looking for material. The list of those who recorded 'Leave it there' (also known as 'Take your burdens to the Lord') reads like a history of gospel music, from the guitar evangelists Blind Willie Johnson, Washington Phillips and Blind Joe Taggart, through to groups of the 1940s and 1950s, such as the Wings of Heaven, the Sensational Nightingales, the Five Blind Boys of Alabama, the Golden Gate Quartet, and the Ward Singers.

LUCIE CAMPBELL

Several of Tindley's hymns appeared in *Gospel Pearls*, the hymnal that was launched in September 1921 at the National Baptist Convention that Dorsey was reluctantly taken along to by his uncle. They were in part responsible for planting the idea of the potential of gospel music in his mind. On the selection panel for that groundbreaking hymnal was Lucie Campbell, a young Mississippi-born woman who had been directing the convention's young people's choir since 1916. She was to become another role model for gospel music writers.

Campbell was a dynamic force in all musical aspects of the National Baptist Convention. A pianist and teacher, she also sat on the convention's music committee and wrote songs, musicals and pageants. From 1919 until her death in 1963 she wrote a new song for the choir to perform at each annual meeting, and these songs rapidly spread throughout the Baptist Church and beyond. In 1930 she and Dorsey met for the first time, and she used her influence to get more people to listen to his songs. Later she was responsible for introducing singers such as Marian Anderson and Mahalia Jackson to the convention.

Like Tindley, she used common speech and described the emotional vicissitudes of the spiritual walk rather than arguing the doctrinal basis for it. In 'Something within me' she expressed the certainty that a change had taken place in her life, but the use of the word 'something' showed that she was happy to remain abstruse. 'Somebody said it's hope, / Somebody said it's peace, / Somebody said joy, / All I know is that nobody can take it away; / Jesus gave it and it's here to stay.'

Her songs were sensuous. The Jordan was chilly. Spiritual passion was hot. 'In the upper room', the song of hers made famous by Mahalia Jackson, was written as if she had actually visited the scene of the last supper with Jesus. In 'Jesus gave me water', which was turned into a big hit by the Soul Stirrers, she seated herself beside the well when Jesus spoke to the Samaritan woman. Through placing herself within these stories rather than merely recounting them as historical facts, she drew her listeners into the biblical truths.

THOMAS DORSEY

Dorsey continued in the tradition of Tindley and Campbell, writing songs often inspired by real-life events that were then rounded off with spiritual wisdom. He wasn't trying to be doctrinally comprehensive. There was very little about the fall, the sacrificial death of Jesus, the resurrection or the final judgment. As with Tindley, the emphasis was on the reality of suffering contrasted with the promise of God's love and care.

By the 1950s, Thomas Dorsey was a revered elder statesman of the gospel world, as well as a working songwriter, choir director, music publisher and convention organizer.

'There will be peace in the valley', one of his best-known songs and, like quite a few of his compositions, 'inspired' by a spiritual, was fairly typical in its approach. The narrator starts off 'tired and so weary', but reassures himself that one day there will be 'no sadness, no sorrow, no trouble'. He uses images of heaven from Revelation, where 'the lion shall lay down with the lamb', and he will be 'changed from this creature that I am'.

The same formula was adhered to in his best-known song, 'Precious Lord, take my hand', where he found himself 'tired', 'weak' and 'worn', but was led by the Lord 'on to the light'. Like Tindley, he was fond of storms, waves and dark skies. In 'When the gate swings open', made

popular by the Ward Singers, he toils 'through the storm and rain'. In 'If you see my Saviour' (recorded as 'Bedside of a neighbour' by groups such as the Dixie Hummingbirds, the Golden Gate Quartet, the Heavenly Gospel Singers and the Norfolk Jubilee Quartet), he finds himself standing at the bedside of someone about to 'cross Jordan's swelling tide'. In 'De old ship of Zion' he is lost 'on an isle in life's dark sea'.

Almost every gospel artist of the era recorded some Dorsey: the Golden Gate Quartet, the Dixie Hummingbirds, the Soul Stirrers, Sister Rosetta Tharpe, Mahalia Jackson, Sister Ernestine Washington, the Fairfield Four. In 1973 Anthony Heilbut produced a double album for Columbia Records with new recordings of Dorsey songs by almost every top gospel artist then alive, from

Sallie Martin and Delois Barrett Campbell to Alex Bradford, Marion Williams and Bessie Griffin. In the sleeve note Heilbut commented:

> Each field of popular music has its major song writers, but Thomas A. Dorsey's domination of black gospel music is quite special. As both the supreme exponent of his craft and a model for later writers, he is gospel's answer to W. C. Handy, perhaps more original than the Father of the Blues, certainly more prolific. By a conservative estimate, one out of four modern gospel standards (as distinguished from hymns or spirituals) is a Dorsey composition.

ROBERTA MARTIN

Roberta Martin was one of the earliest songwriters to be influenced by Dorsey. She'd arrived in Chicago from Arkansas at the age

of ten, studied music at Northwestern and heard gospel music for the first time when she met Dorsey, and later became the pianist for the young people's choir at Ebenezer Baptist Church. Blessed with a powerful contralto voice, she was also gifted as a writer and arranger. She formed her own group in 1933 with the help of Theodore Frye, and two years later named it the Roberta Martin Singers.

This group, eventually nine strong, set new standards for vocal arrangements and piano. There was no bass; each singer was clearly identifiable, and Martin developed a piano style that mixed the raw barrel-house of Arizona Dranes with what she'd learned of European classical music. The chords she came up with had never been used in gospel before, but were soon imitated by a legion of followers.

She began writing and had her first hit in 1943 with 'Try Jesus, he satisfies'. She would go on to write almost seventy

songs and establish a company to publish not only her own songs but any song recorded by the Roberta Martin Singers. Among her best-known compositions are 'He knows just how much we can bear', 'God is still on the throne' and 'Just Jesus and me'.

The Roberta Martin Singers proved to be a great training ground for other performers and writers. Eugene Smith (first tenor) went on to write 'I know the Lord will find a way', a classic example of gospel blues that gospel historian Horace Clarence Boyer reckons made more of a contribution to gospel than if Smith had done what many had urged him to do and founded his own group. Robert Anderson (low baritone), who left to pursue a solo career in the early 1940s, founded his own publishing company and went on to write such songs as 'Prayer changes things', 'Why should I worry?' and 'Oh Lord, is it I?'

KENNETH MORRIS

Another hugely influential songwriter was Kenneth Morris, the author of 'Dig a little deeper', 'Jesus steps right in', 'Yes, God is real' and many other gospel standards. Like Dorsey, Morris had grown up in church and had entered the world of jazz and blues. Trained at the Manhattan Conservatory of Music, he'd performed at the Chicago World Fair in 1934 but fell ill during the visit and so extended his stay. While recuperating he came across the newly developing gospel community. He began attending the First Church of Deliverance where he became choir director and is credited with being the person to introduce the Hammond organ into gospel music (in around 1939) as a partner to the piano.

At Deliverance he met Sallie Martin, who was then managing Dorsey's publishing company.

They became great friends, and when Martin formally broke with Dorsey in 1940 she and Morris formed their own company, Martin and Morris Music. Martin's role, as it had been with Dorsey, was to take her group, the Sallie Martin Singers, on the road to perform the latest songs in the company's catalogue while Morris remained in Chicago to notate, arrange, compose and handle the paperwork. Martin and Morris would build itself up to become the leading publisher of black gospel music, with a catalogue of over 1,500 songs. It would also distribute for other publishing houses, including Clara Ward Publications, Roberta Martin Music Studios and Savoy Music.

Often they would be sent poorly written songs, or poems in need of music, and Morris would polish the best of these into pieces worthy of publication. Also, he wrote and arranged over 500 of his own songs, many of which would become gospel standards. He had his first hit in 1940 when Wings Over Jordan recorded 'I'll be a servant for the Lord', and in the same year he adapted and arranged 'Just a closer walk with thee', a song he'd heard sung by a railway porter when travelling from Kansas City to Chicago. He altered the music, added some verses of his own, and saw it become his number-one title.

Horace Clarence Boyer points out that Morris's lyric-writing formula was to state a problem and then answer it in the final two lines of the verse. Thus in 'Yes, God is real' the problem was the limits of human knowledge, and the answer was the certainty of knowing the reality of God through inner experience. In 'Christ is all' the problem was hardships and sorrow, and the answer was the fact that Christ had paid for all our sin on Calvary.

HERBERT W. BREWSTER

The most outstanding writer to follow Dorsey was the Reverend Herbert W. Brewster, born in Somerville, Tennessee, in 1897. College-educated (he had a BA and a DD) and with an interest in literature, music, drama and theology, he became a minister in Memphis in 1930 and remained at the same church until his death in 1987. He wrote over 200 songs, many of which became gospel standards. Among his best-known compositions are 'Move on up a little higher', 'The old landmark' and 'Surely God is able'.

His songs were wordier than Dorsey's, reflecting his love of poets such as Shakespeare and Longfellow. Because of his training in the study of the Bible, they were also more theologically thorough. He was opposed to frothy displays of religious mania that were not rooted in scriptural understanding. Asked about the requirements of a gospel song, he told Anthony Heilbut: 'A gospel song is a sermon set to music. It must have sentiment and doctrine, rhetorical beauty and splendour.'

He was also committed to social justice. His songs aimed to inspire, encourage and foster self-respect. He was proud that in the 1950s his church became a magnet for precocious white teenagers who wanted to experience for themselves the gospel music they had heard on local radio. It was in the late 1930s that he began writing songs, organizing a church group to perform them. The lead vocalist of the Brewster Singers was a woman with exceptional talent, Queen C. Anderson. Even though she was never able to make a great recording, she was dynamic in performance and would attract visitors to the church. In the mid-1950s Elvis Presley was one of many white teenagers who came to hear her sing.

Every year Brewster would write a gospel music pageant for the church to perform, and many of the songs later covered by gospel acts were originally written for these events. 'Our God is able' was one such song. In 1941 one of his productions, *From Auction Block to Glory*, became the first ever black religious play with specially written gospel music to be staged nationally.

In the mid-1940s he wrote 'Move on up', which Queen C. Anderson would sing at church. In December 1947 it was recorded by Mahalia Jackson and became one of the best-known gospel songs ever. Brewster used the pulsing of phrases in his songs to give a sense of momentum. In 'Move on up' it was 'Gonna meet old man Daniel / Gonna move on up a little higher / Gonna meet the Hebrew children / Gonna move on up a little higher', so that the repeated words seemed like steps on the stairs ascending to heaven. In 'How I got over' a similar pace was set, with the first half of the song being relatively sparsely worded and the second half crammed with visual impressions: 'I'm gonna wear a diadem / in the New Jerusalem. / I'm gonna walk those streets of gold / In the homeland of the soul. / I'm gonna view the host in white; / They've been travellin' day and night, / Coming up from every nation / On their way to the grand coronation.'

Shortly after enjoying the success of 'Move on up' he began writing for the Ward Singers, who over the next decade would record more than twenty of his songs, including 'Surely God is able', 'How far am I from Canaan?', 'Weeping may endure for a night', 'God's amazing love' and 'Tell the angels'. Yet writing songs was only ever a small part of his life. He established theology schools in twenty-five American cities, was involved in the Civil Rights movement, served on the education board of the National Baptist Convention as well as heading its drama department, edited an African American newspaper, wrote books and pamphlets and preached at East Trigg Baptist Church in Memphis for almost sixty years.

In 1982 he was honoured by the Smithsonian Institute in Washington DC, which devoted a seminar to his songwriting and presented his musical drama *Sowing in Tears, Reaping in Joy*. What was celebrated by many people was the fact that Brewster was a herald of the Civil Rights movement. His songs were spiritual, but they also inspired blacks to move upwards and onwards. The material he wrote in the 1940s had become part of the soundtrack of the 1960s.

Interview with the Reverend Herbert W. Brewster (1897–1987), Memphis, April 1983

❀ **Tell me about the sort of people who used to come to East Trigg Baptist Church just to hear the music. I believe a lot of young white people started attending.**

Yes, in the days before integration all the church services were racially segregated and there weren't many whites in attendance. On some occasions the hierarchy of the denominations would come together and have an association. In the late 1930s and throughout World War II we found it very easy for people to get together and found a strong connection between people of all races. But it wasn't easy. I carved out a programme that I called *The Old Time Camp Meeting of the Air*, in which we put together old spirituals and a dash of anthems and so on and we had something for everyone. The groups I used were all made up of young people. They began to flock here from all the universities and colleges. Elvis Presley was in that group of youngsters who came along, and another black boy from around here, B. B. King. That period was known as the Golden Age of gospel. We had great fellowship and co-operation. I had a motto, 'When grace is in, race is out.' I also used to say, 'The ground is level at the cross.' That was very attractive, and people felt comfortable being together, and, of course, it was a great experience for this area of Memphis because nothing like this had existed before.

❀ **Can you remember seeing Elvis in those days?**

Yes, yes. He was among the regular attendance of the youngsters. He hadn't begun his skyrocketing in music. He came and sang along with us.

❀ **Did he sit with the main congregation or did he observe from the balcony?**

There was no separation. Everybody was together. Somebody recently wrote that there was a separation, but there was no separation. I found out that the line of separation between black and white was just a thin line. It was a small thread.

❀ **A lot of the songs sung in the church were ones that you composed.**

I wrote it for the young people and I didn't exclude anybody. We would start out with 'Camp meeting tonight'; that was the song we always came on with. Following that we had the old-time heartfelt religion, songs I had worked out so that the youngsters could relate to them. Then there would be some of my later compositions such as 'The hope of the world is Jesus'. We had a great variety of songs. We changed what we sang each Sunday because we didn't want it to become monotonous. There would be hand-clapping and foot-stomping. People could do whatever they felt like doing.

✿ **Did people 'fall out'?**

A few people that came in would. Our people were not the sort to do that. This church is an educational institution. We have a theological seminary here and we are not the sort of people for rollicking and rolling and that kind of thing. They would clap their hands rhythmically. It's a Baptist church from the old Southern Baptist tradition. This church is not Pentecostal. It's Bible-based and Christ-centred. I have been the Dean of Religion and the head of 7 million people in the National Baptist Convention. I've also been the head of its educational department. I have founded schools. At some time I have had twenty-four colleges under my supervision. This was not for ignorant people. We had people with all kinds of degrees here, but we didn't let education and sophistication drive away salvation as it so often did. When people accused Elvis of being a racist he would point out that much of his inspiration came from attending this church, but we didn't have a lot of razzle-dazzle with no meaning here. Everything had to have meaning.

✿ **Did you present featured vocalists?**

Yes, I did. They came from all over the nation. Mahalia Jackson got her start here. I wrote her music, all Mahalia Jackson. We had the only programme of that kind and the music was brand new, my arrangements were original and were taken directly from the hearts of the people. The real leader of the Camp Meeting Choir was Queen C. Anderson. She was a Memphis girl. Then we had between seventy-five and a hundred people who regularly took part in the singing. We had people like Clara Ward, who was a nationally known singer, and Marion Williams. I taught these people. I wrote most of their music. They would come here for weeks at a time and I would write songs for them while they were here. This was a place of activity in those days.

✿ **When you heard rock and roll, could you hear traces of gospel?**

Certainly. It was evidenced in the rhythm, and there were certain plaintive lines and slurs that were characteristic of early gospel music. Some of the best gospel I ever heard anyone sing was when Elvis sang 'Peace in the valley'.

✿ **What about the way rock-and-roll singers moved?**

Yes – the kind of excitement and the hallelujahs and the shouting. There was a great similarity between the way the youngsters responded to Elvis when he was singing and the way they did in church when we had our sings. He admitted he was touched by those songs and that they became part of his make-up.

We Shall Overcome

THE VOICE OF PROTEST

On Easter weekend of 1960 the Student Nonviolent Coordinating Committee (SNCC), one of the most significant organizations in the Civil Rights movement, held its founding conference in Raleigh, North Carolina. One of the organizers, a white Californian named Guy Carawan, led the gathered delegates in a rendition of what for most of them was an unknown song called 'We shall overcome'. It

The March on Washington in August 1963 was a seminal moment in the Civil Rights movement. Gospel music and adapted spirituals provided inspiration for activists committed to social justice and equality.

would go on to become the best-known song of the campaign against segregation in the South.

Carawan was employed by the Highlander Folk Center, an educational institution established to help Southerners who were engaged in justice and freedom issues. Carawan's specific interest was the use of music in empowering people on marches, sit-ins and demonstrations. It was while at Highlander that he heard 'We shall overcome', a song used by black members of the Food and Tobacco Union during a 1945 strike in Charleston, South Carolina.

These strikers, in turn, had taken some of the words from Charles Albert Tindley's 1901 hymn 'I'll overcome some day' and the music from the folk song 'No more auction block'. The changes were significant. Tindley's hymn pictured life as a battlefield against 'seen and unseen powers' which could be overcome through prayer, Bible-reading and obedience to Christ. 'If in my heart I do not yield,' he wrote, 'I'll overcome some day.' The strikers' version, which was the one Carawan heard and later helped to embellish, was simply about overcoming social opposition through determination and community action.

'We shall overcome' was the first adapted religious song to be picked up by the Civil Rights movement and it triggered a trend. Traditional spirituals were revisited because of their ability to unite, inspire, motivate and challenge. When protestors gathered they found music uplifting and uniting. Given that the majority of them in the South had grown up in Protestant churches, it was natural that they would turn to the church to provide them with material that they knew and could sing. It was in this way that such songs as 'This little light of mine' and 'We shall not be moved' became anthems of the movement.

Spirituals didn't motivate by goading into direct action, certainly not by advocating violent overthrow, but by dignifying determination and by holding up examples of biblical characters who had overcome more powerful enemies by remaining faithful to their convictions. Moses, Noah, Joshua and Daniel were four such heroes who repeatedly cropped up in spirituals: Moses famously leading his people out of captivity in Egypt despite the intransigence of Pharaoh; Noah being rescued from a sinful world in an ark that his detractors scoffed at him for building; Joshua, who brought down the walls of Jericho through the sound of music; and Daniel remaining unharmed in a den of lions because God knew that he was a righteous man who'd been unjustly accused by the jealous henchmen of Darius, King of Babylon.

In each of these cases the lesson was clear: it is better to remain true to God, whatever the opposition, than to capitulate. There was an inner strength that developed when doing the right thing. In the Bible stories God's blessing always came to those who held out on principle rather than those who did what was most convenient or popular. Spirituals such as 'Moses, Moses', 'Didn't it rain?', 'Joshua fit de battle of Jericho' and 'Didn't my Lord deliver Daniel?' might have sounded cute and childlike to secularized white ears, but to African Americans suffering the indignities of segregation and racism they were rallying calls to take tough moral decisions that could involve persecution and suffering.

The other side of the stories that the spirituals told was that the destination of those who took the broad and easy road was destruction. Pharaoh's army drowned in the Red Sea, those who scoffed at Noah were lost in the flood, the citizens of Jericho got buried beneath the rubble, and Daniel's false accusers were thrown to the lions. This communicated the emboldening message that if the powerful chose to use their power for evil, they would one day be brought down. Because of their number or their power, they may appear invincible, but only righteousness is ultimately invincible.

It's impossible to overestimate the importance of such songs in creating the moral imagination of African Americans. The same stories, and the same principles, were carried into gospel music. It is better to suffer for doing what is right than to have a comfortable life doing what is wrong. One person with God is in a majority. Evil deeds will not go unpunished. Good deeds will not go unrewarded. The history of African American people was living proof of these truths.

THE MESSAGE OF EQUALITY

Besides providing the motivation for doing what was right, whatever the cost, the spirituals gave a basis for equality. People were not equal in size, intelligence or beauty, but they were equal in value before God. It was sinful to degrade, abuse or hate anyone made by God in the image of God. There was equality in heaven and the principles of heaven were to be put into operation down below. 'I got a robe, you got a robe / All God's chillun got robes …' The kingdom of God didn't allow for poverty, class structures or factions. The spiritual 'You got a right', collected by James Weldon Johnson in 1925, said, 'You got a right, I got a right / We all got a right to the tree of life.'

Gospel songs emerged that daringly applied this principle to the specific issue of race. In 1946 the Golden Gate Quartet released 'No restricted signs in heaven', with its clear message that segregation was incompatible with the rules of the kingdom of heaven.

> *Knock a-knock, a-knock knock knock knock*
> *Folks were knocking at the pearly gates.*
> *Knock a-knock, a-knock knock knock knock*
> *Askin' 'bout the rooms and 'bout the rates.*
> *Old St Peter, official greeter,*
> *He was present to let them in.*
> *A few looked down, 'cos their skin was brown,*
> *But Pete he hollered with a great big grin:*
> *'Welcome! Welcome!*
> *There are no restricted signs up in heaven*
> *And there's no selected clientele.'*
> **'No restricted signs in heaven',**
> **the Golden Gate Quartet**

Seven years later, James Walker, soon to become a member of the Dixie Hummingbirds, went into a studio in Jackson, Mississippi, and recorded 'Prayer for tomorrow' with his group the Southern Sons. The song's prayer that one day 'everybody will be as one' anticipated not only the vision of the Civil Rights movement but the peace-loving hippie idealism expressed in John Lennon's 'Imagine' almost two decades later.

When the Dixie Hummingbirds recorded it in 1964, at the height of the movement, they muted the notion of Christian discipleship in the original. The Southern Sons had started the song, 'For in thy footsteps, Lord, we'll always follow, / This is my prayer, yes, Jesus, for tomorrow', but the Dixie Hummingbirds had changed this to 'Lord, help us to love one another / Every creed and every colour'. Here the cry of 'Lord' seemed more of an interpolation than a form of address. Significantly, the title was changed to the more general 'Our prayer for peace'.

SINGING FOR SOCIAL JUSTICE

The Civil Rights movement was both a blessing and a curse for gospel music. It drew deserved attention to the vast reserve of moral and spiritual power in the music of the black American church, yet frequently adopted from gospel whatever conformed to a liberal humanistic outlook, and disregarded or altered the rest. In this way the divisions between gospel and soul were virtually erased as increasingly gospel acts found that the way to a much broader acceptance

was to sing about love, peace and unity with a few 'Lordies' thrown in but Jesus left out.

Mahalia Jackson was an uncompromising figure, however. Always concerned with social issues, particularly racism, she was contacted in 1956 by Ralph Abernathy of the newly formed Southern Christian Leadership Conference and asked to sing at an event to mark the first anniversary of the Montgomery Bus Boycott, which had been started by Rosa Parks' refusal to sit at the back of a local bus, the area designated for 'negroes'.

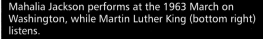

Mahalia Jackson performs at the 1963 March on Washington, while Martin Luther King (bottom right) listens.

Mahalia accepted, and gave a dynamic performance of several songs at St John AME Church of Montgomery, Alabama, in December 1956, at the end of a day of fasting and thanksgiving. From then on she was inextricably linked with the emerging movement for civil rights. The following year she was invited by the SCLC to the Prayer Pilgrimage for Freedom in Washington DC. Here she sang at the Lincoln Memorial as part of a bill that concluded with a speech by Martin Luther King. Her song of choice was 'I been 'buked, I been scorned', an old spiritual acknowledging the twin truths of earthly hardship and heavenly restitution.

> I been 'buked Lord, I been scorned
> I been 'buked Lord, I been scorned
> You know, I been 'buked Lord, I been scorned
> I been talked about, shows you're born.
>
> I'm gonna tell my Lord, when I get home
> I'm gonna tell my Lord, when I get home
> I'm gonna tell my Lord, when I get home
> Just how long they've been treatin' me wrong.
> **Traditional**

King and Abernathy were convinced that Mahalia's voice was a useful weapon in their armoury as they sought to defeat segregation and racism. Just as spirituals had done in the time of slavery, gospel music could use the belief system of their aggressors. Just as it was hard for the police to beat protestors when they were kneeling in prayer, so it was hard for ostensibly Christian politicians to paint the Civil Rights movement as 'Communist' when gospel music was so much a part of its presentation.

'ALL GOD'S CHILDREN'
Essentially the Civil Rights movement tried to

Martin Luther King, pictured here in 1965, used the language and rhythm of gospel in his classic speeches.

hold white America to account. It wasn't seeking to introduce new ideas but to point out that the foundational beliefs – in freedom, democracy and the value of the individual – had not been applied fairly to all. The teachings of the Bible – about loving one's neighbour, caring for the alien, and regarding everyone as an image-bearer of God – likewise hadn't been applied universally. Martin Luther King's genius lay in taking the teachings revered by the white majority and preaching them back at them. 'We aren't engaged in any negative protest and in any negative arguments with anybody,' he said in his final speech. 'We are saying that we are determined to be men. We are determined to be people. We are saying that we are God's children and that we don't have to live like we are forced to live.'

King loved not only the rhetoric of the King James translation of the Bible but the cadences of hymns. His most famous speech, delivered at the Lincoln Memorial in August 1963, was full of references to the sort of biblical imagery that gospel music delighted in – 'the storms of persecution', 'trials and tribulations', 'all God's children', 'the cup of bitterness', 'the table of brotherhood' – and ended with a reference to the spiritual 'Free at last'. Mahalia sang two songs that day. She revisited 'I been 'buked, I been scorned' and added 'How I got over'. Her old friend, the Chicago broadcaster Studs Terkel, said later: 'Whoever was there can never forget that moment. Of course there was the address of Dr King; his plea for sanity for mankind, for liberation for all. But preceding him, at his request, was Mahalia Jackson.'

GOSPEL AND THE FOLK MUSIC REVIVAL

The fact that gospel had such a natural affinity with civil rights led to a reappraisal by the younger generation of whites who in all other respects had washed their hands of church culture. These were the college-educated 'baby-boomers' who were searching for liberation in every area of their lives and associated Christianity with conformity, repression and the preservation of the status quo. However, there

The Newport Jazz Festival played an important role in introducing gospel music to young, affluent, white audiences.

was something in gospel music that chimed with their quest for authenticity, freedom of expression, ecstatic experience and social equality.

The folk music revival, spearheaded by people like Pete Seeger, took gospel music and spirituals seriously even though many of those involved (again, like Seeger) were atheists. John and Alan Lomax, a father-and-son team of collectors, travelled the byways of America in order to make field recordings of music that had been passed down through the generations but had never made it onto the printed page or magnetic tape. They feared that these songs would disappear as television and radio spread, and they treated gospel as another American folk music on a par with country blues, Appalachian ballads and work songs.

It was through the preservation work of Seeger and the Lomaxes that gospel began to enter the repertoires of young singers such as Bob Dylan ('Gospel plow'), Joan Baez ('All my trials'), Peter, Paul and Mary ('Children, go where I send thee'), and Johnny Cash ('Swing low, sweet chariot'). It no longer seemed incongruous to sing a spiritual among a collection of protest songs or, indeed, to have Mahalia Jackson perform at a festival that also featured Chuck Berry. The introduction of gospel to the Newport Jazz Festival was indicative of this mood.

Countercultural types who appreciated Miles Davis, Phil Ochs or the Paul Butterfield Blues Band could also appreciate the Ward Singers, Sister Rosetta Tharpe and the Dixie Hummingbirds.

Harry Smith, an eccentric archivist who made up recorded anthologies of overlooked American music by copying rare discs, had a powerful influence on many key performers of the early 1960s. In 1952 he released a three-double-album collection, *The Anthology of American Folk Music*, which became not just a great resource for those looking for unusual songs to cover but a practical guide to how to write from

Mahalia Jackson on stage at Newport in 1958. She tried to make her perfomances as much like church as was possible at an open-air festival.

the heart and soul. Smith divided the 112 songs into four sections – songs, ballads, social songs, and labour songs. In the social-song section he put a number of gospel recordings, including two by the preacher J. M. Gates ('Must be born again', 'Oh death, where is thy sting?'), 'I'm in the battlefield for my Lord' by the Reverend D. C. Rice and his Sanctified Congregation, and Blind Willie Johnson's 'John the Revelator'.

By the time of the protest marches, those on the radical left felt comfortable with gospel. They may not have endorsed the doctrines, but they admired the passion and the spirit of hope. They were also aware that a century before, when spirituals were relatively young, they frequently contained political aspirations couched in biblical language. The chariot that was 'a-coming to take you away' spoke of escaping to the

Northern states as well as of going to heaven. The river that needed crossing was the Ohio as well as the Jordan. The spirituals, created in secrecy and loaded with implicit meanings, could be subversive.

The singing may have seemed spontaneous but was often prepared in advance by a core leadership. Activists trained at the Highlander Folk Center in Monteagle, Tennessee, were told what types of song roused flagging spirits and inspired unity. Both the Congress for Racial Equality (CORE) and the SNCC had gospel-style groups known as the Freedom Singers, who would perform at major events. Solo singers, often known only in a particular region, would also perform. Fannie Lou Hamer, for example, whose singing of 'Amazing grace' inspired Judy Collins, was known mainly in Mississippi and so would appear on marches through that state.

ADAPTING THE MESSAGE

The difference between the songs sung by Mahalia Jackson and those used on the freedom rides, marches and mass rallies was that the spirituals were almost always adapted to fit current events. The titles would be modified – 'Woke up this morning with my mind on freedom' was taken from 'Woke up this morning with my mind on Jesus'; 'Keep your eye on the plow' (also known as 'The gospel plow') became 'Keep your eye on the prize' – extra verses would be composed and topical names would be inserted.

As a member of the SNCC Freedom Singers in Albany, Georgia, Bernice Reagon Johnson, the founder of the *a cappella* ensemble Sweet Honey in the Rock and now a professor of history at American University, helped transform spirituals and gospel songs. 'Over my head' (sometimes

Harry Smith (1923–91) was an eccentric ethno-musicologist whose *Anthology of American Folk Music* collected together rare recordings of gospel, folk, blues and other roots music. The albums became resource material for young folk musicians in the 1960s.

Civil rights marchers, pictured here in the shadow of the Capitol Building in Washington DC, found that gospel songs embraced a shared vision of dignity, justice and hope.

known as 'Up above my head'), the gospel song made popular by Sister Rosetta Tharpe, she altered during performance. The traditional words were 'Over my head / I see trouble in the air … I really do believe there's a heaven somewhere', but Johnson changed it to 'Over my head / I see freedom in the air … There must be a God somewhere'.

In 1987 she explained the process of adapting African-American traditional songs. 'From this reservoir activist song leaders made a new music for a changed time,' she said.

Lyrics were transformed, traditional melodies were adapted and procedures associated with old forms were blended with new forms to create freedom songs capable of expressing the force and intent of the movement.
Again and again, it was to the church that the movement activists came for physical protection and spiritual nurturing – the very structure developed by the Afro-American community for the survival of its people. The church provided the structure and guidance for calling the community together; it trained the singers to sing the old songs and gave them permission to create new ones.

The Reverend C. T. Vivian, another participant in the movement, said that although spirituals seemed a natural fit, there were times when the traditional lyric was inappropriate for particular circumstances.

> When we started seeking songs to use at mass meetings, the only thing we had among us that had any sense of life to it was church music. And some of the church music didn't fit at all. For instance, I was giving a speech once, and the choir followed with 'I'll fly away'. Now that didn't fit at all. In fact it was a direct contradiction to what I was saying. How much different it could have been if they had followed with a movement song that was also religious.

Among the most popular songs were those that celebrated determination, that pledged to continue fighting, whatever the opposition, because the cause was right. Songs such as 'We shall overcome', 'Ain't gonna let nobody turn me round' and 'We shall not be moved' reflected the stubbornness of the Old Testament heroes and heroines who wouldn't budge from fighting God's cause.

Songs about freedom and heading for the Promised Land were popular. Sometimes the word 'freedom' was in the original song, but at other times it was a convenient two-syllable replacement for 'Jesus'. 'I'm in love with Jesus' might go down well in the church, but 'I love freedom' made far more sense on a march. 'I'm gonna sit at the welcome table' took on a new meaning against the background of blacks being refused seats in white restaurants. At church, 'This little light of mine' meant letting the light of the gospel shine in your life, but on the streets of Alabama it meant being unafraid to stand up for justice. 'Great day for me' was written about salvation, but in a civil rights context it was understood to be about the goal of desegregation.

A typical adaptation would be 'Oh freedom', which was worked on by members of the SNCC. The traditional first verse, which was retained, was:

> Oh freedom, oh freedom, oh freedom over me
> And before I'll be a slave, I'll be buried in my grave,
> And go home to my Lord and be free.

The rest of the verses introduced other concepts in their first lines ('No more weeping', 'No burning churches','No more Jim Crow', etc.), while the second and third lines were retained from the spiritual.

The movement's song catalogue increased as the focus of the operations changed from sit-ins and freedom rides to marches and voter registration rallies. Significant legislation began to be introduced in 1964, with the Civil Rights Act outlawing discrimination in employment and public accommodations and the 1965 Voting Right Act. By the time of the Civil Rights Act of 1968, attention was turning towards improving living conditions and trying to eliminate hunger and poverty in the black community.

STAPLE SINGERS

Gospel groups emerged whose approach was better fitted to the developing mood about civil rights, Vietnam and personal freedom than it was to worship, teaching and evangelism. The paramount example was the Staple Singers, a family group led by guitarist Roebuck 'Pops' Staples. Although their guitar-based sound was fairly unusual in gospel in the 1950s, their material wasn't. Their biggest hit back then was a version of the traditional hymn 'Uncloudy day'.

By the early 1960s, though, they had imbibed the spirit of restlessness and questing that was

Roebuck 'Pops' Staples (1914–2000) performing with two of his daughters at the LA Coliseum in August 1972.

affecting the college generation and recorded 'message songs' that identified them with the folk protest genre. Mavis Staples would later say: 'We made the transition to protest songs when we heard about Dr Martin Luther King and visited his church. Pops called us into his room and said, "If this man can preach this, we can sing it and out a beat under it." '

In 1963, newly signed to the Riverside label, they became the first black group to record a Bob Dylan song when they cut a version of 'Blowin'

in the wind'. After three albums with Riverside, they signed to Epic, where they became even more committed to songs of protest. In 1965 they recorded 'Why am I treated so bad?', and in 1967 the Buffalo Springfield song 'For what it's worth', which detailed dissension on Sunset Strip between the police and club-goers.

The trajectory of the Staple Singers' outlook can be told by their album titles: *Swing Low, Sweet Chariot* (1961), *This Little Light* (1964), *Freedom Highway* (1965), *Soul Folk in Action* (1968), *The Staple Swingers* (1971), *Be What You Are* (1973), *Unlock Your Mind* (1978), and *Hold on to Your Dream* (1981). Allegiance to

the gospel style and the gospel message gave way to imperatives to be free, soulful and self-fulfilled. The Civil Rights movement, rather than broadening the narrow fundamentalist scope of gospel, had replaced it with the gospel of being yourself.

Another songwriter who mined the same seam was Curtis Mayfield. Raised in Chicago with a knowledge of gospel music, he wrote songs for his group, the Impressions, that employed the imagery of spirituals to sell the doctrine of self-improvement. 'Keep on pushin'', released in 1965, became an anthem for young black Americans. It sounded like a gospel song and used the same vocabulary. There was a reference

The suited man on the right stands on the spot where Martin Luther King was shot dead on 4 April 1968. In the distance are rooming houses, one of which was used by the gunman to fire his fatal shot.

to Mahalia Jackson's 'Move on up a little higher', an utterance of 'Hallelujah!' and an injunction to persist in fighting for their cause. However, the strength called on was no longer divine but 'my strength', and the reason to carry on was not because it was a calling but because 'it don't make sense / Not to keep pushin''.

Aware of the way his songs had inspired the Civil Rights movement, Mayfield wrote 'We're a winner', directly addressing African Americans and urging them to follow their leaders. Again the song referred to 'Move on up' as well as to 'Keep on pushin''. Released in 1967, it was in the best-seller charts when Martin Luther King arrived in Memphis in April 1968 to address striking sanitary workers.

King was assassinated on 4 April 1968 on the balcony of a Memphis motel. The previous night he had delivered a powerful speech at the Masonic Temple in which he referred to the power of the movement's prayers, words and

songs. He specifically mentioned 'Over my head' and 'We shall overcome'. As he got ready to go out for a meal with a local minister, he spoke to Ben Branch, a member of the twenty-five-strong Operation Breadbasket Band, some of whom had also been invited. 'Ben,' he apparently said, 'make sure you play "Precious Lord" at the meeting tonight. Sing it real pretty.' Minutes later he was on his back, dying from a single bullet.

The request was borne in mind when it came to organizing King's funeral. Mahalia Jackson delivered the song at Ebenezer Baptist Church. The event marked the end of an era and the plunging of America into a period of deep unrest and insecurity. Gospel music, too, was entering uncharted waters. Black artists now had an almost 50 per cent share of the charts. In the month of King's death, Otis Redding, Aretha Franklin, James Brown and Sly Stone all had singles in the top ten. Each of them had begun their musical education singing gospel.

Hallelujah, I Love Her So

BEYOND CIVIL RIGHTS

Marvin Gaye grew up singing gospel in his father's church in Washington DC. When his father travelled to other cities to preach, Marvin would often accompany him to deliver a solo that would win over the older women in the congregation. As a teenager he began singing doo wop, the popular vocal music of the time,

Marvin Gaye performs before a massive audience at the 1968 Miami Pop Festival, held at Gulfstream Park in Hallandale, Florida.

Marvin Gaye's classic 1971 album *What's Going On* embraced gospel, soul and the social conscience of the Civil Rights movement.

but his father disapproved. He referred to it as the 'devil's music'.

His father was even more disapproving when Marvin joined a professional group, the Moonglows, and later signed a solo contract with Motown Records in Detroit. He wanted to know why his son was wasting his precious God-given talent on worthless songs about love.

Once he had acquired wealth, fame and acclaim, Marvin developed an interest in being prophetic rather than merely entertaining. Like his father, he wanted to preach. Like his younger self, he wanted to sing gospel, but he wasn't always sure which gospel he wanted to sing. He found the solution he was looking for on the album *What's Going On*. In a brilliant way he combined the sentiment and style of gospel with current social concerns over the environment, violence and urban decay. One of the tracks on the album, 'Holy holy', was just stand-out

original gospel, from Marvin's own pen.

There had always been a tension between gospel music and secular pop. It was evident in Thomas Dorsey's vacillation between church music and blues in the 1920s, the way in which Rosetta Tharpe couldn't make up her mind whether to stay with gospel or go out to the nightclubs in the 1940s, and the recurring temptation faced by quartets like the Dixie Hummingbirds and the Golden Gate Quartet to become the next Mills Brothers or Ink Spots.

It made sense that the music industry would try to lure gospel musicians away from working exclusively in the church. Gospel acts knew how to sing and perform, they knew how to work audiences, but the language of their songs inevitably limited their appeal. The moguls argued that if only they would harness their skills to lyrics of a more earthly nature they could become world-beaters. Their incomes and their influence would increase. Left in their natural state, they were destined to become the secret of a few.

The church's argument was that the purpose of gospel music wasn't to make money or increase fame. It existed to convey teachings, facilitate worship and spread the good news of salvation through Jesus Christ. If someone was gifted as a singer, writer, musician or performer, it was precisely that: a gift. The gift was given by God for a specific purpose. If you used it to bring glory to yourself rather than to God, you were committing a sin.

Although presented as a black-and-white issue, in practice there was wriggle room. Many gospel stars awarded themselves the same sorts of perk as their secular counterparts. Few of them gave the impression that they sacrificed, fasted and prayed in order to bring God greater glory. When they spoke of their success it was usually in terms of records sold and churches wrecked; not souls saved or spiritual lives deepened.

There were also dalliances with secular culture that seemed to be tolerated. When gospel stars began appearing in nightclubs, it was explained as a penetration into godless culture rather than an act of selling out. Rosetta Tharpe told *Jet* magazine that she was 'brought up to believe night clubs were bad, wrong, and immoral. I don't see it that way now. I have long wanted to reach a larger public and I think I am doing it this way. I might help some of the club patrons spiritually. Who knows?' In May 1956 Clara Ward told *Color* magazine: 'I now feel that God intended for his message to be heard not solely by those who attend churches, but also by the outsiders who, in many cases, never attend a house of worship. For that reason the Ward Singers have taken our gospel singing into the Apollo Theater in New York City.'

GOSPEL AND POP

Similarly, there were gospel acts who would never have entertained the idea of 'leaving the church' but who nevertheless recorded pop standards. Mahalia Jackson cut versions of 'What the world needs now' and 'The green leaves of summer', the Golden Gate Quartet recorded 'Careless love' and 'Dipsy doddle', Clara Ward recorded 'Hang out your tears to dry', The Beatles' 'Help' and 'Zippety doo dah', and the Caravans managed to justify recording 'The white cliffs of Dover'.

Others drifted towards the popular 'message songs' of the 1960s, which at least seemed compatible with Christian concerns for peace,

justice and freedom. Marion Williams recorded Bob Dylan's 'Blowin' in the wind', as did the Caravans; the Soul Stirrers recorded Pete Seeger and Lee Hays's 'If I had a hammer', and the Staple Singers covered Curtis Mayfield's 'People get ready' and Burt Bacharach and Hal David's 'What the world needs now'.

The problem was in part created by the rigid secular/sacred divide that was characteristic of African American churches. Although all Christians agree that, in the words of the Westminster Confession, the 'chief end of man is to glorify God and to enjoy him for ever', there is often disagreement as to how God should be glorified and how he can be enjoyed. Some think God is glorified and enjoyed only during worship, prayer and evangelism. Others think he can also be glorified and enjoyed through cultural activities, social action and a good life well lived.

When things are harshly divided into sacred and secular, the Christian artist is denied the opportunity to explore such subjects as love, friendship, money, food, nature, family, work and leisure. The only approved way to incorporate such things is to spiritualize them. Such thinking forced gospel singers to act as though their lives comprised only devotional activities.

Some singers became frustrated at the narrowness of this outlook. The concerns of the Civil Rights movement challenged them. They knew that the God they worshipped had opinions about injustice and racism, but they felt constricted by the expectations of the genre. If they were to condemn racism or police brutality in a song, it would be considered out of order. They were to be spiritual, not political.

The songs of people like Bob Dylan and Pete

THE CASH BOX

VOLUME XV

JULY 10, 1954

NUMBER

In 1949 Jerry Wexler (left) coined the term 'rhythm and blues' to describe black American music. He later said he wished he'd called it 'rhythm and gospel'.

Jerry Wexler, Ahmet Ertegun and Miriam Abramson, who run Atlantic Records, sit before a gallery of their stars, all of whom won top Rhythm and Blues honors in *The Cash Box* Disk Jockey Poll. Ruth Brown was voted "The Most Programmed Female Vocalist". The Clovers were "The Most Programmed Vocal Group", The Drifters were named "The Up and Coming Vocal Group". And Joe Turner received two honors. His "Honey Hush" was "The Most Programmed Record" while he himself was voted "The Most Programmed Male Vocalist." Quite a lineup for one record firm.

Seeger illustrated how moral issues could be raised in song. Unlike gospel singers, they didn't claim to have all the answers, but they succeeded in putting relevant questions on the public agenda. 'Blowin' in the wind' and 'The times they are a changin'' tackled the moral issues of the day and used biblical language that gospel singers recognized and could identify with. These new folk artists also had the advantage that they were being listened to by the young.

Some musicians reluctantly accepted the division between sacred and secular and so deserted gospel for R&B. Some had already lost the faith of their childhood, some wanted fame at any price and others felt confined by gospel music's parameters. Because this period happened to coincide with the rise of teenage consumerism and the massive expansion of the recording industry, these musicians of gospel heritage found themselves at the cutting edge of exciting new developments in Western popular music. The sound of gospel was to make an undeniable contribution to the sound of the 1950s and 60s.

RHYTHM AND BLUES

When the legendary producer Jerry Wexler was a reporter working at *Billboard* magazine in 1949 he coined a term to describe what had up until then been known only as 'race music' – defined as music created by black Americans for black

Americans. The term he came up with was 'rhythm and blues' (R&B), although he later commented that a more accurate description would have been 'rhythm and gospel' because the new music consisted of the rhythm and beat associated with blues along with the harmonies and vocal styles of gospel.

Clyde McPhatter, best known as the lead singer of the Drifters, was from a gospel group known as the Mount Lebanon Singers and all his early records were essentially secularized versions of gospel. The influential Hank Ballard ('Work with me, Annie') was raised singing gospel in Bessemer, Alabama, and went on to perform R&B with his group, the Midnighters. One of his most popular songs, 'The twist', which triggered off an international dance craze when recorded by Chubby Checker, was actually written in 1956 by Joseph 'JoJo' Wallace of the Sensational Nightingales, who'd thought it was too risqué to be performed by his gospel group. Wallace passed it to the former gospel singer Little Joe Cook, who had a recording contract with Okeh, but Cook turned it down. Wallace then gave it to Hank Ballard.

ROCK AND ROLL

Black gospel was the favourite music of almost all the early rock-and-roll pioneers. Elvis Presley loved the Southern gospel of the Blackwood Brothers and the Statesmen Quartet, as well as the black gospel that he heard at first hand at East Trigg Baptist Church. Elvis's producer, Sam Phillips, was also a huge fan of gospel and never failed to listen to Reverend Brewster's Sunday evening radio programme.

Little Richard was a pioneer of rock and roll who was steeped in gospel and unashamedly borrowed from it to create his unique style.

Jerry Lee Lewis, Carl Perkins and Johnny Cash – Elvis's fellow artists at Sun Records in Memphis – were all inspired by gospel. When Perkins and Lewis got together with Elvis for an informal singing session at Sun studios in December 1956, their repertoire was dominated by gospel – 'Just a little talk with Jesus', 'Lonesome valley', 'I shall not be moved', 'Peace in the valley', 'Down by the riverside', 'Farther along', 'Precious Lord', 'Jericho road'. Cash had wanted to start his career by recording gospel, but Phillips wasn't interested, because the gospel recordings made by Sun had not been a commercial success.

The two most powerful black forces in early rock and roll – Chuck Berry and Little Richard – both emerged from the Southern church with a good knowledge of gospel. Berry was brought up in Antioch Baptist Church, St Louis, Missouri, where his parents were choir members. He has claimed that his earliest musical memories are of them singing hymns at home. In his autobiography he wrote: 'Looking back I'm sure that my musical roots were planted in me, then and there.' His mother would sing hymns as she cleaned around the house, and the words of Watts and Wesley became the foundation of his vocabulary. 'Sometimes she'd emphasize a passage in a song and the change in her volume and expression would frighten me. It was as if she'd suddenly discovered Jesus standing in the house enjoying the song.'

Little Richard (real name Richard Penniman) captured the world's attention with his ecstatic style of singing and his gobbledygook language. Both had origins in his experience of church in Macon, Georgia. He knew the Baptist Church through his mother and the Holiness Church through his relatives. He sang in a children's gospel group, the Tiny Tots, and later with a family group, the Penniman Singers. He idolized Brother Joe May and imagined himself as a powerful preacher who could make people well through music.

When Specialty's Art Rupe signed him in 1955 the label was best known for gospel, but Rupe was looking for singers who could take the church music in a secular direction. Little Richard auditioned with two gospel songs that caught the attention of Robert 'Bumps' Blackwell, the black producer Rupe had hired to discover new talent. Blackwell knew that this was the singer who could do something new with the gospel sound. Blackwell later said: 'I could tell by the tone of the voice and all those churchy turns that he was a gospel singer who could sing the blues.'

END OF THE GOLDEN AGE

The purity of gospel music was under threat from both sides. There were gospel producers wanting to import the sound of R&B and R&B producers wanting to take advantage of the best that gospel could offer. It's no coincidence that this marked the end of gospel's Golden Age, as record sales began to drop for the first time. In 1955 *Billboard* reported a 25 per cent drop on the previous year's sales of gospel records. The paper concluded that 'gospel devotees' were finally battening down, believing that there should be 'no connection between their music and any other kind of music, even classical, and, furthermore, want no association with these other fields'.

Among black musicians there was a discussion as to whether gospel had become too commercial or whether commercial music had become too influenced by gospel. Brother Joe May felt that 'so-called rhythm and blues is nothing more than an off-shoot of good gospel song', and argued that a failure to understand this 'may cause a general undermining of all true gospel singing everywhere'. Lavern Baker hit back by saying that it was gospel that was copying R&B. Clara Ward's response was: 'If anyone is guilty of taking a beat, then it's the current rhythm and blues artists, because most of them are former gospel singers.'

THE DEVELOPMENT OF SOUL

The secular music that sounded most like gospel became known as 'soul' in 1961. This, of course, had immediate spiritual connotations. The soul is the spiritual principle embodied in human beings and recognized as being the deepest part of any individual. The term 'soulful' had been coined in 1860 to mean 'full of or expressing feeling or emotion'. A decade later the *Cincinnati Gazette* thought that the Fisk Jubilee Singers sounded as though they were 'breathing forth the soul'.

RAY CHARLES

Ray Charles was the first major black performer to take the elements of gospel to create secular music. Vocally he was clearly indebted, as were his backing singers, the Raelettes. He idolized men like Alex Bradford, Ira Tucker of the Dixie Hummingbirds, Jess Whittaker of the Pilgrim Travelers, Archie Brownlee of the Five Blind Boys of Mississippi and Claude Jeter of the Swan Silvertones. In his autobiography, *Brother Ray*, he wrote: 'These guys have voices which could shake down your house and smash all the furniture in it.'

But what initially shocked black Americans was not that he sang in the style of a church singer but that he took songs beloved by Christians and rinsed out all the divine references. 'This little girl of mine' was a rewrite of 'This little light of mine', 'Lonely avenue' he took from 'How Jesus died' by the Pilgrim Travelers, and his breakthrough hit 'I got a woman' (written with his trumpet-player Renald Richard) was based on a gospel song heard on a car radio. 'Hallelujah, I love her so' blatantly took the language of spirituals and crossed it with the language of earthly passion. This was such a controversial move at the time that some radio stations refused to play it. Charles's producer Jerry Wexler knew exactly what was taking place. He admitted that it was nothing less than 'the secularization of gospel, turning church rhythms, church patterns and especially church feelings into personalized love songs'.

JAMES BROWN

Another performer who minted pop from gospel was James Brown. He'd sung in a choir and was a member of the Ever Ready Gospel Singers, whose first recording was the classic 'His eye is on the sparrow'. Brown took the drama of the black pulpit and turned it into show business. He would drop to his knees like a penitent when singing 'Please please me', and had a routine where he would appear to collapse from the emotion of performing and have to be removed from the stage by handlers, only to return a few moments later with rejoicing. It was an enactment of death and resurrection.

Soul music took the passion that gospel directed to God and directed it towards a lover. In doing so it enlarged the potential of the love song. Traditionally love songs had been trite and sentimental, but with the advent of soul there was the potential to go deeper and wider. Anyone who had grown up singing gospel was aware of an extensive range of emotions that could be brought into play when expressing God's love for us or our love for God. Soul singers took this knowledge and applied it to the expression of feelings between people.

ARETHA FRANKLIN

Aretha Franklin, another protégé of Jerry Wexler, did for the women what Ray Charles had done for the men. She was the daughter of a celebrated Detroit preacher, the Reverend C. L. Franklin, who was educated at one of the Reverend Brewster's theological schools, made records of his sermons and was deeply involved in the Civil Rights movement. She learned to sing at church, and went with her father on his revival tours, where she would perform gospel material. C. L. Franklin was a close friend of Clara Ward, and when Aretha first recorded, in 1956, she sang songs that Ward had made popular, and imitated her style.

Aretha left gospel for pop in 1960, but didn't really get into her stride until 1966 when Wexler produced her and, in his own words, 'took her back to church'. This didn't mean a journey back to gospel music, but a return to the gospel sound. Instead of trying to be a pop singer, she sang secular songs with gospel intonations, and the hits started coming: 'I never loved a man', 'Do right, woman', 'Respect', 'Chain of fools', '(You make me feel like) a natural woman'. She became known as the Queen of Soul, and in 1972 she did return to gospel music itself when she recorded the live album *Amazing Grace* with James Cleveland's Southern California Community Choir.

The showmanship of James Brown owed a lot to the preachers and singers he had seen in church.

She started the concert by announcing that she hadn't left the church, because the church was always inside her. She was implying that church wasn't necessarily a sacred space but rather a state of mind. As long as you had that gospel feeling, you were in church wherever you were. Whatever the church community may have thought of her career pattern, the album sold 2 million copies in America, making it the best-selling gospel album ever.

Soul music in the 1960s was dominated by church exiles. Solomon Burke had once been a preacher, Otis Redding, Marvin Gaye, Aretha Franklin and Nina Simone were the children of preachers, and Sam Cooke, Lou Rawls, Wilson Pickett and Johnny Taylor had been in gospel quartets. Even the music of Motown, 'the sound of young America', as record-company owner Berry Gordy promoted it, was heavily indebted to the music heard in Detroit's churches, from the choral-style backing vocals to the persistent slap of the tambourines.

As gospel filtered into the outside world through the medium of soul, the old-time quartets found themselves marginalized. Once they had seemed fresh and original, a secret of the black church, but now their sound was being imitated around the world. The old groups were finding it increasingly hard to survive and few young people wanted to start new ones.

Aretha Franklin is the daughter of a famous preacher, and through her father she met most of the leadng gospel singers of the 1940s and 1950s.

Interview with Ray Charles (1930–2004), London, July 1982

❀ **Why did your generation of musicians leave the church?**

I don't think it's a matter of 'leaving the church'. In certain areas of America there are certain things that just happen. In the Southern part of the United States, which is quite conservative, children went to church. *All* children went to church. So it's not like you were *in* church and then you *left*, as though you were a true church member. That wasn't the case. All kids went to church in the South when I was coming up. You just did. There

was no such thing as not going to church. So I was raised in a Baptist church, and naturally I have a lot of the influences from that, but what I wanted to do was to play jazz music, so obviously I couldn't do that in the church.

❀ **What was the attitude of the church towards blues music?**

I have no idea. Church music is church music and blues is blues. Some people want to connect up the two, and I guess that in a way they are connected in some sense because they were both used for communication purposes. In other words, you would both sing your messages. You could do it with religious songs or with the blues. In that sense it was communication. But the blues is the blues and church music is church music. I never thought that outside of the feeling they were that close.

❀ **Didn't the church look down on the blues and refer to it as 'the devil's music'?**

Yes. They say the 'reels' or the blues is devil's music and one of the reasons that even today I won't record a religious album is because I was taught as I grew up that you don't serve two gods. If you're gonna play the blues, you play the blues. If you're gonna do religious music, then you do religious music. Of course, I still have the same feeling. It may be antiquated, I don't know, but I feel the same way today.

❀ **You say that you can't serve two gods. What is the 'god' of the blues?**

What I meant was – don't split yourself. It wasn't saying that you have two gods. It was saying that if you're gonna play the blues, play the blues. There's nothing wrong with that. If you're gonna play religious music, do that. There's nothing wrong with that. But you don't do both. Some of the music played in churches nowadays is a little too jazzy as far as I'm concerned. I don't knock the people that do it but I don't feel it's for me. I like the old Baptist hymns. They had rhythm too. Man, you would go to a Sanctified church, a Holiness church, and they had all the rhythms in the world! They'd dance you out of this room! It wasn't that they didn't have rhythm, it's just that I think that there are certain things that don't go. I think there ought to be a difference between what is supposedly God's music and contemporary music. There ought to be a difference between the church and the concert hall. That's the way I feel.

❀ **There is often a highly emotional response to gospel music. People speak of 'falling out' and being 'filled with the Spirit'. Is that to do with the rhythmic quality of the music?**

Well, churches can be very warm. I've seen people fall out at concerts too. Music can do a hell of a thing to people! If I want to, I can whip the crowd into a frenzy and make them almost crazy with the music. Just with music. I can do that if I want to. But I don't do that because I don't like it and I don't think it's necessary to get people to a point where they're almost mad. What I try to do is get the people to a pitch and then do something at an easier tempo or something light-hearted.

❀ **Was it this excitement that led you to fuse gospel, jazz and blues?**

No. I just like music. I'm a musician. I was born with music in me in some kind of a way. Somehow or another it got into my body and I was going to play music, period. Regardless.

❀ **There was nothing specific in gospel that attracted you?**

No. Gospel was a kind of music just like the blues

was a kind of music, country and western was a kind of a music, and classical is a kind of music. It's all different and I like all of it.

❀ **Some of your early songs were adapted from spirituals. Is it true that 'You better leave that woman alone' was taken from 'You better leave that liar alone'?**

Yes.

❀ **And 'Talkin' 'bout you' was also taken from a spiritual?**

That's right. That's another one. 'This little girl of mine' was taken from 'This little light of mine'.

❀ **What about 'I got a woman'?**

That could fit a lot of songs because that's an old standard sixteen-bar phrase. It's like a public-domain type of chord structure. You could find a lot of songs with that.

❀ **I read that it was based on 'When I'm lonely (I talk to Jesus)'.**

I don't know about that. It's a possibility. I know that the chord structure is done in a lot of old spiritual tunes.

❀ **Did you face criticism when you incorporated blues lyrics with the gospel sound?**

Some. There were people who thought it was sacrilegious or something. But I must say, in all fairness, that the few people who wrote to me weren't bothered by it at all. Some preachers around the country did sermons on my music. They would use my songs in the place of the text they usually preached on.

❁ **It's often said that in soul music the love for God is replaced by love for a man or woman.**

You can look at it that way. I'll accept that. I think that's a fair statement. They are looking for love, hope and faith in God, as you say, or love, hope, faith and durability in a woman.

❁ **James Brown took the performance style of a black preacher and incorporated it into his act.**

I know James Brown's music but what he did or didn't do I can't tell you. At one time I think he was singing in a spiritual group – a quartet or something like that. That might be the key. Most black people, especially those born in the South, were in the church. You don't have to be me or James Brown or Otis Redding. All of us was in the church. Aretha Franklin. All of us. Out of the church, man. That's it.

❁ **Why didn't they stay in the church?**

You'd have to ask them that. I can't speak for other people. I had something I wanted to do and I couldn't do what I wanted to do in the church. I wanted to play jazz music and you just don't play jazz music in church. That's all. Simple as that.

❁ **Do you think that if the church had accepted jazz it would have led to a new style of church music?**

No. I don't think any of us would have done that. We were taught as children, 'Deliver to Caesar what is Caesar's. Give unto God what is God's.' There was no way we, or should I say 'I', would have played jazz in church. To me that would have been an abomination. I wouldn't have done it. If I go into a church I'm deadly serious about it. But everybody has to stand alone at the time of judgment.

Riding the Mighty High

When Mahalia Jackson died in January 1972 her body lay in state at Greater Salem Baptist Church in Chicago. Over 50,000 mourners filed past the open coffin, where she was dressed in a long blue gown with gold threads, wearing white gloves and clutching a Bible opened to Psalm 20. The next day, at the Aerie Crown Theater, her first funeral took place in front of a congregation of 6,000. Martin Luther King's wife Coretta Scott King was there, the great jazz singer Ella Fitzgerald and Sammy Davis Jr gave eulogies, the Reverend C. L . Franklin preached and his daughter Aretha sang 'Take my hand, precious Lord'.

Three days later there was a second funeral in New Orleans, the city of Mahalia's birth. It took place downtown at the Rivergate Convention Center. The funeral cortege consisted of twenty-four limousines. She was

The Queen of Gospel lies in her coffin while the Queen of Soul sings in her memory. Aretha Franklin at Mahalia Jackson's funeral in 1972, singing a Thomas Dorsey song.

honoured in word and song by the governor of Louisiana, John J. McKeithen, Moon Landrieu the mayor of New Orleans, comedian and political activist Dick Gregory, soul star Lou Rawls and gospel singer Bessie Griffin. She was later buried in Providence Memorial Park in Metairie, Louisiana, a suburb of New Orleans.

There was a sense that as the mourners said goodbye to Mahalia they were also saying goodbye to gospel. No one believed that gospel music would ever again have so skilled a practitioner and so great an ambassador. For millions of people around the world Mahalia *was* gospel. 'This great woman is gone from us,' said Ella Fitzgerald. 'I tell you, there's not another singer like her in the world.' Brother Joe May died four months later, Clara Ward a year later and Rosetta Tharpe in October 1973. The pantheon of gospel greats was thinning out.

Of the quartets still extant, few of them had their legendary line-ups intact. Archie Brownlee of the Blind Boys of Mississippi was dead, as was Sam Cooke of the Soul Stirrers. The Golden Gate Quartet had moved to Paris, the Pilgrim Travelers had broken up, Julius 'June' Cheeks had left the Sensational Nightingales and Claude Jeter of the Swan Silvertones had become a preacher. The groups that hung on were emulating funk and disco trends in often embarrassing ways. Quartets that had once set trends with their matching suits were now middle-aged men in thinning Afros, flared trousers and platform shoes.

Gospel music was something that pop openly plundered. The Rolling Stones used the Mighty Clouds of Joy and Dorothy Love Coates as support acts in America. The Beatles had Billy Preston add his gospel chords to 'Let it be'. Paul Simon recorded with the Dixie Hummingbirds and Claude Jeter on his first album after the dissolution of Simon and Garfunkel. It had been the jazz-rocker Al Kooper in the mid-1960s who had introduced Paul Simon to the music of the Swan Silvertones. Jeter's improvised line 'I'll be a bridge over deep water if you trust in my name', in their recording of the traditional spiritual 'Oh Mary, don't you weep', inspired one of Simon's most enduring compositions. He acknowledged his debt by giving Jeter a cheque for $1,000 and an invitation to sing on the 1973 album *There Goes Rhymin' Simon*. Thus, according to *The Guardian*'s obituary of Jeter, 12 March 2009, it can be said of Jeter that 'he is perhaps best remembered as the singer who inspired Simon and Garfunkel's classic "Bridge over troubled water"'.

JAMES CLEVELAND: CROWN PRINCE OF GOSPEL

The loss of Mahalia Jackson left gospel music without a figurehead, someone who was respected within the church community but equally respected outside. Other than Thomas Dorsey and Sallie Martin, who were alive but not known as performers, the only colossus in gospel was the songwriter, singer and choir director James Cleveland, but he didn't have an endearing personality, and his homosexuality, if it had become public knowledge, would have destroyed his career.

Cleveland was a Zelig-like character who'd known everyone of importance in gospel music from Dorsey and Martin onwards. He'd been a boy soprano at Pilgrim Baptist in Chicago in the 1940s when Dorsey was director of music. As a paper boy he delivered to Mahalia Jackson, and if she was out he'd pop over to her beauty salon, where, according to Cleveland, he would 'just sit around and listen to her hum songs while she was straightening hair'. By the age of sixteen he was writing, and one of his earliest songs, 'Grace sufficient', was recorded by the Roberta Martin Singers. When two of Martin's singers – Norsalus McKissick and Bessie Folk – left to form the Gospelaires, Cleveland took their place.

At the age of fifteen he joined the Thorne Crusaders and damaged his voice straining for the high notes, leaving it with a uniquely gravelly quality that came to distinguish him. In 1954 he became a member of the Caravans under Albertina Walker, and was later joined by Dorothy Norwood, Cassietta George and Inez Andrews. The Caravans recorded songs of his, such as 'The solid rock' and 'The old-time religion', and turned them into hits. After the Caravans he was with several other groups, including the Meditation Singers, the Gospel All-Stars and the Gospel Chimes, displaying a talent not only for writing but for taking old songs and arranging them with his driving piano and growling voice.

The turning point in his career came in 1960 when he made his first record with a choir. Although he would still sing with groups – his own group, the Cleveland Singers, featured Billy Preston on organ – his emerging talent, and the one he would be remembered for, was directing mass choirs. He formed the Gospel Singers' Workshop (now the Gospel Music Workshop of America) in 1968. It was a hipper version of Dorsey's National Convention of Gospel Choirs and Choruses, attracting the generation of musicians reared on rock and soul. Like Dorsey, Cleveland used the organization's annual conventions to build a choir that would sing his new songs.

Cleveland became the most high-profile male gospel musician in America, commanding high fees and able to sell out huge venues. He was the gospel singer that secular folk had heard of. He toured Europe with Liza Minnelli, appeared with his church choir on Elton John's 1976 album *Blue Moves*, contributed to Quincy Jones's soundtrack for the TV series *Roots*, won four Grammy awards and, in 1981, became the first gospel artist to have a star on the Hollywood Walk of Fame.

He became known as the Crown Prince of Gospel, and lived a life befitting the title. His mansion home in Los Angeles was decorated with red wallpaper and had crystal chandeliers; he wore expensive gold rings, owned a restaurant and was always surrounded by attractive young men. When *Ebony* magazine interviewed him he was happy to boast of having a hundred suits in his closet, fifty pairs of shoes, and a bespoke overcoat made from the fur of a Persian lamb. His answer, when asked how he could justify living in such luxury as a 'man of God', was: 'I don't feel religion was meant to make pleasure less enjoyable.'

SHIRLEY CAESAR: FIRST LADY OF GOSPEL

His female counterpart (in musical stature rather than in lifestyle) was Shirley Caesar, who became known as the First Lady of Gospel. Like Cleveland, she was born before the war, started her career in the 1950s, and had sung with the Caravans. When Mahalia died, and the search was on to find someone to fill her shoes, Caesar and Albertina Walker were the names most frequently mentioned. Neither of them was happy to be called the Queen of Gospel, because they believed that only one person could ever rightfully hold that title, and she had gone. Caesar's epithet came about accidentally. Her label, Roadshow Records, had never recorded a gospel artist before and so they titled her debut album *First Lady* in recognition of this fact.

Like Mahalia, she had a strong personal faith and believed that gospel music had a sacred purpose. She wouldn't dilute the religion in her music to increase sales, and has, over the years, increased her preaching, theological study and charity work with Shirley Caesar Outreach Ministries. Less committed singers (such as Sam Cooke) often found themselves on the receiving end of one of her sermons. If she ever thought that audiences were becoming more appreciative of her style than attentive to her message, she would become concerned. In her autobiography she wrote: 'My primary purpose as a Christian and as a gospel singer has always been to reach as many people as possible with the message of Jesus, regardless of race, gender, demographic location, or socioeconomic status.' When she was with the Caravans her nickname was 'the bishop'.

Raised in disadvantaged conditions in Durham,

Shirley Caesar performs at the AARP 50th anniversary 'Songs of Soul and Inspiration' concert at the Philips Arena in Atlanta, Georgia, in 2008.

North Carolina, as the tenth of thirteen children, her gospel-singing father died when she was seven and then her mother suffered health problems that left her a semi-invalid. To raise extra income for her family, Shirley began singing gospel at the age of thirteen as Baby Shirley Caesar, touring with a preacher known as One Leg Leroy and taking a spot on his television show broadcast from Portsmouth, Virginia.

Her break came at the end of her first year in college in 1958, when she saw the Caravans in concert at Memorial Auditorium, Raleigh, North Carolina. The line-up at the time was Albertina Walker, Inez Andrews, Sarah McKisick and a pianist. Caesar boldly wrote a note to Walker offering her services as a fourth vocalist, and handed it to Dorothy Love Coates of the Gospel Harmonettes to pass on for her. There was no immediate response, and Caesar left the arena assuming that her letter had been scrapped.

Later the same day the Caravans were performing in the neighbouring town of Kinston. The determined young Caesar followed them there, and this time forwarded a note to them through an usher that simply said: 'Please ask Shirley Caesar to sing a solo.' The plea got through. Albertina Walker invited her onto the stage, where she sang Thomas Dorsey's 'The Lord will make a way somehow', to great approval from the audience.

This did not escape Walker's attention, and not long afterwards the Caravans were sending Shirley Caesar a note, asking her to join the group. The combination of four powerful vocalists made the Caravans one of the biggest draws in gospel. Each girl delivered songs in her own style. 'Lord, keep me day by day' was Albertina Walker's. 'Mary, don't you weep' was

Inez Andrews'. Caesar's special number was 'Sweeping through the city', and she would dramatize her performance by running through the auditorium as if she had a broom in her hand and was ready to sweep it clean.

Her light alto voice with rapid vibrato contrasted with Andrews' piercing alto, and the high point of a Caravans concert came when the two singers followed each other in a sequence of show-stopping songs. She also developed a preaching style of delivery that made it natural for her to tell stories, testify and extract responses from an audience. During the choruses of 'Hallelujah, it's done' she would ad lib homilies, and later in her career she scored big hits with mini-sermons such as 'Don't drive your mama away' (1969) and 'No charge' (1975).

She left the Caravans in 1966 to concentrate on preaching, became a singing evangelist for a short time and then in 1968 formed the Shirley Caesar Singers. Mahalia's death propelled her to the front line. Although not as innovative, emblematic or well known, she had a similar sense of integrity and was committed to living the life she sang about. In 1974 she recorded two albums with James Cleveland that set the seal on her new position. They were *The King and Queen of Gospel*, volumes 1 and 2.

Over the years she moved from the exclusively black church audience to embrace the white church audience. Her music became more progressive as a result, but she never rounded off the sharp edges of her message. Crossover songs that talked about 'him' rather than 'Jesus' would not be a part of her show. 'I have never wanted to do that and find it distasteful when others do,' she said. 'As gospel singers, we should not try to camouflage who we are singing about. If we are taking a stand for the Lord, then we should be emphatic about it.'

Words were important to her and she agonized over adding horns, drums, guitars and keyboards lest the sound should obscure the lyric. When a fan accused her of becoming too 'worldly', of making music for people to click their fingers to, she wrestled with the issue before deciding to return to her older, less cluttered sound. She figured that if people had to 'get past the music' in order to get to the message, she must be doing something wrong. The result was *Live in Chicago*, an album that dominated the *Billboard* gospel chart throughout 1989, remaining in the top spot for fifty weeks.

James Cleveland took a similar view of the drift towards what the industry was describing as 'rock gospel'. He saw it as a distraction from the music's main objective. It drew attention to subsidiary elements of style and away from what the songs were really about. 'Gospel music expresses love for Christ and it cannot be sung as rock gospel or rock music,' he said. 'In true gospel music, the message is paramount, not the music. In rock gospel, the music is more important than the message.'

THE MIGHTY CLOUDS OF JOY

Firmly in his sights when he made these comments were the Mighty Clouds of Joy. Although nowhere near as influential as the Dixie Hummingbirds or the Soul Stirrers, they had sold far more records than these greats. In the 1970s they had become one of the most talked-about groups. In his gospel encyclopaedia *Uncloudy Days*, Bill Carpenter argued that they were 'the most successful gospel quartet in history'.

Like Cleveland, they had come from a traditional gospel background and had cut their first record in 1960. By 1964 they had added organ and drums, and two years later they began using bass. 'You have to be able to change,'

By the 1970s, James Cleveland was the most powerful gospel singer in America. He was referred to as 'the Crown Prince of Gospel'.

The Mighty Clouds of Joy toured with the Rolling Stones and emulated the look of a Motown group.

reasoned lead singer Joe Ligon. 'You can't just say: "We'll sing just one style, and that's all we can do." A lot of my friends started out in this business, and when the music changed and they couldn't change with it, the audience left them.'

They emulated groups like the Four Tops and the Temptations, which were having such huge success with Motown, wearing colourful stage costumes, growing their hair into Afros and sporting beards and moustaches. The Soul Stirrers had brought gospel into the age of movement following the flat-footed performances of the jubilee era. The Mighty Clouds of Joy ushered in the age of choreography.

Their songs became less spiritually explicit as they tried to couch their faith in contemporary language. 'Ride the mighty high', for example, sounded like a drug song, but they assured their Christian followers that it was really about 'praising the mightiest high of all – the Lord'.

Ironically, a year after they released their version it was covered by Jerry Garcia of the Grateful Dead, one of rock music's leading advocates of the transforming power of LSD. They also recorded Carole King's 'You've got a friend', presumably hoping that audiences would think that the friend in question was Jesus.

Johnny Martin of the Mighty Clouds of Joy responded to Cleveland's criticism in an interview. 'It's easy for him to say that rock isn't gospel,' he said. 'He's making plenty of money, and his records, since they are choir-oriented, are always being played on the radio. In our case, being a quartet, we need hit records to survive. The average station that plays gospel doesn't play quartets. They play choirs.'

THE WILLIAMS BROTHERS

The Williams Brothers were another quartet attempting to fuse traditional gospel words with contemporary rock sounds. Originally known as the Sensational Williams Brothers, the group was made up of Doug, Melvin and Leonard Williams and Henry Green. Doug Williams has said they were heading in this direction before the Mighty Clouds of Joy. 'Even though we never get credit for that, it was there,' he said. 'Even before we started recording and were just doing concerts, our arrangements were different from regular quartets. The word "contemporary" was not even in existence in gospel music at that time.'

The three Williams brothers in the group were the sons of Leon 'Pop' Williams, who in the 1940s sang with the Big Four Gospel Singers. His two eldest sons had been in a gospel group during the 1960s, and when he discovered that his other sons had fine voices he trained them to sing. A stickler for detail, Pop Williams made sure that

they were professional in everything, from the way they moved to the way they conducted themselves in public when they were off stage.

From 1973 onwards, following their debut album *Holding On*, the Williams Brothers had a string of gospel hits – 'Jesus will fix it', 'Jesus made a way', 'If it wasn't for the Lord', 'If I don't wake up', 'A mother's love', 'I'm just a nobody' and 'Sweep around your own front door'. They recorded their album *Blessed* for the Word label, but the label didn't want to release it, so it was offered to Malaco. When Malaco released it in 1985 it became an immediate hit, staying in the gospel charts for eighty-nine weeks. They went on to launch their own label, Blackberry Records, and when Leonard stopped singing with the group Doug and Melvin embarked on solo projects.

Despite the creation of 'rock gospel' neither the Mighty Clouds of Joy nor the Williams Brothers ever had a major pop hit. The Clouds came close with 'Mighty high', which reached number two on the *Billboard* disco chart in 1975, and 'Jesus will fix it' was the number one record in Atlanta for a short period during 1973. The only group to really cross over was the Edwin Hawkins Singers with 'Oh happy day' in 1969, and, surprisingly, it wasn't because of any flirtation with rock and roll, funk or soul. Nor was it because of any dilution of message. After all, this was a song that had the line 'Oh happy day / When Jesus washed my sins away'.

'OH HAPPY DAY'

In 1968, Hawkins, who had founded the Northern California State Youth Choir in the early 1960s, had recorded an album called *Let Us Go into the House of the Lord*. It was done on a two-track recorder at Hawkins' expense, and 500 copies were pressed. The idea was to sell them in the San Francisco area to recoup expenses. He never imagined it would even get played on the radio, let alone that it would become a huge international hit.

The song was loosely based on words by the eighteenth-century British hymn-writer Philip Doddridge, a contemporary of Isaac Watts and Charles Wesley. Doddridge's hymn started:

> *O happy day, that fixed my choice*
> *On thee, my Saviour and my God!*
> *Well may this glowing heart rejoice,*
> *And tell its raptures all abroad.*
> **Words by Philip Doddridge**
> **(1702–51)**

Hawkins came across the words in an old hymnal owned by his mother. He wrote a new tune for it, and in rewriting the lyric he eventually retained only the three words 'Oh happy day' from Doddridge's original. It was a classic gospel technique of composing; the sort of thing that Dorsey had done for years with spirituals.

The recording, featuring Dorothy Morrison on lead vocal, had a call-and-response pattern, with the choir sounding as joyful as the lyric. The only music to be heard was Hawkins' gently rolling piano and the occasional slap of a tambourine. It sounded contemporary without having made any concessions to current pop.

A DJ at a local bay area radio station (KSAN)

The Edwin Hawkins Singers had the biggest gospel hit ever with 'Oh happy day' in 1969.

began playing it, and before long radio stations in other US cities picked up on it. When word got out that this was an independent recording, the major labels made bids to release it and give it the national push that it needed. This was how Hawkins came to sign a deal with Buddha Records, the New York label run by Neil Bogart, in April 1969. The Northern California State Choir was renamed the Edwin Hawkins Singers; the record was put out and went to number four in the US charts and number two in the UK charts. With eventual sales of over 7 million, it became the best-selling black gospel single of all time.

The reasons for its success are hard to fathom. There had been many great gospel songs before, and none had crossed over. There had been many attempts to succeed in the mainstream market. It may have benefited from the uniquely 'spiritual' feel of the times. Young people were exploring altered states of consciousness, Eastern religions and the occult. The Jesus movement was starting in California and religious issues were being examined in the songs of such prominent artists as The Beatles, Bob Dylan and The Who. Within a short time there would be such hits as 'Jesus Christ Superstar', 'Spirit in the sky', 'My sweet Lord' and 'Amazing grace'.

The success of the single immediately projected Hawkins onto the world stage. From playing churches in the San Francisco area, he found himself on *American Bandstand* and the *Smothers Brothers Comedy Hour*, and in concerts, supporting such acts as the Jackson 5 and the Supremes. His recording of 'I'd like to teach the world to sing' was used in a Coca-Cola campaign.

He capitalized on the success of 'Oh happy day' by recording 'Every man wants to be free', another song that appealed to the hippy spirit. Like 'Oh happy day', it won the Grammy for 'Best Soul Gospel Performance'. His record label thought it a good idea to have him back up the young hippy folk singer Melanie on her single 'Lay down (candles in the rain)', and it proved to be a commercially astute move. The single went into the top ten in 1970.

While some observers thought it marked gospel's coming of age, there were others who thought that gospel had given up too much to get there. Hawkins' response was very similar to the one given by Thomas Dorsey in the 1930s, Rosetta Tharpe in the 1940s and Clara Ward in the 1950s. 'We preach, and the Bible teaches, to take the gospel into all the world,' he said. 'But when it all comes down, we [Christians] don't want to do that with our music. The church world is quick to criticize that. I think sometimes that it is out of jealousy. Someone has succeeded, and people don't like it. A lot of that goes on.'

A barrier that was slowly coming down, though, was the barrier between contemporary Christian music (white Christian rock and pop) and black gospel. Just as white rock fans helped to put 'Oh happy day' into the charts, the fans of white Christian rock were appreciating the music of the Edwin Hawkins Singers. This openness would soon lead to a very different type of gospel singer – one for whom 'crossing over' didn't mean 'going secular' but being welcomed by both the black and white music-loving audiences.

CHAPTER

14

Jesus Is the Answer

The 'love and peace' era of the late 1960s also involved spiritual questing and the birth of the Jesus movement. Pop music became more open to references to God, Jesus and the Spirit.

WINNING THE WHITE AUDIENCE

On 30 April 1976, the gospel singer Andrae Crouch took to the stage in front of a crowd of 13,000 young people in a field outside of Wilmington, Kentucky. This was the Ichthus Festival, a conscious Christian response to the Woodstock Festival of 1969, which had come to define the aspirations of the 'love and peace' generation. Christian 'Jesus rock' bands like the Archers and the J. C. Power Outlet played, as well as solo singer Randy Matthews. Crouch was the only black person to perform. He was probably the only black person in the field that day.

The crowd's response was enthusiastic. It didn't seem to them that he was playing a different genre of music. The guitars, bass, drums and keyboard sound was very familiar to them, as were the songs he was singing – 'Jesus is the answer', 'Soon and very soon'. This sounded like Jesus rock played by a musician who happened to be black.

In his trailer dressing room before going on, he'd been asked by a journalist how he was now regarded by gospel traditionalists. He said,

Some of the gospel singers have approached me for help
because they think I know the secret of getting into the

white field. They want to know what I can do for them. They usually think of it as a new business opportunity rather than a ministry, which is really sad. They want to know what the formula is for gaining acceptance with a white audience. Or they want me to get them on a record label which would give them the sort of exposure that I've had.

Crouch, born in California in 1942, was the first black gospel singer to play to a primarily white audience. He would soon be joined by Jessy Dixon, who was born in Texas in 1938. Although their styles were very different – Dixon was a stand-up vocalist and performer, Crouch a keyboard player and songwriter – they were both committed to an evangelical form of Christianity, had roots in the black church, had learned to sing and play as children, and were warmly accepted by young white Christians.

JESUS ROCK

Jesus rock was initially closely aligned with the Californian Jesus movement. It was partly the response of former hippies who still loved their rock music and saw no reason why it couldn't be used to express Christian truth, and partly

an effort by the traditional church to use forms of communication acceptable to the young. Although it never created any chart hits or impinged on the consciousness of the average *Rolling Stone* reader, it did lead to the creation of the genre known as 'contemporary Christian music'.

Initially Jesus rock was controversial for the same reasons that Thomas Dorsey's gospel music had been controversial in the 1930s. Some felt it was 'worldly' and that rock music was tainted because of its association with drugs, sex and lack of self-control. Others speculated that the very rhythms of rock were somehow capable of opening up the consciousness to spiritual attack by demons. However, the young audience for whom it was intended had no such reservations. It wanted music that was culturally relevant and spiritually affirming, emotionally exciting and mentally challenging.

Solo artists like Larry Norman, Keith Green and Randy Stonehill, along with bands such as Lovesong, the Resurrection Band and Liberation Suite, began playing at Christian rock festivals. Very soon there was a Christian music subculture with its own record labels, recording studios, magazines and radio shows. Naturally, the fans who liked white rock also liked soul and Motown, and knew that rock and roll was really R&B. The music industry was no longer segregated, so it made sense for contemporary Christian music to embrace black musicians.

This was how things were when Crouch and Dixon made their impact. Even though they were from the black church, they found a home in the white church, among people who wouldn't have heard of James Cleveland or Shirley Caesar. Some black church members thought that they

were betraying their roots, that in order to win over the wealthier white audiences they had compromised their sound.

Certainly neither of them produced the raw sound of the country church, but this was because their generation was exposed to a wider range of music rather than because of a rejection of roots. Crouch was a lover of jazz, R&B and rock. Dixon had sung ballads in clubs and had trained as a concert pianist at college. Neither of them had been cosseted in a gospel-only environment, and the music they made reflected powerful personal Christian commitment lashed to the best of the sounds of their era. Crouch even took the unprecedented step of including two white musicians in his group, the Disciples.

According to Crouch, it was a combination of musical adventurousness and a disappointment in the shallowness of preaching that caused a lot of his generation to reject the limitations of the older style of gospel. 'I think we lost a lot of good talent because the preachers and ministers didn't really preach the Word and get them to fall in love with Jesus,' he said. 'Many of them also left because they wanted a lot more than C to F and F to G chord progressions in their music. They wanted to hear what it would sound like if they used strings or horns. They were just music lovers. Yet people made them feel that if they sang anything else they were out of the church.'

ANDRAE CROUCH

Crouch was born in Compton, Los Angeles, where his father, Benjamin, ran a cleaning business. Preaching was in his genes. His great-uncle, Samuel Crouch, was one of the early leaders of the Church of God in Christ, the denomination that had produced Arizona Dranes and Sister Rosetta Tharpe. Benjamin Crouch was a street preacher in his spare time, and took his family to Emmanuel Church of God in Christ, where Samuel, by then a bishop, was pastor. Benjamin then trained for the ministry and had become pastor of his own church in Pacoima in the San Fernando Valley by the time Andrae was at junior high.

At this church, Christ Memorial, Crouch first organized a choir. Already a pianist he fell in with a group of teenagers from other churches that he'd met at district youth meetings and put together a group that they named the COGICS (Church of God in Christ Singers). Almost all the members would go on to make their mark in music. Gloria Jones became a solo artist and a writer for Motown. She had a son with the British rock star Marc Bolan of T Rex, and was driving the car in which he was killed as it careered off the road and hit a tree in 1977. Edna Wright was part of the girl trio Honey Cone, which had a string of R&B hits in the early 1970s, and Billy Preston was to become a solo artist as well as a popular session musician with the likes of The Beatles, The Rolling Stones, Elton John, Ray Charles and Eric Clapton.

After dropping out of college, Crouch was employed by Teen Challenge, a Christian organization that worked with drug addicts, and attended Bible college in the afternoons. During this time he drew the addicts into a choir and helped them make an album using some material he'd written. This was the first time any of his songs had been recorded. They included

'The power of Jesus', 'I cannot tell it all', 'Some day I'll see his face' and 'Hallelujah, I am free'.

His experience with the Addicts Choir accustomed him to working with people of different races and also convinced him that music had the potential to help in the healing process. When counselling, he would frequently use his songs to comfort, encourage and build up. At college he would set Bible verses to music as a memory aid, a technique he had first used with algebraic formulae while at high school. This technique would profoundly affect his songwriting.

Although his group, the Disciples, formed with Billy Thedford and Perry Morgan, was based at Crouch's home church, it didn't make its mark through working the traditional gospel circuit. The first engagements he mentions in his autobiography *Through It All* were a short tour in Hawaii, an appearance at Disneyland and a concert at a white Church of the Nazarene in Los Angeles. In 1968 he was approached by Ralph Carmichael, a white record-company owner who had worked as an arranger for artists like

Andrae Crouch was unique among gospel artists in building his reputation almost exclusively with white audiences.

Bing Crosby, Nat 'King' Cole, Ella Fitzgerald and Peggy Lee. Regarded as one of the innovators of contemporary Christian music, he had formed Light Records in 1966 with the aim of producing the sort of music that would appeal to the 'Jesus people'.

Crouch signed with Light, the first black musician to do so. His initial albums for the label were quite mild, lacking both the earthiness of gospel and the dynamism of rock. They sounded like a melange of church music, easy listening and contemporary pop. In 1974 he found his feet with the first studio album he had produced (with drummer Billy Maxwell), *Take Me Back*. This was a new and vibrant gospel sound complete with guitars, keyboards, synthesizers, brass, drums and bass, using different vocal combinations on almost every track.

His 1978 album *Live in London* is regarded as his best from the period. Recorded at a theatre, it sounded like a church service, and Crouch took the opportunity to exercise his preaching skills between numbers. This was to be his last album with the Disciples. From here on he was just Andrae Crouch, recording more albums for Light before switching to Warner Brothers in 1981. Lyrically, he continued to explore spiritual themes, but his music was becoming indistinguishable from the sort of soul funk being created by Stevie Wonder and Earth, Wind & Fire.

In 1982 his career as a gospel performer came to a juddering halt. Driving in Los Angeles one day, he was stopped by police, who discovered what they believed to be traces of cocaine in the car. When his apartment was searched they found equipment traditionally associated with drug-users. He was charged with possession of cocaine and other dangerous drugs and released on bail. The charges were later dropped, but it was enough to send shudders through the Christian music industry. It looked as though the secular direction of his career was being paralleled by a secular direction in his life. (Crouch's explanation was that the powder in the car was chicken soup and the drug paraphernalia found at his home belonged to a friend.)

Burned out from a heavy touring schedule and chastened by the arrest, he ducked out of the limelight for a decade to concentrate on arranging, studio work and composing for film and television. His ability to score vocals, probably undervalued in the lyrically sensitive world of contemporary Christian music, was highly regarded in the recording world. He arranged the backing vocals on such hits as Michael Jackson's 'Man in the mirror' and Madonna's controversial 'Like a virgin' (although he refused to appear in the video), worked with the legendary Quincy Jones on the soundtrack of *The Color Purple* (he co-wrote the rousing 'Maybe God is trying to tell you something') and did choral arrangements for the movie of *The Lion King*.

When he returned to gospel in 1994 it was with a stunning album, *Mercy*, that contained the best of what he'd always been able to do. The vocal arrangements were impeccable and the words dealt imaginatively with the theme of repentance and forgiveness. Instead of the finger pointing at the congregation, the finger was pointing at Crouch. He was confessing his own shortcomings and standing amazed that God would have anything to do with him, let alone come to him with grace. It won him two Grammys.

The following year he took over as pastor of Christ Church, his father having recently died. He continues to sing and record but doesn't tour as frequently or for as long. In 2004 he was awarded a star on the Hollywood Walk of Fame, joining only two other stars from the world of gospel music – James Cleveland and Mahalia Jackson.

JESSY DIXON

Jessy Dixon had much more grounding in traditional gospel circles. He played piano for the Clara Ward Singers and Brother Joe May, spent five years with James Cleveland's group, the Gospel Chimes, and directed the renowned Thompson Community Singers in Chicago. In the late 1960s he founded his own group, the Jessy Dixon Singers, and gained a reputation for his experimental arrangements. He was referred to within gospel circles as Mr Progressive, and when James Cleveland passed away in 1991 he was considered his natural heir.

Dixon was a powerful and charismatic performer. Handsome and debonair, usually wearing a trim moustache and a well-cut suit, he would work with two or three backing singers. His commitment to gospel was all the more powerful because his conversion had taken place after singing gospel for over twelve years. He had been one of those who hadn't walked the straight and narrow but who suddenly saw the truth of what he'd been singing about.

Dixon had spent his career almost exclusively on the black gospel circuit until Paul Simon spotted him performing in New York. Simon, who had already drawn attention to gospel by using the Dixie Hummingbirds and Claude Jeter on record, recruited Dixon for a forthcoming tour.

This exposure introduced Dixon to the white audience. Simon not only used his vocals behind his songs but gave him a spot in which he'd

Jessy Dixon had his roots in the old gospel world of Clara Ward and Thomas Dorsey, but became popular with white rock audiences.

perform two or three gospel numbers, usually 'Operator', 'What do you call him?' and Andrae Crouch's 'Jesus is the answer'. This association lasted through the 1970s, and the Jessy Dixon Singers were featured on the albums *Still Crazy after All These Years* and *Live Rhymin'*.

In 1977 Dixon left Savoy Records, the label he had recorded with since 1964, and joined Andrae Crouch on Light Records. Andrae and his drummer Billy Maxwell produced his first album, *It's All Right Now*, and a string of albums followed, making him a popular figure in contemporary Christian music circles. In 1993 two things happened that brought him to an even larger and more culturally diverse audience. First, he wrote a song, 'I am redeemed', that was destined to be his 'Precious Lord'. Released as a single, it stayed in the top ten of the gospel charts for five years. It was a beautifully simple song with theology acceptable to Christians of any denomination. In concert Dixon would ad lib in the breaks, showing that his amazement at being saved hadn't dimmed over the decades.

BILL AND GLORIA GAITHER: WHITE GOSPEL

Secondly, he was invited by Bill and Gloria Gaither to take part in their Homecoming events. The Gaithers were superstars in the white gospel firmament, not just as performers (the Bill Gaither Trio, the Gaither Vocal Band) but as the authors of such gospel standards as 'Because he lives', 'The King is coming' and 'He touched me'. The Homecoming events, started in 1991, brought together the cream of Southern gospel and contemporary Christian music.

The format was quite simple. The Gaithers would sit on stage surrounded by some of the biggest names in white gospel, and a sort of singing party would ensue, watched by an auditorium of people. The show would move from city to city, and often country to country, and would result in a new album and DVD each year. Although not as high profile as the tours made by

rock legends, they nevertheless out-grossed many of them. For example, the 2004 Homecoming tour made more money than Elton John's US tour of the same year.

Inviting Dixon to participate was a gamble because he originated neither from contemporary Christian pop nor from Southern gospel. Accomplished as he was, his reputation wouldn't have been familiar to the typical audience member of a Homecoming concert. However, the gamble paid off because Dixon rapidly became a star of the show. He never compromised his style, but was more than happy to sing songs with a country flavour, to have established Southern gospel singers backing him and to be the only African American on the show. The Homecoming series took him to new audiences in America and around the world.

It's easy to see why he was so enthusiastically welcomed. He's an impeccable performer whose training under men like James Cleveland taught him the art of stagecraft. He knew exactly how to stand, walk, hold the microphone and give appropriate facial expressions. There was enough sanctified dancing to impress the Pentecostals but enough controlled expression of personal faith to reassure the evangelicals. He's a gracious ambassador of gospel, and one of the few still performing who is a living link with the illustrious past of Thomas Dorsey, Sallie Martin, Mahalia Jackson, James Cleveland, Clara Ward, Roberta Martin and Brother Joe May.

THE WINANS

Andrae Crouch played a pivotal role in taking the gospel music of a new generation into the white world of rock festivals, evangelistic events and mainline churches. He not only did it with his own music but alerted Light to other artists capable of making the same journey. In 1981 he tipped them off about the Winans, now the greatest dynasty in contemporary gospel. The original Winans were four sons of David and Delores Winans from Detroit, Michigan, but since they started recording they've been joined by almost all the rest of their kin, most notably by CeCe and BeBe Winans, and more recently by their own children, nieces and nephews.

The Winans were raised on traditional gospel (the parents had met in a choir organized by James Cleveland, and the COGIC church they attended had been founded by their great-grandfather) but their personal preference

was contemporary R&B. So when they began recording they developed a style that owed little to the great quartets of the past. Their three albums with Light between 1981 and 1984 made them stars in contemporary Christian music, and then a further four albums for Quincy Jones's secular label, Qwest Records, saw them crossing to the R&B and pop charts.

Unlike most gospel artists, they were able to work easily with their secular counterparts. The urban soul hit 'Choose ye this day' was recorded with Vanessa Bell Armstrong, 'Ain't no need to worry' with Anita Baker and 'Love has no color' with Michael McDonald. Their album *Live at Carnegie Hall* was produced by Teddy Riley, the

The old and the new: Aretha Franklin performing with Bebe Winans in Los Angeles, 2008.

167

man credited with fusing R&B and hip hop to create new jack swing, and R. Kelly, the singer behind the hits 'I believe I can fly' and 'Bump 'n' grind'. It made the pop, CCM, gospel and R&B charts.

TRAMAINE HAWKINS

The career of the Winans took a trajectory similar to that of Tramaine Hawkins, another recruit to the Light label. She had recorded with a local Californian group, the Heavenly Tones, when she was only ten years old, and cut her first album with them for Savoy in the mid-1960s, James Cleveland producing the sessions. At the end of the 1960s she was part of Edwin Hawkins' choir and appeared on 'Oh happy day'. In the early 1970s, under her single name of Tramaine Davis, she recorded and toured with Andrae Crouch as part of the Disciples.

Shortly afterwards she joined the Love Alive Choir, directed by Edwin Hawkins' brother Walter. The two got married, and she became the star singer on albums that Hawkins and his choir recorded for Light as well as on the singles 'Changed' and 'Goin' up yonder', which were instant radio hits.

Tramaine Hawkins went solo in 1980, recording her debut solo album, *Tramaine*, for Light, following it up three years later with *Determined*. In 1985 she made the controversial move of recording a techno-funk song, 'Fall down (Spirit of love)', for the A&M label. It made the number-one spot in *Billboard*'s dance chart, but upset people who felt it wasn't right to create songs about the Holy Spirit as dance tracks for sexually charged club audiences. 'Church people tend to be very picky about things that they consider

sacred,' she commented at the time. 'But even though some of my work may have offended some people, the music has brought souls to Christ.'

She has continued to pursue a career somewhere between the revival circuit and the dance floor, attracting musicians like Carlos Santana and Jimmy McGriff to play on her gospel albums, signing a deal with Columbia and even recording a 'duet' with the late Mahalia Jackson on 'I found the answer' through the wonders of digital technology. Many regard her as the greatest female voice in gospel music today. 'I was placed on earth to sing music that uplifts, that soothes, that consoles,' she once said. 'I'm just doing what God wants me to.'

Tramaine Hawkins has been recording since the mid-1960s, but still manages to retain a cutting edge.

Interview with Jessy Dixon, Jerusalem, July 1978

❀ **How do you feel about performing in Jerusalem?**

It's one of the highlights of my career. I've always wanted to come here just to be close to where the Lord walked and where he worked so many miracles. It's almost unbelievable. To be able to come here and sing about him is a great honour. I consider myself to be a PR firm for Jesus Christ because a PR firm builds up and promotes someone's name and image.

❀ **Your break came when you were spotted by James Cleveland.**

Yes. He came to San Antonio, Texas, where I was raised, and he heard me sing because I was the opening act at his concert. He told me that if I ever came to Chicago he'd like to help me. I left college during my second year of studying music and James took me on the road as part of his show. James would have me stand up and sing and then I'd play piano and Billy Preston would play organ while James sang.

❀ **How did you go on to develop?**

I was around people who were writing songs and it inspired me to write. I was around James Cleveland and Roberta Martin, Dorothy Norwood, Robert Anderson, Dorothy Love Coates. It was an experience that I cherish, because I had no business being there, and if it hadn't been for James I would never have gotten into these circles. Aretha Franklin was there. She would come with her father, who was a travelling preacher. I met Mahalia Jackson and was asked to play for her because my style was different to musicians out of Chicago. She would invite me to her home and share stories with me. It was a great experience and helped me know what gospel was all about.

❀ **Did James Cleveland teach you how to work an audience?**

Yes. I was taught how to perform on stage because it's completely different from singing in church. You have to learn to use a microphone – how to use it in your hand; how to leave it in the stand. You have to learn how to move around in an audience and how to bow. You have to learn how to walk on stage – everything.

❀ **What happened after you left James Cleveland?**

James had me record a song I wrote called 'There is no failure in God'. We were in the studio recording it, and I was doing the lead, and Herman Lubinsky, who owned Savoy Records, came into the studio and said he'd like me to record it on my own. It was just like that. James was trying to get his own career together, so I took the offer up.

❀ **That became the Jessy Dixon Singers?**

The first records I made were with a choir. That's how the Dixon Singers evolved. I took the choir to the Apollo Theater in Harlem and found it too much to have thirty voices away from home for ten days. It was too expensive for the promoters and not enough money for the singers. They did it out of love for me. So I had to get a smaller group and so I had two girls.

❀ **What have been the big steps in your career since then?**

The first was coming to the Lord. When I accepted the Lord as *my* Lord I felt myself making other steps with my music. Before then my ambition had been to make progress in the gospel market.

When I found that I didn't want this as much as I'd thought, it almost blew my mind. I almost considered going back to school or becoming a music teacher.

❁ It seems unusual for a gospel singer to become a committed Christian in mid-career.

I'd chosen gospel as a career without thinking of it as more than a career. Then I realized that in order to truly progress I'd have to give my whole self to it rather than just my talent. I was giving it my soul, I was giving it my body, but then I realized I really had to know who it was I was singing about.

❁ It's hard to understand how you could sing the gospel but not apply it to your own life.

I felt that being religious was enough, that being religious took care of the commitment that was required. At the back of my mind I felt that there had to be more. It was like the Peggy Lee song 'Is that all there is?' I kept trying to put my finger on what it was.

❁ How did your conversion affect your music?

Because it affected my whole life it affected my music, which was a great part of my life. I wanted to sing again. I wanted to sing because I was learning about the person I was singing about, learning to have fellowship with him. Suddenly I wanted to hear everything about Jesus as if I had never heard it before, which I guess I never had. I had never really listened with my heart. To listen with your mind is not enough. Some of the songs I had sung earlier in my career I could no longer sing. Some of them were completely unbiblical. Some of them weren't really gospel once I knew what gospel really was. Some of them made you feel sorry for yourself. Some of them encouraged you to be content with where you were. The more I get to know the Lord I realize that so much of what we consider to be inspirational gospel music really isn't. In fact, it hurts people.

❁ Had you always read the Bible?

Not that much. I would read it and compare my life to it but it would condemn me so I would close it up.

❁ How did the connection with Paul Simon come about?

I was wondering whether the Lord wanted me to continue to sing. Then an invite to perform at the Newport Jazz Festival came out of the blue. It was at that festival that Paul Simon heard me. His producer then called me and asked me if I'd like to bring my group on tour with him. I did!

❁ How has touring with Paul Simon and appearing on the *Rhymin' Simon* album helped your career?

It's helped me get to audiences that were previously ignorant of gospel singing. Some have told me that all they knew about gospel was Mahalia Jackson. For me this has been like pioneering new territory.

❁ You play a lot to white audiences now. Do you feel that you've deserted the black church?

Not at all. I feel that white audiences deserve to hear what we've been hearing all along and have perhaps taken for granted. It's time for it to be done because if we don't do it someone else is going to take it.

15

Shakin' the Rafters

GOSPEL CHOIRS

Over 150,000 fans were crammed into a temporary enclosure in London's Hyde Park on 2 July 2005 to witness the spectacle of Live 8, an awareness-raising event organized by Bob Geldof to highlight issues surrounding the G8 conference then taking place in Scotland. A further 50,000 watched the event nearby on giant screens. Madonna took to the stage wearing a white top and matching baggy trousers, clutching the hand of the Ethiopian refugee Birhan Woldu, and asking the crowd, 'Are you ready to change history?' The first song in her three-song set was 'Like a prayer', her 1989 hit that likens sexual attraction to the

The London Community Gospel Choir performs with Madonna at Live 8 in Hyde Park, London, in July 2005.

power of prayer. Behind her, to her right, also dressed in white trousers and shirts, was the fifty-strong London Community Gospel Choir.

The choir, carefully choreographed, followed the arrangement that Andrae Crouch had worked out for the single, providing a rich backdrop for Madonna's vocal. The power of their voices, the dazzling contrast of white cotton against dark skin, and the precision of their movement as they gestured with their outstretched arms and then clasped their hands together as the song reached its resolution gave the opening number the visceral impact she was clearly hoping for. Reviewers were ecstatic.

The employment of a gospel choir to bring a feeling of transcendence and a sense of the spectacular is increasingly common in secular affairs. If the unchurched public was asked what single image comes to mind at the mention of gospel music, it would surely be the black gospel choir swaying in time to the rhythm of a song, mouths open wide, eyes raised to heaven. It's an image reinforced in movies (*Sister Act*, *Preacher's Wife*), in advertising (Nivea in the UK) and on record (Michael Jackson, Madonna, Elton John). When Bruce Springsteen performed his song 'The rising' in front of the Lincoln Memorial in the presence of Barack Obama two days before Obama's inauguration he was backed by a full red-robed gospel choir. The choir has become emblematic of gospel in the way that a quartet would have been fifty years ago. Guided tours of Harlem take bus loads of visitors to Mount Moriah Baptist Church on a Wednesday to hear the ARC (Addicts' Rehabilitation Center) choir during their Hour of Power, or to Abyssinian Baptist Church on a Sunday to 'experience the soul-stirring power of gospel music'. The House of Blues offers a 'gospel

brunch' where you can 'Praise the Lord and pass the biscuits'! Gospel music is packaged as a cultural experience.

Choirs have existed for as long as gospel music, but, because of the large numbers of singers involved, they weren't able to tour as extensively (if at all), and they made records much later than the jubilee groups, quartets and soloists. Before Thomas Dorsey's innovations the premier showcase for choirs was the National Baptist Convention, which, beginning in 1919, had the songwriter Lucie Campbell as its musical director. Long before taking up this office, she had been involved with choirs, once organizing a 1,000-voice choir made up of singers she'd contacted around Memphis.

Before gospel music, large choirs were organized to exemplify orderliness, restraint and the attainment of classical European musical values. Choristers studiously avoided the swaying, clapping and dancing now associated with gospel choirs. Churches chose choir directors who'd been trained at music conservatories, because they wanted their choirs to embody social progress. They believed that this form of singing, because it was dependent on co-operation, co-ordination and conformity, could aid them in their cultural advancement.

Consequently, choirs prided themselves on singing works such as Handel's *Messiah*, Bach's cantatas, Haydn's *Creation* and Mendelssohn's *Elijah*. Olivet Baptist Church in Chicago had a Choral Study Group, organized, it said, 'to create a desire for better music among Chicago Negroes and to render musical numbers of the higher type'. Bethel AME Church Choir, also in Chicago, performed Friedrich von Flotow's opera *Martha* in 1921, with orchestral accompaniment by

A specially assembled 125-voice adult choir performs 'The rising' with Bruce Springsteen at the We Are One Barack Obama inaugural celebration, Lincoln Memorial in Washington, 18 January 2009.

J. EARLE HINES

Prof. James Earle Hines & His Goodwill Singers
The St. Paul Baptist Church Choir of Los Angeles

James Earle Hines is seen on his album cover, back left.

musicians from the Chicago Symphony. Pilgrim Baptist Church, where Dorsey would eventually become music director, had a twenty-seven-piece orchestra to accompany its choir during Sunday worship. Clearly, their idea of cultural progress was to move away from the fervour of the plantation meeting huts and closer to the calm reflection of the opera houses and concert halls of Europe.

One of the significant contributions of Dorsey's revolution was its reaffirmation of the African aspects of music, the things that didn't come so naturally to Europeans. The suggestion was made that rhythm, movement and improvisation, far from being infantile, might simply be a different set of skills. This attitude initially affected the choruses, the smaller groups that sang at weekday events but not at the Sunday worship services,

but it soon spread to the main choirs. Eventually it became *de rigueur* for choirs to sing contemporary songs, to unleash emotion and to stray from the text 'as the Spirit led'.

WINGS OVER JORDAN

The first professional black choir in America was the Wings Over Jordan Choir founded in 1935 in Cleveland, Ohio, by Glenn T. Settle, the minister of Gethsemane Baptist Church. In 1937 Settle went with his singers, then the senior choir of his church, to local radio station WGAR to try to interest it in a show that would appeal to black listeners. The programme director, Worth Kramer, happened to be a fan of spirituals and was attracted to the idea. At that point Settle had nineteen singers. Kramer added a further sixteen, drilled them for several weeks and then gave them their own Sunday morning show. Short speeches by black leaders, authors and academics were included.

In 1938 the CBS network (of which WGAR was a recent affiliate) picked up the show and broadcast it nationwide on 107 stations and on short-wave radio around the world. It became so popular that over 5,000 letters were flooding in every week. Rather than the 'art songs' that choirs were expected to sing, they performed unaccompanied spirituals – 'I'm a-rollin'', 'Over my head', 'Take me to the water', 'Amen', 'Swing low, sweet chariot' – although still in a formal fashion. The choir was instantly recognizable by its low, almost spooky humming, and by the soprano solos of Mildred Pollard on numbers such as 'I'm going to sit at the welcome table' and 'He's all in all to me'.

By 1940 the members of the group had all abandoned their day jobs and were touring the country in a bus, giving concerts to non-segregated audiences at $1,500 a time. The profits were ploughed into a scholarship scheme for black students. During the war they worked for the United Service Organization, performing for American troops in Europe. In 1947 their contract with CBS Radio ended, but the group continued to tour, visiting Japan in 1953 and Korea in 1954.

ECHOES OF EDEN

The demise of their spot on national radio coincided with the rise of St Paul Baptist Church Choir in Los Angeles under the directorship of James Earle Hines (not to be confused with jazz pianist Earl 'Fatha' Hines). Originally from Atlanta, Hines had studied at the Cosmopolitan School of Music in Cincinnati and had briefly been a member of the Wings Over Jordan Choir.

As part of the Goodwill Singers he'd worked for the National Baptist Convention, encouraging the growth of choirs in affiliated churches. In 1946 he was recruited by Pastor John C. Brabham to direct the choir at St Paul Baptist Church in downtown Los Angeles.

This choir, initially known as the Echoes of Eden Choir, was to become the prototype of the modern gospel choir, with hand-clapping, powerful solos and the use of polyphony and antiphony. The repertoire was taken from a mixture of sources – traditional hymns ('Yield not to temptation'), spirituals ('Every day will be Sunday') and the contemporary gospel songs of people like Kenneth Morris ('My God is real') and Thomas Dorsey 'If we never needed the Lord before (we sure do need him now').

The choir of the Abyssinian Baptist Church in Harlem, popular with congregants and tourists alike.

The sound of the St Paul Baptist Church Choir was very different from that of the Wings Over Jordan Choir. Hines was a consummate showman who could create mass hysteria among audiences. Gospel historian Anthony Heilbut believes that he set the standard for church-'wrecking' that the quartets sought to follow. After Hines, argues Heilbut, 'it became clear that gospel involved more than singing. If you didn't move the people out of their seats, into the aisles, and – ideally – leave them flat on their backs, you had not scored.'

He led the choir with his baritone voice, and would frequently set up call-and-response exchanges with them. On recordings it's possible to hear gasped cries of 'Amen' and 'Can I get a witness?', showing that he had broken with the tradition that tried to rid choirs of 'wild excitement' (as Bishop Daniel Payne described it). There was a new sense of rhythm and an escalating feeling of excitement. Choirs were looking back and capturing some of the excitement and passion of the rural churches of the South.

The R&B singer Etta James was one of those who attended the church during this dynamic period. 'Everyone loved our church,' she wrote in her autobiography. 'We had one of the biggest, baddest, hippest choirs anywhere ... Our choirmaster, Professor James Earle Hines, was my first and heaviest musical mentor, the cat who taught me to sing. Fact is, I wanted to sing just like him.'

Such was the reputation of the church that black celebrities such as the boxer Joe Louis, the actress Hattie McDaniels (*Gone with the Wind*) and the singer Nat 'King' Cole would drop by on a Sunday night. From 1947 to 1950 Capitol Records made several live recordings of the choir, which were released as singles. Local radio station KFWB, based in Lincoln Park, featured the choir on a weekly show that had an audience of one million and reached into seventeen states.

The National Convention of Gospel Choirs and Choruses had assembled a mass choir each year that would perform a selection of the latest gospel songs. Recordings of the performance were sold to participating churches. This was considered to be the only viable way of selling choral records without the publicity gained by regular radio broadcasts or the benefit of an outstanding personality like J. Earle Hines. Significantly, the Wings Over Jordan Choir and the St Paul Church Choir of Los Angeles only made one long-playing record apiece, both records being made in 1953.

ABYSSINIAN BAPTIST CHOIR OF NEWARK

During the early 1960s things began to change. In 1958 Savoy Records issued a record by the Young People's Choir of the Abyssinian Baptist Church of Newark which couldn't have sold too well, because the label didn't touch a choir for another three years. In 1960 John Hammond, the organizer of 1938's *From Spirituals to Swing* event, took a risk on recording the same church's senior 100-voice choir for Columbia Records. The choir director at the time was the flamboyant Alex Bradford, who happened to be a Savoy artist. This resulted in contractual complications that were resolved only when Savoy conceded that Bradford could conduct the singers and use songs he'd written, but couldn't appear on the recording as a performer. The result was a twelve-track LP, *Shakin' the Rafters*, which captured the choir's energy, enthusiasm and frequently faltering vocal leads.

Inset: Alex Bradford and the Bradford Singers, undated.

Main photo: In September 1962, members of the cast of *Black Nativity* – which tells the story of the birth of Christ in terms of Negro spirituals and traditional jazz – performed in the new Coventry Cathedral, UK. At the organ is Joe Washington and at the piano, Alberta Carter.

The Abyssinian Baptist Choir was to become the vocal training ground for a number of highly successful soul singers, including Cissy Houston (mother to Whitney), Dionne Warwick, Judy Clay and Madeline Bell. When Bradford toured Europe in 1962 with *Black Nativity*, the 'gospel song play' written by poet Langston Hughes, he brought Bell with him as part of his group, the Alex Bradford Singers. She stayed behind in London, becoming one of Britain's most in-demand session singers (she's the high female voice on the Rolling Stones' 'Gimme shelter') as well as a founder member of the chart act Blue Mink ('Melting pot').

BLACK NATIVITY

Black Nativity, premiered in December 1961, would eventually take gospel to Broadway, and the cast was effectively a small choir. Hughes got his inspiration by visiting Harlem churches late on Sunday nights. His description of the power of those services captures the essence of the gospel music experience, one which he was able to translate to the stage. 'I usually arrived about ten at night when services were in full swing,' he wrote. 'I was never bored. Song and a sense of drama swirled around me. A mingling of ancient scripture and contemporary problems were projected with melodic intensity and rhythmic insistence. Every night I was drawn into the circle of oneness generated by the basic beat of the gospel tempo.'

ANGELIC CHOIR

In 1961 Savoy recorded three choirs, one of which was the Angelic Choir from the First Baptist Church of Nutley, New Jersey. This couldn't have sold well either, because the following year A&R director Fred Mendelsohn came up with the idea of putting them in the studio with one of his more experienced artists, James Cleveland, in the hope that Cleveland would be able to bring out the best in them.

Cleveland was best known as a former member of the Caravans. He'd also recorded with the Gospel Chimes and had lent his name to recordings by the Gospel All-Stars, a female group from Brooklyn. In its own right the Angelic Choir was not outstanding, but Cleveland made it an accessory to his own voice. He adopted

PICCADILLY
THEATRE

"BLACK
NATIVITY"

by
LANGSTON HUGHES

PROGRAMME ONE SHILLING

Programme for *Black Nativity* at the Piccadilly Theatre in London.

the role of the preacher, sometimes speaking in hushed tones, sometimes straining his gruff voice to sing, while the choir was like a responsive congregation.

The first album, *This Sunday in Person*, was recorded in July 1962, a single, 'Redeemed', was recorded two months later, and then in December a follow-up album, *James Cleveland with the Angelic Choir*, volume 2, which featured a spoken version of the old hymn 'How great thou art' with Billy Preston on keyboards. The breakthrough recording turned out to be the third album, *Peace Be Still*, recorded live in September 1963. This was the recording that made it clear that choirs could compete with soloists and quartets. Anthony Heilbut later said that these three albums with Cleveland and the Angelic Choir were 'the best documents of church services on record'.

THE CLARK SISTERS

Savoy responded to the success of the Angelic Gospel Choir by recording more choirs, including the Christian Temple Choir, the Voices of Tabernacle Chorale, the Christian Tabernacle Choir and the First Church of Love, Faith and Deliverance Choir. One of the most significant choirs the label signed was the Southwest Michigan State Choir, directed by the formidable Mattie Moss Clark from Detroit. Two days after Cleveland had recorded *Peace Be Still* Clark and her choir laid down tracks for the album *Wonderful, Wonderful*, which included the single 'I thank you, Lord'.

Clark was an Alabama native who'd relocated to Detroit after the war and had become a powerful figure in the COGIC music scene, both as president of the denomination's National

Music Department and as a songwriter, arranger, singer and pianist. She had been responsible for important innovations in choral singing, introducing three-part harmony and taking the music away from traditional pipe-organ instrumentation. She wrote on a Hammond organ, the keyboard introduced to gospel by Kenneth Morris in the 1930s, and this meant that her songs worked best for choirs if they too used a Hammond organ.

Before her death in 1995 she had recorded thirty-five albums, written over a hundred songs, founded the Clark Conservatory School of music and, through her work with COGIC, discovered a number of future gospel acts, including Edwin Hawkins and Andrae Crouch, both of whom appeared in her Midnight Musicals at the annual convention. Her other great legacy was her five daughters – Jacky, Twinkie, Denise, Dorinda and Karen – who found fame in the 1970s and 1980s as the Clark Sisters, the paramount female gospel group of the era.

The Clark Sisters began as choir singers, their mother schooling them so well that they could always be called on to demonstrate a song to the rest of the choir. As a group, they incorporated many of the tricks they'd learned from Mattie to create music that fused most contemporary forms of black music. In 1983 they had a surprise mainstream hit with 'You brought the sunshine', the first gospel song to make the charts since 'Oh happy day'. It was later used in a TV commercial for Sunny Delight orange drink.

James Cleveland moved to Los Angeles in 1963 to pastor the New Greater Harvest Baptist Church. He was eventually fired from this position for neglecting preaching in favour of music, and so in November 1970 he founded

The Clark Sisters are the daughters of Mattie Moss Clark – director of the Southwest Michigan State Choir, songwriter, arranger, singer and pianist. The girls, pictured here in 2006, had a mainstream hit in 1983 with 'You brought the sunshine'.

his own church, Cornerstone Institutional Baptist Church, with seating for 2,000, and took with him the choir from his previous church. This choir was built up into the Southern California Community Choir (SCCC). Although he worked with other choirs – the Voices of Tabernacle, the Charles Fold Singers, the Gospel Music Workshop of America Mass Choir, the Salem Inspiration Choir, the Prayer Tabernacle Choir – it was with the SCCC that he had his greatest success.

Jessy Dixon, Cleveland's old protégé, also worked with choirs in the 1960s, starting with the Chicago Community Choir, with whom he first recorded for Savoy in 1964. Promoters outside of Chicago wanted to book the choir,

but it became impracticable both logistically and financially to tour or even to do a string of dates in another city. Dixon solved the problem by retaining three female vocalists, who became the core of the Jessy Dixon Singers.

THE TOMMIES

He also had an association with the Thompson Community Singers, led by the Reverend Milton Brunson, writing songs for the choir and playing piano on its hit single 'Rise and walk'. The Tommies, as they were always known, were formed by Brunson when he was at high school in 1948. Based at St Stephen's Church, they named themselves after the pastor, the Reverend Eugene Thompson, and kept the name after

Brunson became ordained and founded the Christ Tabernacle Missionary Baptist Church.

The Tommies recorded for Vee-Jay in the 1960s and Hob and Nashboro in the 1970s. But it wasn't until the 1980s, when they signed to Word, that they really broke through. Their album *Miracle Live* reached the top ten in *Billboard*'s gospel chart in 1984, and they followed up this achievement with five albums that all reached the top spot – *There is Hope* (1986), *If I Be Lifted* (1987), *Available to You* (1989), *Open Our Eyes* (1990) and *My Mind is Made Up* (1992). In 1995 they received a Grammy for the album *Through God's Eyes*. Brunson died suddenly in 1997, and the choir was taken over by his widow, JoAnn.

JOHN P. KEE

The most notable choir leader over the past twenty years has been John P. Kee, a broad-shouldered, husky-voiced replacement for James Cleveland, who is known to his fans as the Prince of Gospel. From Durham, North Carolina, Kee studied music at college and later worked with prominent musicians in the world of jazz, funk and folk. In the 1980s he played at Jim and Tammy Bakker's notorious PTL Club and had songs covered by Edwin Hawkins ('Jesus lives in me') and the New Jerusalem Baptist Choir ('Show me the way').

In 1981 he founded the sixty-voice New Life Community Choir, recruiting members from the lower echelons of urban society. He began recording with them in 1989, and has since produced ten albums with them, as well as producing six albums with the Victory in Praise Mass Choir, which he formed in 1990.

As contemporary gospel quartets lost the distinctiveness they'd had in the 1940s and 1950s, it was the choirs that still sounded most obviously gospel to untrained ears. This led to their being employed in all kinds of commercial ventures to signify joy, enthusiasm or a vague sense of spirituality. The Georgia Mass Choir, started in 1983 by the Reverend Milton Biggham – now director of Savoy Records in its new incarnation as the gospel imprint of Malaco Records – performed six times during the 1996 Olympic Games in Atlanta. They were also featured on the soundtrack of *The Preacher's Wife* and have appeared on *Good Morning America* and *Saturday Night Live*.

One of the most outrageous uses of a gospel choir came in 2007, when the cosmetic company Nivea commissioned a TV commercial in Britain for its skincare products, featuring a female gospel choir praising the power of certain creams to reduce cellulite. The advert started with the lead singer looking directly into the camera and announcing, 'This be the dedication to the resurrection of this sweet mother-lovin' ass.'

Ken Burton, a music director approached to put the choir together, rejected the offer and later campaigned against it. 'The campaign features a gospel choir in a church setting,' he told London's black community newspaper *The Voice*. 'All the elements of worship are present – the singing, the responses from the congregation and the lifting of hands. Corporate companies always like to use black people in these "buffoon" portrayals. Why can't we see adverts involving gospel choirs in dignified settings? Why do they always have to act like fools?' A spokesperson for Nivea's public relations company said that the campaign wasn't meant to offend. 'It was aimed at all women of different shapes and sizes,' she said. 'The use of gospel music was intended to create a fun and joyful atmosphere.'

One of the most remarkable examples of the merging of the corporate and the choral is Britain's London Community Gospel Choir (LCGC), founded in 1982 by the Reverend Bazil Meade, an immigrant from the Caribbean island of Montserrat. Not attached to one church or even one denomination, the members of LCGC were recruited from a number of London churches. The first prominent home-grown gospel act in Britain, it started modestly, mainly playing church events, but after national television appearances it caught the eye of the secular music and business world.

Over twenty-five years later LCGC is a highly successful business operation offering a wide range of services as well as recordings and merchandise (mugs, teeshirts, key rings). Clients don't have to book the whole choir. They can book units as small as five singers and a keyboard-player, depending on their needs. In its publicity LCGC says it will perform at corporate events, after-show parties, conferences, schools, cabaret clubs, weddings, funerals, prisons, theatres, concert halls and churches. The choir is described as 'controversial, professional, energetic, inspiring and Spirit-filled'.

Members organize music workshops in schools, sing back-up on studio recordings, accept commissions to compose new gospel-inspired pieces and offer 'gift experience day vouchers' that allow members of the public to meet with and sing with them. They have performed, either in concert or in the studio, with over sixty major international music stars, including Michael Bolton, Eric Clapton, Elton John, Paul McCartney, Jessye Norman, Tina Turner and Madonna. In the corporate world they have been used by major companies, including Coca-Cola, Disney, Toyota, T-Mobile, Swatch, Nintendo and Christian Dior.

Not surprisingly, the repertoire of the LCGC is eclectic, ranging from spirituals and gospel to 1960s soul and contemporary R&B. They are similarly flexible in their appearance. If you hire them for a wedding, for example, you can choose whether you'd like them dressed in red choir robes, black robes with gold edging, red shirts with black trousers, baby-pink shirts with black trousers, white shirts with black trousers, or dressy wedding outfits. Happy couples can choose from a list of thirty-eight songs, ranging from traditional gospel ('Oh happy day', 'Amazing grace' or 'This little light of mine') to pop (The Beatles' 'All you need is love', Marvin Gaye's 'How sweet it is', Bob Marley's 'One love' or Robbie Williams' 'Angels').

NOEL ROBINSON AND GRAHAM KENDRICK

Gospel choirs have proliferated in Britain since the 1980s. Although they almost all owe something to the classic choirs of the past, they have developed a different sound, because the cultural origins of their members are more likely to be in Britain, Africa or the Caribbean than in America. They are also more likely to have been influenced by the white praise and worship movement pioneered by writer–singers like Matt Redman, Stuart Townend, Noel Richards and Graham Kendrick than by the spirituals collected by James Weldon Johnson or the work of Mahalia Jackson and James Cleveland.

Noel Robinson was undeniably affected by

praise and worship. He grew up influenced by the Afro-Caribbean gospel music of London Pentecostal churches and commercial R&B. He was taught to play guitar by his father and was soon playing as a session musician. However, his career path was determined by a fortuitous meeting with Graham Kendrick, who hired him to play on his tours. Suddenly Robinson found himself playing to white audiences and discovering a genre of music that hadn't yet taken root in the black church.

Kendrick's songs could be performed by a group but could also be sung along to by any size of congregation. They gained prominence as the charismatic movement burgeoned in the 1970s and worshippers became more emotional in their displays, often dancing, swaying and raising their arms. Songs of his, such as 'Shine, Jesus, shine', 'Knowing you' and 'The Servant King', became established favourites as overhead screens featuring the words replaced hymnals, and 'worship bands' replaced pianos and organs. To critics it was lightweight 'happy-clappy' music that turned worship into an entertainment spectacle. To proponents it was a rebirth of hymnology comparable to what had taken place in the eighteenth century and proof that God's Spirit was at work in a new way.

Robinson believes that some of his Afro-Caribbean rhythms rubbed off on Kendrick. Certainly some of Kendrick's phraseology and sing-along approach rubbed off on Robinson. He formed a group, Nu Image, made up of a band and what was effectively a small choir of four sopranos, four altos and two tenors, who performed in a similar way to Kendrick, leading congregations rather than putting on a show for them to admire. Among his best-known songs are

'You are my healer' and 'Your mercies endure'.

Similarly, London-based Muyiwa and his group of musicians and backing singers, Riversongz, centre on praise and worship songs. Muyiwa was born in Nigeria, and became known in Britain through being a presenter on Premier Radio and elsewhere through being the host of *Sounds of Africa* on Lufthansa Airlines' in-flight entertainment. His material, including songs such as 'Lift his name on high' and 'Oh Lord our God', is at times reminiscent of Andrae Crouch, but with more influence from contemporary soul and R&B.

Sometimes choirs are the product of a particular church, such as the Ruach Ministries Choir headed by Bishop John Francis, which operates from Brixton, south London. There are also regional choirs, such as the Urban Choir in Manchester and the One Voice Community Choir in Preston. In 2005 many of these choirs were brought together under the directorship of David Daniel and singer/arranger Tyndale Thomas to produce a heavily TV-advertised album titled *The Best Gospel Album in the World Ever* for the Virgin label.

British record companies have frequently tried to find ways of mass-marketing gospel music. In the late 1980s Virgin tried to make a star out of vocalist Lavine Hudson, who had briefly appeared with the LCGC. However, there was always a collision between Hudson's openly evangelistic aims and the record company's desire to turn her into a phenomenon. She made only two albums and has since retired from public appearances.

In 2001 and 2003 the television company GMTC organized the GMTV Gospel Challenge in an attempt to find Britain's best new gospel acts. The first competition was won by Raymond & Co., a group of three girls fronted by Isaiah-Raymond Dyer, a former prisoner who had converted while awaiting sentencing on a charge of armed robbery. The album they made as a result of the recording contract awarded to the winner went on to win a MOBO award. In 2003 GMTV's challenge was won by a duo from Birmingham, Hutchinson and Gayle.

There are now even gospel choirs where no religious commitment of any kind is required. The music is regarded not as a ministry but as a style of singing which produces pleasure for those who perform. In 2006 the Academy of Contemporary Music in Guildford, Surrey, put together the ACM Gospel Choir under musical director Mark De-Lisser. In 2008 it reached the semi-finals of a BBC television competition, *Last Choir Standing*. Out of the twenty-nine members in the group at this time only five were non-whites.

Clearly, for some people, a gospel choir is no more than an exotic experience, an aural parallel to the enchantment of a medieval castle, the grandeur of a stately home or the splendour of a Hawaiian beach. But for millions of believers a gospel choir is still an expression of unarticulated praise and a representation of inner joy. Like everything else in gospel, choirs are undergoing a process of reinvention. The sounds that once seemed safe and reassuring are being lashed to the beat of the inner city. In many cases the gowns are coming off and the teeshirts are coming on. Hip hop is being made holy and rap is being redeemed.

CHAPTER

16

Stomp

KIRK FRANKLIN AND NU NATION

The diminutive figure in the long white jacket, white trousers and black shoes addressed the camera: 'For those of you that think gospel music has gone too far, who think we've got too radical with our message, well, I've got news for you. You ain't heard nothin' yet! And if you don't know – now you know. Glory, glory!' What followed over the next three minutes was one of the most progressive gospel videos ever made, one that would noisily usher in a new era of streetwise urban spiritual music.

The choir, God's Property, were wearing teeshirts and jeans, some of them with sweaters knotted around their waists, gyrating on catwalks to a riff sampled from Funkadelic's 'One nation under a groove', with their arms pumping in time. Cutaway shots showed dancers flipping through the air. The bulk of the song, 'Stomp', was carried by the choir, with Kirk Franklin, the man in the white suit, anticipating the lines and urging them on. The second verse was rapped by Salt

Kirk Franklin has been the figurehead of a movement to create gospel music for the age of hip hop, breakdancing and urban soul.

(Cheryl James of Salt-N-Pepa). 'I keep the live beat bumping / Keep it jumping / Make the Lord feel something.' When it was all over, a Bible reference was all that was left on the screen: Romans 10:9. Anyone looking it up would have read: 'If thou shalt confess with thy mouth the Lord Jesus Christ, and shalt believe in thine heart that God hath raised him from the dead, thou shalt be saved.'

The gist of the song was that God is so amazing that he makes you feel like dancing. Thinking of his goodness and faithfulness makes you want to stomp, stomp, stomp. Franklin implied in the spoken introduction to the song that he'd been accused of being too direct in his message, but of course the concern of traditionalists in the church would not have been the explicitness of his words but the genre-blurring nature of the music. Franklin is a gospel singer by heritage and attitude but his sound on this record was a blend of gospel, funk, hip hop and R&B. In other words, it didn't sound distinctively gospel. The album containing 'Stomp' – *God's Property* from Kirk Franklin's Nu Nation – sold 3 million copies and made the top of the R&B charts. It broke all kinds of records, and became the best-selling gospel album ever. The video was played in heavy rotation on MTV.

The *God's Property* project wasn't, strictly speaking, a Kirk Franklin album, but Franklin used it to promote his vision of a new type of gospel that was urban in sound and realistic in the way it dealt with the problems facing the young. His next album, 1998's *The Nu National Project*, built on this vision. On the first track he again presented himself as someone accused, this time in the form of a courtroom drama where a judge summarized the charges against him:

'Charge number one: Trying to take the gospel to the world. Charge number two: Making gospel music too secular. Charge number three: Tearing down the walls of religion.'

The truth is that in many ways Franklin is nothing more than an old-style gospel singer who has worked with some of the contemporary music of his day in much the same way that Thomas Dorsey did in the 1930s and Rosetta Tharpe did in the 1940s. His debut album, *Kirk Franklin & the Family*, released in 1993, owed a lot to his work with gospel choirs in the Dallas/Fort Worth area and sounded at times like something Andrae Crouch would record. His lyrics were always direct, affirming, and orthodox in theology.

SEEKING THE LOST

The main difference with Franklin is in the variety of music that he draws on, the professionalism with which it's executed, and the street savvy that he brings to his lyrics. Previous gospel singers, however innovative, have tended to write for the already saved. Franklin addresses the lost and assumes that they must be a little like he was when growing up on the streets of Dallas in the 1970s and 1980s, feeling rejected and lonely, getting drawn into early experiences of sex and drugs, wondering if it was possible to be given a fresh start.

Thomas Dorsey grew up admiring Ma Rainey, Bessie Smith and spirituals. Franklin, it would appear, grew up liking Michael Jackson, Prince, Andrae Crouch and the Edwin Hawkins Singers. His work is a synthesis of these inspirations, but he doesn't seem to have compromised the subject matter of his songs or to have worked in secular situations simply because the money was better. His attitude is uncompromising and his directness has become part of his appeal. Nu Nation is his vision of a movement of young people who are equally uncompromising: 'a generation of believers that are tired of keeping silent', as he stated in the sleeve notes to his album *The Nu Nation Project*.

'A DUDE WHO IS SERIOUS ABOUT THE LORD'

Born in Dallas in 1970, Franklin has become the prototype of a new breed of gospel performer. He was raised in the church but led an erratic life, walking on both sides of the road, as he has put it. He recounts so many rededications of his life in his 1998 autobiography *Church Boy* that it's hard to fathom his spiritual state at any given time. He dates his conversion to a point in his youth when a friend of his was killed. He prayed a prayer of dedication, but his confessed fecklessness, drug-taking and addiction to pornography lay in the future.

Born to a single mother, he was brought up by a great-aunt, and had a hard time at school. He was neither an academic high achiever nor a sporting success. He believed he was unpopular because of his height, his artistic interests and the fact that he attended church. He was abused by the man his mother eventually married, and at eighteen he fathered an illegitimate child of his own. Matters were made worse when he discovered rampant hypocrisy in the church. His minister told him not to worry about his promiscuous sexual behaviour.

Music was the one consistent factor in his life, and it was what kept him clinging to the church even when his life spiralled out of control. He learned to play piano, enjoyed seeing visiting gospel groups and made fumbling attempts to compose. He became music director at Mount Rose Baptist Church, played piano for other churches, and sang with various gospel groups, the most consistent of which was the Humble Hearts.

During his late teens his reputation as a choir director built, and in 1990 he was invited to direct a mass choir at the Washington DC convention of the Gospel Music Workshop of America (GMWA), the organization that James Cleveland had started in 1968. It was Cleveland's last convention. He was obviously in bad shape, and six months later he was dead. Although no one was aware of it at the time, there was a changing of the guard.

The fact that he'd directed at the GMWA was a boost to Franklin's reputation, especially back home in Texas. It led to more invitations to run workshops for choirs. Two years after the trip to Washington DC he pulled together a group of seventeen friends he'd met through various churches and choirs to form a new group he named the Family. To show what he felt they could do, he recorded them in performance singing ten of his best songs.

Copies of the resulting tape were given to gospel singers passing through Dallas and mailed out to major record companies. A copy ended up on the desk of Vicki Lataillade, owner of a newly founded gospel label called Gospo Centric Records. She'd been involved in gospel music for her whole professional career, promoting artists of the calibre of Andrae Crouch, Tramaine Hawkins, the Clark Sisters and Edwin Hawkins. She loved what she heard on the tape and made Franklin an offer. It wasn't the best he'd received, but he was impressed with her concern about spreading the gospel message. He felt that he'd rather be with a company that made spirituality a priority than with one that looked only at numbers.

Gospo Centric took the tape as it was, cleaned it up in a studio and released it as *Kirk Franklin & the Family* in June 1993. In December the first single from the album, 'Why we sing', had topped the gospel charts. A year later R&B stations began to pick up on it. In January 1994 the album went gold and climbed the R&B charts until it reached number six. It even reached number fifty-eight in the *Billboard* 200.

Kirk Franklin & the Family was a relatively traditional gospel album with a choral sound and featured vocalists. Songs such as 'He's able', 'Silver and gold' and 'Call on the Lord' wouldn't have been out of place during gospel's Golden Age. It was with his 1996 album, *Whatcha Lookin' 4*, that he began to experiment with a more contemporary sound. It outsold his debut album, making it to number three in the R&B charts and twenty-three in the *Billboard* 200. He was doing something unprecedented in gospel music in making albums that topped the gospel and CCM charts, as well as getting high positions in the R&B charts and *Billboard* 200. His next four albums would all reach the top twenty in all four charts.

Some within the church community remained suspicious, fearing that he was essentially an R&B singer who'd chosen to use religious lyrics to capture a share of an adjacent market. Shirley Caesar gave a measured and sensible answer when questioned about Franklin's authenticity. 'There were times when I would look at him and I would frown on it, because I was not used to that kind of gospel,' she said. 'But when the

Clark Sisters and the Hawkins Family came out, they called that contemporary. Twenty years later it's traditional, compared to what we're listening to now. So give it another fifteen years and what he's doing will be traditional.'

The difference between Franklin and earlier artists accused of smooching with secularism, like Rosetta Tharpe and Clara Ward, is that Franklin is fearless with his message and has a heart for troubled youth. If non-church organizations employ him, or if secular artists want to sing with him, it's always very much on terms that Franklin has set. Despite his flamboyance on stage where he dances and spins, it doesn't seem that he is given to ostentation. In 2007 he told *Jet* magazine:

> I don't try to live the life of a celebrity. I choose not to adopt a celebrity personality. I am just one of God's children. I am not elite. I'm trying to keep important what God sees as important. God isn't up there in heaven happy when I go platinum. He's up in heaven happiest when I catch a red-eye to go and see my children play soccer. So I'm trying to keep my focus on the things that matter most. As imperfect as I am, as jacked up as I am, I really want to be a dude who is serious about the Lord and I want to mirror Christ in any way that I can. I am just trying my best to make God happy.

Franklin has helped redefine gospel, opening the way for a new generation of performers who want to be as implicit or explicit about their faith as each song demands but who no longer want gospel to confine them in their musical exploration or determine the kind of venues they perform in. The majority of them want to compete with all the other singers in the R&B arena rather than be given special treatment in a sideshow known as gospel.

MARY MARY

Franklin paved the way for acts like Mary Mary. They comfortably enjoy success as mainstream R&B artists and gospel singers without having to produce separate product for each market. 'It's definitely contemporary,' says Tina Campbell. 'It's music that everybody in any style of music can relate to. It's universal, but the lyrics are undeniably gospel. You're not confused with what we're talking about. I don't think gospel or being a follower of Jesus dictates a certain chord, or a certain kind of instrumentation. I think your words define where a song goes.'

Mary Mary are two sisters, Erica and Tina (once Atkins, now Campbell, having both married men with the same surname), born into a Christian home in Los Angeles, where their father was a youth minister and their mother a choir director and evangelist. They sang in choirs, appeared on the *Bobby Jones Gospel Show* on BET and later studied music at college. They also began to write songs. One, 'Dance', was used in the 1998 movie *Dr Dolittle*, and another, 'Let go, let God', was on the 'Inspirational' soundtrack album released with the movie *The Prince of Egypt*.

In 2000 they were signed as recording artists to Columbia, whose most notable gospel successes had been with Mahalia Jackson in the 1950s and Tramaine Hawkins in the 1990s. Their debut album, *Thankful*, went platinum, and the first single, 'Shackles (Praise you)' became an instant club hit. 'Shackles' had a similar theme to Franklin's 'Stomp' – take the shackles off my feet and I'll be able to dance for the Lord – and was the first single to duplicate its success, becoming the top gospel seller as well as making it into the R&B top ten.

Singers Mary Mary perform during the Stevie Wonder 10th annual House Full of Toys benefit concert in Hollywood, 2005. Mary Mary are typical of the new breed of gospel acts which combine contemporary sound with uncompromising lyrics.

Their approach on *Thankful* and subsequent album releases remained consistent. The sound was contemporary R&B with occasional injections of rap and gospel, but the attitude of the subject matter was always unerringly Christian. As with Franklin's work, it differed from old-style gospel in that it wasn't written in coded language for the chosen few. It tackled the same topics that were being tackled by their R&B contemporaries, yet with faith, prayer and the presence of God as a non-negotiable base line. 'We deal with all the same things, the same inner conflicts, relationships, life, business, family, all of that stuff,' Erica told *Essence* magazine. 'We just have a different source.'

YOLANDA ADAMS

Another gospel artist walking the same path is Yolanda Adams, who, until her 1999 album *Mountain High … Valley Low* for Elektra, had recorded traditional gospel for gospel labels. For her first release on a secular label she enlisted the help of several mainstream producers, including Jimmy Jam and Terry Lewis, best known for their effect on early 1980s R&B with their band Time and then for producing Janet Jackson. The new material fitted comfortably in the contemporary R&B/pop landscape, but in every song there was a twist that would turn the listener's attention heavenwards. One of the most played singles from the album was 'Yeah', written by Erica and Tina of Mary Mary. *Mountain High … Valley Low* went platinum and earned Adams a Grammy.

'Gospel is being played on hip-hop stations, not just R&B and Adult Contemporary stations,' Adams noted in 2005 on the release of her second studio album on a secular label, *Day by Day*.

It's being played everywhere because people need inspiration all the time. It's not something that we think about and say: 'This is what we're going to do for the secular market and this is what we're going to do for the gospel market.' All you do is walk in to your producers and say that you want to make great music. That's how we do it.

Her songs remain staunchly gospel in outlook, although

Yolanda Adams performs at the Songs of Soul and Inspiration Concert celebrating the 50th anniversary of AARP in 2008 at the Philips Arena in Atlanta, Georgia, USA.

less reliant on the phrases of old-time religion. As with Mary Mary, she's more likely to suggest practical advice in making sense of life or to sing of Christ as her lover than she is to paraphrase a Bible story or rework an eighteenth-century hymn. Of the songs on *Day by Day* she said:

> I take the listener on a journey with me from my prayer time to the time where I'm contemplating a business decision. It's about things that we deal with day by day, not just the spiritual but the natural. There's a song about relationships. Women of all colours want to know: How can I get over this heartbreak? How can I get over this hiccup in my life? On this album, I tell them.

Tye Tribbett (centre) performs in Central Park, New York, 2009.

TYE TRIBBETT

New Jersey based Tye Tribbett and his Greater Anointing Choir display a similar energy and spiritual commitment to Kirk Franklin. The son of a preacher and a choir director, Tribbett displays aspects of both of these gifts, but in a very twenty-first-century way. His female choristers are also furious dancers, his musicians play brass, guitars, drums and keyboards and his concerts are part biblical pronouncement and part musical spectacular. Although he grew up in a more traditional environment and was schooled in the Tri-State Mass Choir and the Music and Arts Seminar run by Edwin Hawkins, you're more likely to discern traces of Jay-Z or Michael Jackson in his music than Mahalia or the Dixie Hummingbirds.

Like Franklin, he has a keen grasp of what it takes to make a splash in the modern media age and he is one of the few gospel artists to be recognized by his mainstream contemporaries. He has performed on bills with the likes of

Tim McGraw, Luther Vandross and Elton John, and, like Mary Mary, was a contributor to *The Prince of Egypt* 'Inspirational' album. He writes songs such as 'All hail the King' for his church audience and 'Good in the hood' for the others. 'We're going to get into a lot of trouble,' he once predicted. 'But I'm ready. I sing about issues that are going on. I'm not lying. My point is that I'm going to make it a little uncomfortable. That's what Jesus did.'

KIM BURRELL

Kim Burrell is another artist who had a traditional gospel upbringing but who now draws on more contemporary influences. Raised in Houston, Texas, she came up through James Cleveland's Gospel Music Workshop Choir and made her recording debut in 1995 with the album *Try Me Again*. Her style has been described as 'jazz gospel'. She's performed with singers like R. Kelly, Harry Connick Jr, George Clinton and Stevie Wonder, and has probably had more effect

Kim Burrell was trained by James Cleveland and has been cited as an influence on both Beyoncé and Mariah Carey.

on today's female R&B singers than any other contemporary gospel artist. Among those citing her as a significant influence on their music are Jessica Simpson, Beyoncé, Faith Evans and Mariah Carey.

All of these new gospel artists have struggled with the division between secular and sacred that has been fundamental to gospel history. Traditional gospel belonged within the church and only dealt with issues relating to conversion, prayer, worship and obeying the Commandments. It had nothing to say to the outside world other than 'Repent and be saved'. For any non-believer rejecting this, there was very little to relate to in gospel other than the style and the passion.

Traditional gospel music implicitly regarded the political, social and personal – the secular

life – as being on a lower level and so not worthy of comment. Life was divided into the spiritual and the secular, and the secular was, by and large, seen as something to flee from. The new generation of gospel artists has an implicit belief that the division is wrong but hasn't always been able to articulate why this is so.

Tina of Mary Mary comes close when she says: 'We're first natural, then spiritual' – meaning that we are created beings before we are redeemed sinners. Gospel music has a history of emphasizing the second over the first. She goes on:

There is a whole lot in secular music that has to do with us all just being human. There's a lot of it I can relate to. I can relate to love songs. I can relate to songs talking about the kind of upbringing that I had, or the violence in the world. I'm not against music that isn't gospel. I listen to all kinds of music. It's all a part of my life. It's just that if you're a Christian there are some things that are inappropriate, some areas you should limit.

DONNIE MCCLURKIN

Donnie McClurkin, older than Kirk Franklin by a decade, has been his more traditional counterpart. He has stuck closer to the traditional lyric format while stretching out musically. Yet, mainly due to a plug from Oprah Winfrey on her show, his debut solo album, *Donnie McClurkin*, flew off the shelves in 1996, and two of the tracks, 'Stand' and 'Speak to my heart', became

huge radio hits. His follow-up album, *Live in London*, similarly experienced a sales surge, when R&B DJs played the track 'We fall down' in support of the Reverend Jesse Jackson, who in January 2001 was discovered to have fathered a child with a woman who wasn't his wife.

'We fall down', which has since become McClurkin's signature tune, simply says that we all suffer or make mistakes, but we all have the choice to pick ourselves up. This was a particularly poignant message for McClurkin, as he'd suffered a dysfunctional family background at the hands of abusive parents who were addicted to alcohol and drugs. After the funeral of his two-year-old brother he was raped by an

Donnie McClurkin, seen here performing in 2008, is a more musically traditional counterpart to Kirk Franklin.

uncle, and years later by the son of that uncle. He has spent much of his life picking himself up.

McClurkin became a figure of controversy when he confessed to an ongoing struggle with homosexual attraction. His confession was unsettling for the black church because he announced what many people knew to be true, which was that the American gospel music world was heavily populated with male homosexuals. It outraged the liberal media because he was claiming that homosexual practice was inconsistent with Christian purity and that those tempted by homosexual behaviour could be 'healed'. In 2007 Barack Obama was criticized for allowing McClurkin to sing on behalf of his campaign for President. Obama responded by

admitting that he'd been unaware of McClurkin's views, which were contrary to his own, and redressed the balance by recruiting an openly homosexual pastor as well.

Although he still records, he tours less frequently because, like Claude Jeter, James Cleveland, Andrae Crouch and John P. Kee before him, he has found more fulfilment in preaching, being based in one place and singing primarily to his own congregation. In 2002 McClurkin founded Perfecting Faith Church in Freeport, New York, where he became the senior pastor. This megachurch attracts a thousand worshippers to its services, and McClurkin finds himself offering advice to many celebrities from the music industry.

There is something more traditional too about Byron Cage. When he performs with his nine-voice group Purpose you can hear the effect of his musical upbringing in various mass choirs. When he performs alone you realize that this minister of music at Ebenezer AME Church in Fort Washington, Maryland, sees his music as ministry rather than entertainment. On stage he is a worship leader rather than a performer.

A surprising number of the new generation of male gospel singers are ministers, the sons of ministers or both. The old pattern was to retire from the stage and take over the pulpit, but the new pattern is for those who have church-based ministries to stay there and use the church as a base for an expanded ministry. Smokie Norful ('All about you', 'Where would I be?'), who has a theology degree and has been ordained by the AME, is minister at Victory Cathedral Worship Center in Romeoville, Illinois, and records for EMI. Marvin Sapp ('Never could have made it', 'You are God alone') pastors Lighthouse Full Life

Smokie Norful performing on a rainy day in New York's Central Park, 2009.

Center Church in Grand Rapids, Michigan, and has made seven albums over the last twelve years.

RECONCILING THE SACRED AND THE SECULAR

The advent of Kirk Franklin was a huge tonic to the gospel music industry. He became a figurehead and an indication of the way forward. He demonstrated that there was no good reason why gospel should be marginalized and showed

Israel Houghton with his award for Best Pop/Contemporary Gospel Album at the 52nd Annual Grammy Awards at the Staples Center in Los Angeles, California, in 2010. Houghton describes his music as 'cross-cultural, cross-denominational and cross-generational'.

that it wasn't necessary to compromise to reach a mass audience. His single 'Lean on me' was recorded with R. Kelly, Bono, Mary J. Blige and Crystal Lewis, and yet it was an upfront expression of John 13:35.

The sales of gospel music increased from $381 million in 1995 to $538 million in 1996 and experienced a similar percentage increase the following year. Franklin's Tour of Life, which he made with Fred Hammond (formerly of Commissioned) and Yolanda Adams, was the 'most commercially successful tour in gospel music history', according to *Ebony* magazine.

For the longest part of its history, gospel music could be defined not only by the colour of the artists' skins and the content of the lyrics but by certain arrangements, combinations of instruments, vocal tricks and choices of chords. Although it could range from the close harmonies of the Golden Gate Quartet to the spine-tingling falsetto of Claude Jeter, there was always a recognizable gospel sound just as there was a recognizable jazz sound.

Recording artist Tonex released the first gospel album to have a parental advisory warning. This was a step too far for most gospel fans.

'gospel reggae' of Christafari and the mixture of neo soul, funk jazz and rock that characterizes the British group Four Kornerz. Although their intention is to evangelize, and the words of their songs are inspired by the New Testament gospel, they incorporate nothing of the musical vocabulary of gospel music as it has developed over the years. Surely there must come a point when the disconnection from the tradition is so great that it can no longer be considered a part of it. If a jazz musician started sounding like Bob Marley it would be considered a departure from rather than an advance in or a contemporary manifestation of jazz.

Israel Houghton, who benefits from being the worship leader at the Houston megachurch of popular TV evangelist Joel Osteen, typifies this break with the past. Whereas gospel music in the past tended to be by blacks for blacks, with whites invited in to listen, the music of Israel and New Breed, which mingles rock and worship, sees no barriers. Houghton believes his music is 'cross-cultural, cross-denominational and cross-generational. We want to reach everybody.' Asked if this is a betrayal of his gospel heritage, he says:

I was never purely a gospel artist or a black gospel artist. I think of it in terms of worship and praise. That is what I am a lot more comfortable being associated with.

We're living in an interesting time where Christians are still attempting to categorize things and put them into boxes that they've been used to. What's amazing is that the world has worked around this. MTV has figured how to do 'mash-ups' where cultures collide and make everybody like what they hear. The secular industry loves crossing boundaries.

Today there is music classified as gospel that no longer has that generic sound. Rather than merely being influenced by contemporary secular music, it has taken it as it is and simply injected a lyric drawn from the Bible or from Christian experience. The question that will face gospel historians of the future is whether this new Christian music is yet another branch or twig on the gospel tree that was planted back in the days of slavery or whether it more appropriately belongs to the much broader category of contemporary Christian music.

Cases in point are the 'gospel hip hop' of groups like 29th Chapter, Jahaziel and Lecrae, the

Sometimes the boundaries crossed are too great, as with the controversial young gospel star Tonex, whose flamboyant and erratic career has often seemed more like that of Prince than that of a minister of song. He was Grammy-nominated for his 2004 album *Out of the Box* and had won six Stellar Gospel Music Awards, but in 2005 he divorced his wife of five years and was later sued by his record company for breach of contract. Worse was to come. In 2006 he released an album on iTunes called *Oak Park: 92105*, which was distinguished by being the first gospel album ever to carry a parental advisory warning. He'd previously released it in 2003 on his own website.

He followed this up in 2007 with a privately released song called 'The naked truth', which used obscene language and had lines such as 'I got out alive nigga … (I'm) the genius, the faggot, the weirdo, the hobo, the homo, the magnet …'. This was so far from the great gospel lyrics of the past that his record label dropped him, and the longsuffering church community decided that while it would tolerate musical progression there were some limits that had to be acknowledged. Tonex offered a profuse apology but the damage was already done.

BLENDING OLD AND NEW

The new gospel sounds have never completely wiped away the old. Shirley Caesar still tours and gives maternal advice to stars like Yolanda Adams. Jessy Dixon is more visible than ever before. The Blind Boys of Alabama had their career rejuvenated in the 1990s when they recorded for Peter Gabriel's Real World label and found themselves welcome guests in rock venues and jazz clubs around the world. They discovered a way of blending the old and the new that prevented them from becoming merely a museum piece, cutting a version of 'Amazing grace' that set the words of John Newton's hymn to the music of 'The house of the rising sun' and making a gospel song out of The Rolling Stones' number 'Just wanna see his face'.

A few of the old groups from the 1940s and 1950s – the Soul Stirrers, the Dixie Hummingbirds, the Sensational Nightingales, the Jackson Southernaires – continue without a single original member. Back catalogues are kept alive by record companies like Document, which releases old material with archive-like precision. The twenty-first century has seen the publication of some of the best-researched biographies of various Golden Age greats, including Jerry Zolten's *Great God A'mighty* (2003), about the Dixie Hummingbirds and the 'rise of soul gospel music', and Gayle Ward's *Shout, Sister, Shout: The Untold Story of Rock-and-Roll Trailblazer Sister Rosetta Tharpe* (2007).

The new artists are respectful of their predecessors. They believe they are facing the same criticisms that faced the Fisk Jubilee Singers in the 1870s, Thomas Dorsey in the 1930s, Mahalia Jackson in the 1940s and Andrae Crouch in the 1970s and also that they're presenting the same message. Kirk Franklin speaks for them all when he says that he's trying to bring about a re-evaluation of gospel music. 'It's not corny and it's not hokey,' he says. 'We're not just running around with choir robes on, yelling and screaming. It's not about that any more. Gospel needs an edge so that it will receive the same kind of respect that other types of music get.'

Bibliography

Allen, William Francis, with Ware, Charles Pickard and Garrison, Lucy McKim, *Slave Songs of the United States: The Classic 1867 Anthology* (Mineola: Dover Publications, 1995)

Berry, Chuck, *Chuck Berry: The Autobiography* (London: Faber & Faber, 1988)

Blakey, D. N., *Revelation Blind Willie Johnson: The Biography* (n.p.: Lulu, 2007)

Boyer, Horace Clarence, *The Golden Age of Gospel* (Chicago: University of Illinois Press, 2000)

Caesar, Shirley, *The Lady, The Melody, and The Word: An Autobiography* (Nashville: Thomas Nelson, 1998)

Carawan, Guy, and Carawan, Candie, *Sing for Freedom: The Story of the Civil Rights Movement Through its Songs* (Montgomery: New South Books, 2007)

Carpenter, Bill, *Uncloudy Days: The Gospel Music Encyclopedia* (San Francisco: Backbeat Books, 2005)

Charters, Samuel, *The Legacy of the Blues* (London: Calder & Boyars, 1975)

Crouch, Andrae, *Through It All* (Waco: Word, 1974)

Cusic, Don, *The Sound of Light: A History of Gospel and Christian Music* (Milwaukee: Hal Leonard, 2002)

Darden, Robert, *People Get Ready: A New History of Black Gospel Music* (New York: Continuum, 2004)

Dorsey, Thomas, *Great Gospel Songs of Thomas Dorsey* (Milwaukee: Hal Leonard, 1988)

Equiano, Olaudah, *The Interesting Narrative and Other Writings* (London: Penguin, 1995)

Franklin, Kirk, *Church Boy: My Music and My Life* (Nashville: Word Publishing, 1998)

Genovese, Eugene D., *Roll, Jordan, Roll* (New York: Vintage Books, 1976)

Gillett, Charlie, *The Sound of the City* (London: Sphere Books, 1971)

Gray, Michael, *Hand Me My Travelin' Shoes: In Search of Blind Willie McTell* (London: Bloomsbury, 2007)

Guralnick, Peter, *The Last Train to Memphis: The Rise of Elvis Presley* (London: Little, Brown, 1994)

Guralnick, Peter, *Searching for Robert Johnson* (New York: Plume, 1998)

Harris, Michael W., *The Rise of Gospel Blues: The Music of Thomas Andrew Dorsey in the Urban Church* (New York: Oxford University Press, 1992)

Hayes, Cedric J., *A Discography of Gospel Records 1937–1971* (Copenhagen: Karl Emil Knudsen, 1973)

Heilbut, Anthony, *The Gospel Sound: Good News and Bad Times* (New York: Limelight Editions, 1985)

Hiss, George L., *The Joe Bostic Story* (Milton Keynes: AuthorHouse, 2007)

Jackson, Jerma, *Singing in my Soul: Black Gospel Music in a Secular Age* (Chapel Hill: University of North Carolina Press, 2004)

Johnson, James Weldon, and Johnson, J. Rosamond, *The Books of American Negro Spirituals* (New York: Viking, 1969)

Lomax, Alan, *The Land Where the Blues Began* (London: Methuen, 1993)

Lornell, Kip, *Happy in the Service of the Lord: African-American Sacred Vocal Harmony Quartets in Memphis* (Knoxville: University of Tennessee Press, 1995)

Oliver, Paul, *The Meaning of the Blues* (New York: Collier Books, 1963)

Owen, Nicholas, *Journal of a Slave-Dealer* (New York: Houghton Mifflin, 1930)

Poe, Randy, *Squeeze My Lemon: A Collection of Classic Blues Lyrics* (Milwaukee: Hal Leonard, 2003)

Reagon, Bernice Johnson, *We Who Believe in Freedom* (New York: Anchor, 1993)

Reagon, Bernice Johnson, *If You Don't Go, Don't Hinder Me: The African American Sacred Song Tradition* (Lincoln: University of Nebraska Press, 2001)

Sackheim, Eric, *The Blues Line: Blues Lyrics from Leadbelly to Muddy Waters* (New York: Grossman Publishers Inc., 1969)

Schwerin, Jules, *Got To Tell It: Mahalia Jackson Queen of Gospel* (New York: Oxford University Press, 1992)

Stowe, Harriet Beecher, *Uncle Tom's Cabin* (Ware: Wordsworth Editions, 1995)

Tosches, Nick, *Where Dead Voices Gather* (London: Jonathan Cape, 2002)

Turner, Steve, *Hungry for Heaven: Rock'n'roll and the Search for Redemption* (Downers Grove: InterVarsity, 1995)

Turner, Steve, *Trouble Man: The Life and Death of Marvin Gaye* (London: Michael Joseph, 1998)

Turner, Steve, *Amazing Grace: The Story of America's Most Beloved Song* (New York: Ecco, 2002)

Van Rign, Guido, *The Truman and Eisenhower Blues: African-American Blues and Gospel Songs, 1945–1960* (New York: Continuum, 2004)

Wald, Gayle, *Shout, Sister, Shout: The Untold Story of Rock-and-Roll Trailblazer Sister Rosetta Tharpe* (Boston: Beacon Press, 2007)

Ward, Andrew, *Dark Midnight When I Rise: The Story of the Fisk Jubilee Singers* (New York: Amistad, 2001)

White, Charles, *The Life and Times of Little Richard* (New York: Harmony Books, 1984)

Wolff, Daniel, *You Send Me: The Life and Times of Sam Cooke* (New York: Quill, 1995)

Zolten, Jerry, *Great God A'mighty! The Dixie Hummingbirds – Celebrating the Rise of Soul Gospel Music* (New York: Oxford University Press, 2003)

Index

Index of songs

15 rounds for Jesus 15

A

B

C

D

E

F

G

H

Index of names

Acknowledgments

Alamy: pp. 12, 135 Pictorial Press Ltd; p. 46 Photos 12; p. 175 Ted Pink

Bob Laughton: pp. 53, 71, 178

Bridgeman Art Library: p. 18bl American School, (18th century)/American Antiquarian Society, Worcester, Massachusetts, USA

Corbis: p. 47; pp. 3, 185 Carlos Barria/Reuters; p. 11 Phillipe Lissac/Godong; pp. 20–21 Louie Psihoyos/Science Faction; p. 26 Julio Donoso/Sygma; pp. 27, 38 Lebrecht Music & Arts; p. 30 Hulton-Deutsch Collection; pp. 34, 35, 41, 65, 96, 108, 125, 129, 136b, 146, 150, 155, 160–61, 177tr Bettmann; pp. 42, 56, 105 Underwood & Underwood; pp. 75, 88mr, 91, 110, 142, 145 Michael Ochs Archives; pp. 78–79, 106, 107 Terry Cryer; p. 119 Ted Williams; p. 132 Allen Ginsberg; p. 133 Flip Schulke; p. 138 Henry Diltz; p. 153 Andrew Goetz; p. 163 Lucy Nicholson/Reuters; p. 173 Jason Reed/Reuters; p. 189 Gene Blevins; p. 192 Molly Riley/Reuters; p. 195 Reuters; p. 196 Paul Mounce

Getty: pp. 6–7, 14, 67, 69, 70, 74, 88tl, 93, 95, 98, 101, 131, 158 Michael Ochs Archives; p. 18tr Kean Collection; pp. 18br, 22, 36–37, 37br Hulton Archive; pp. 49, 58, 81, 82, 84, 111 Frank Driggs Collection/Hulton Archive; p. 50 Gai Terrell/Redferns; p. 59 GAB Archive/Redferns; p. 76 Express/Hulton Archive; p. 77 Ron Case/Hulton Archive; p. 85 Gjon Mili//Time Life Pictures; p. 87 Charles Peterson/Hulton Archive; p. 92 Graphic House/Hulton Archive; p. 112 RB/Redferns; p. 114 Tim Mosenfelder; p. 128 Bob Parent/Hulton Archive; pp. 130, 141 Charlie Gillett/Redferns; p. 156 David Redfern/Redferns; p. 167 Michael Caulfield/WireImage; p. 168 Gilles Petard/Redferns; p. 171 MJ Kim; p. 180 Monica Morgan/WireImage; pp. 190, 193 Rick Diamond/WireImage

Lebrecht Music and Arts: pp. 8, 29, 31, 33, 39, 73, 83, 139 NYPL Performing Arts

Lloyd Yearwood: pp. 54, 86

Rex Features: p. 40 Roger-Viollet

Steve Turner: pp. 13, 28, 52, 63, 64, 94, 99, 115, 118, 120, 136tl, 147, 165, 174, 191, 194

Topfoto: p. 177 (main)

Lion Hudson
Commissioning editor: Paul Clifford
Project editor: Miranda Powell
Proofreader: Rachel Ashley-Pain
Designer: Jonathan Roberts
Picture researchers: Jessica Tinker; Jenny Ward
Production: Kylie Ord